TRUE NORTH

THE AUTHOR STARTING UP GRAND RIVER IN FEBRUARY

TRUE NORTH

By

Elliott Merrick

University of Nebraska Press
Lincoln and London

First Bison book printing: 1989
Most recent printing indicated by the first digit below:
1   2   3   4   5   6   7   8   9   10

Library of Congress Cataloging-in-Publication Data
Merrick, Elliott, 1905–
    True north / by Elliott Merrick.
        p.   cm.
    Reprint. Originally published: New York: C. Scribner's Sons, 1933.
    ISBN 0-8032-3140-7 (alk. paper).—ISBN 0-8032-8164-1 (pbk: alk. paper)
    1. Labrador (Nfld.)—Description and travel. 2. Adventure and adventurers—
Newfoundland—Labrador—History—20th century. 3. Merrick, Elliott,
1905–   . 4. Explorers—Newfoundland—Labrador—Biography. I. Title.
FI136.M36   1989
971.8'203—dc19   CIP 88-38068

Reprinted by arrangement with Elliott Merrick

CONTENTS

ILLUSTRATIONS

. . . *If the engine whistles, let it whistle till it is hoarse for its pains. If the bell rings, why should we run? We will consider what kind of music they are like.* Let us settle ourselves, and work and wedge our feet downward through the mud and slush of opinion, and prejudice, and tradition, and delusion, and appearance, that alluvion which covers the globe, through Paris and London, through New York and Boston and Concord, through church and state, through poetry and philosophy and religion, till we come to a hard bottom and rocks in place, which we can call reality, and say, This is, and no mistake; and then begin, having a point d'appui, below freshet and frost and fire, a place where you might found a wall or a state, or set a lamp-post safely. . . . Be it life or death, we crave only reality. If we are really dying, let us hear the rattle in our throats and feel cold in the extremities; if we are alive, let us go about our business.*

HENRY DAVID THOREAU.

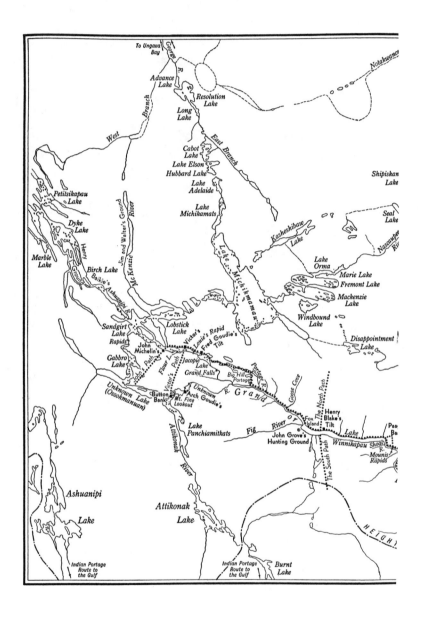

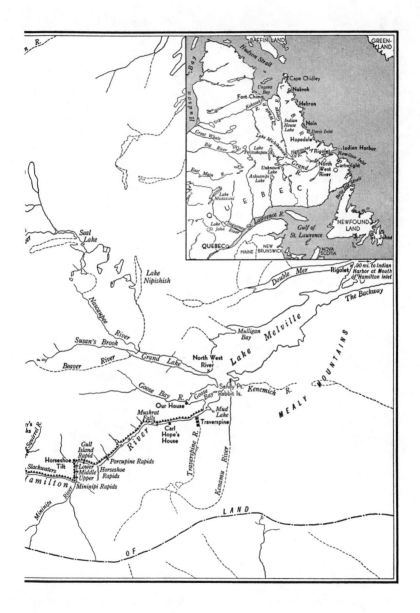

PART I

AWAKENING

Each June from the educational grist mills come thousands of sad young men who do not take to the great American religion of business, who dislike being sandwich men with signs on their backs that read, "My life is for sale to the highest bidder." They are malcontents who do not know what they want, but they know they do not want to devote their lives to business success with the wholeheartedness necessary to achieve that aim. For if they do not desire business success, how can they work for it?

There are thousands of them and each has his battle to fight alone. Some of them are artists without an art—a most ludicrous spectacle. Some of them are spoiled children, a few are dilettants. But most of them are very sincere. They have no aptitudes that can readily be converted into cash, or if they have they do not know it. They have glimpsed the futility of devoting one's life to getting rich and at the same time seen the nobility of a lifetime given to some serious purpose that is pursued for its own sake, not money. If only they could find some work worth doing and incidentally make a living at it. They are not lazy; they would rather be ditchdiggers than salesmen. They do not think themselves any better than the millions who toil in the cities. They merely think it wrong that they should add their mite to the overwhelming power of the system that rules us; that to make a living they should work for something in which they do not believe. They speak haltingly of "Truth" and "Beauty" and "Nature," but soon learn that

3

to speak thus is to be ridiculous or ridiculed, it matters not which.

Over them towers the inevitable necessity to earn their bread. Almost to a man they go into business. It is all they are fitted for, though they have spent four years getting themselves unfitted for it. In the struggle to reconcile their own prostitution with their own aspiration they are tried. Their yearnings are crushed or crystalized.

I happen to have been one of them, and after two years of outwardly conforming, possessed of a good job and excellent prospects, the internal struggle still raged.

Every morning I raced for the train and my breakfast rose in my throat. Past all the green grass and the flower gardens of the suburb, hurrying, hardening my mind to forget them, not to see them. The morning breeze whispered in the leaves and the sky was blue and dotted with fleece.

Why should a person leave all this all day, month after month, for the roaring city? Why should it be considered lazy-man's dilettantism to work in the sunshine all day long, digging, building a house, fishing, or sailing a boat? And to labor in the frenzied city of stupid ants at a task patently not worth the doing—oh, that was praiseworthy and natural. Who turned the world upside down anyway? Who, like an evil fairy in a book, switched all the values, calling the true values shams and the shams truth?

Every morning the fight began all over again. The first waking moments were like childhood, with a fresh mind that loves the bright, vivid earth simply because it is beautiful. Sunshine or rain were all the same, each beautiful in its way, interesting, stimulating, intoxicating.

Each day the hours squeezed in like the sides of a vise.

4

The hostile men, the ugliness, the nervous weariness, the hypocrisy of business all hammering the refrain, "Nothing is beautiful for its own sake. The earth is to be squeezed for what can be got out of it." I used to think: this great stone desert, these mammoth buildings, the subways, the screaming ads, the glittering, slippery tumult of cars and buses and white faces, the Ritz, the Yale Club, the slums, the dirt and smell and ugliness, the water mains and lights, the City Hall, the Mayor, the police, the street sweepers, the smoke,—who wants them? Not I. How did they come so to run us, to be so inevitable? Why do we stand for it, what is it doing to us? Why am I working for it, paying for it?

Going home on the train, thoughts whizzed much the same. Who wants a little box of a house in a suburb, a little wife, a little car with a little garage to put it in, and little hope? Well, why am I working for all this? If I am finally beaten into believing that selling brass pipe for Bing and Bing, Inc., is of any vital importance to the universe, what honor is there in that? Shall I live enmeshed in such a hopelessly organized society that I am dependent upon and helpless before a butcher, a baker, a politician, a judge, a president, an industrial boom, an international trade arrangement, a European imperialist, and a wobbly foreign exchange? All this is not so much to me as the fall of one autumn leaf. Why should I be tossed around in the magicians' hats, talking politics, reading the papers, bewildered and lost in a maze of irreconcilable, incomprehensible, uncontrollable forces? It were better to be slightly more independent. Each man has only one lifetime, and in that space he gets what he wants most; not what he thinks he

5

wants or would like to want, but what he really wants. Do I want a superfluity of material comforts and possessions, a dwelling loaded with conveniences, foods from all over the world, the power to ride and not walk, electric lights, good clothes, cement sidewalks, water out of a faucet, public parks and all that? Are they worth what they cost? Do I want to bend my whole life to a system of law, convention, taboo, evolved solely to enable millions of people to live packed together like sardines in a can? Hardly.

I prefer mud to cement sidewalks, and water out of a bucket to water out of a faucet. The breeze and the sunshine, a suit of rags, a vista that includes no house, no man; these are worth paying for.

One muggy night just before a thunderstorm, I sat up in bed and hammered my fist on the wall and screamed in my mind, "I'm getting out." And I got out.

My wife and I live in Labrador. She came here just as I did, looking for something, Heaven knows what. I found her here; she loves this land for its own sake, not for mine. And that is good.

For two years we worked for the Grenfell Mission, she as a trained nurse and I as school teacher, wood hauler, boat's crew, etc. We have been out on the bare-rock coast amongst the Newfoundland fishermen, where the snow sometimes flies even in August and the schooners scud into the harbor on stormy evenings and fold their wings like tired birds. Winters we have worked at the head-of-the-bay settlement in the spruce woods country where the trappers live and the Indians come to trade at the post. The half-white trapper people are, with a few exceptions, Scotch-Eskimos. The great grandfathers or grandfathers of the present families came out here to work for the Hudson's Bay Company. Gradually they became trappers on their own and took unto themselves Eskimo women, built log houses far from the post and set about making a living out of the wilderness. They made stoves out of rocks, covered the roofs of their houses with lapped birch bark, chinked the logs with moss, built their own boats, knit their own trout and salmon nets, often had to use deadfalls instead of traps, and many times when they lacked guns or powder or shot hunted a living with bows and arrows and snares. On the one hand there is abundant nature, rivers swarming with trout and salmon and pike, a coast where the codfishing is the best in the world, an inner wilderness where mink and marten, fox, otter, beaver, ermine, muskrat, bear, caribou, partridge and rabbit are plentiful. On the other hand there is hostile nature with her awesome, deadly might when one is alone far in the country on winter nights, with her sudden storms and killing cold, never giving up her treasures easily. All the tales of these lives are like music; a minor theme of elemental, bitter suffering finally realized in one resounding harmonious chord whose beautiful major notes are fortitude and strength to live through, or die like a man.

Our friends the scattered families that inhabit the bay are a unique race with oddly combined cultures; Scotch Presbyterian in religion, old English in speech and many customs, Eskimo when it comes to seal fishing and dog driving, Indian in their ways of hunting and their skill with canoes ascending the big rivers bound for the trapping grounds far in the country. Sometimes it seems as though they had taken for their own the best qualities of the three races, the Eskimo laughter-loving happiness, the Indian endurance and uncanny instinct for living off the country, the Scotchman's strength of character and will.

At first glance some of the families might seem poor, ragged wretches, exiled to a lonely, toil-bitten existence in a cruel land. But we came to know them fairly well at the end of two years and we found that though their lives are bitter hard, there is another side to it. The *Toganish Squish* [Doctor Girl], as the Indians call her, made long dog team trips in winter and slept many nights on the floor in log houses where there was sickness or trouble or childbirth. In pain and in joy, in those moments far in the night when a soul is itself, she came to know them as only a doctor or a doctor girl can. In the school perhaps I came to know the children a little. And in the hot woods in summer carrying heavy logs while the blood from the fly bites ran into our eyes, and out at the seal nets early in spring, and going down the 180-mile bay in open boats, and snowshoeing over the hills in winter hunting meat, I came to know the men.

And both my wife, whose name is Kay, and I began to feel that these were happier, finer people than we had ever known before. The primitive hard life seems to produce character as civilized existence cannot. Many times under the twinkling eyes of some wrinkled old woman who could neither read nor write, or in the presence of some scarred, kindly old trapper we felt abashed, almost like children. We who had come "to help the people" found ourselves constantly being helped by them. All we could do was to aid them with material things such as medicine, books, food, clothing and they would not accept even these unless they

8

felt that we were friends. Whereas to us they were a song, an inspiration. They were kinder and stronger than we, and wiser in the business of living. It seemed, as it always does, that no one can truly aid any one else by *doing* anything. Each of us is alone and cut off from every other human being in the world of material things and actions. It is only by *being* something that we can touch another's hand.

A few of these people are even aware of the situation. A trapper admitted to me, rather sheepishly in a moment of rare confidence, that although "the people from away" seemed to accomplish some marvelous feats such as making guns and radios, he could not see that the few who had come to this bay, the Methodists, the sportsmen, the Catholic priests who visit the Indians once a year and even the mission workers, were all so "wunnerful fine." He looked at me with his head on one side, expecting me to grow angry. I told him he was quite right and that he and his people were infinitely superior in character and honesty, happier and wiser how to truly live than the men in the cities. He considered this the windiest of flattery.

As for happiness, it is not often one meets a person who has a good life and knows it, but I have met one here. It is Bert Blake, a thick-set, pronouncedly Eskimo trapper with a jolly grin and a weathered face. He knows more of the country way back in than any other hunter. When he was sixteen he ran away from home to go with Mrs. Hubbard by canoe and portage to Michikamau and clear down the George River to Ungava Bay. He has trapped and hunted and explored through hundreds of miles of country known only to a few Indians, and they won't tell about it. The lakes and rivers and forests and barrens that stretch away

9

almost forever are as much his home as his house by the shore of the bay. He speaks the Montagnais dialect as though he were one of them, and once a year when these Indians come out of the woods they always camp beside his house and defer all questions concerning civilized mysteries to him. The other half-white trappers jokingly call him "The Old Chief," and wherever he travels, whether it is guiding a prospector, or with a little fleet of trappers' canoes bound up the river in the fall, he is the unassuming, natural leader.

Bert and I had been snowshoeing all one December day over the Goose Bay hills, hunting partridges and porcupine. When we stopped at noon to boil the kettle we sat on balsam brush before a fire and he told me how, on the long trip to Ungava, they were in rapids going down the George for nearly two weeks, never knowing what the river would be like below them, and often the banks were cliffs and they couldn't get ashore and they couldn't go back, so they had to run on down, though it looked almost like suicide; and how they lost the pump for Mrs. Hubbard's pneumatic mattress and he had to blow it up with his mouth every night; and what the ruins of the long-abandoned Hudson's Bay post on Michikamau looked like when he passed them last summer on an eight-hundred-mile canoe and portage trip.

"I been in the country trappin' every winter since I were twelve," Bert said. "And out of the last thirty summers I only missed three in the bush. Seems like you like this kind of trippin', b'y. Well, there's nothing for me like travellin' a new river, seein' the beeg heels close in behind and the bends open up ahead, breathin' cold sunshine and seein' new country every day."

Swinging home in the sudden winter dusk, Bert had a singed porcupine across his back and I had six partridges in the bag. As we stepped and stepped and stepped, he ahead and I behind, across a wide white marsh that looked, in the fading light, as limitless as an ocean, we commenced to realize that we had walked nearly thirty miles. A lovely sunset stained the sky, one of the sad, tugging kind that set one thinking of all the lonely, beautiful country off there a thousand miles to Hudson's Bay that no one has ever seen; and the snowy glades in the spruces where the rabbits dance on moonlight nights, the rocky coves ringed with birches, the gorges and bare mountains, the barrens and rivers and forty-mile lakes. Sometimes it draws like a magnet. Several times I caught Bert turning for a look himself.

Suddenly we stopped and sat down on our snowshoes in the middle of the marsh and watched the stars come out. Bert lit his pipe, and when the stars were bright he pointed with the stem to the Big Dipper and said, "My Lard, I wish't she was full of tea."

He laughed quietly, as though it were an old, old joke that must have pulled him the last few miles of many a long day's walk. When we were twisting our feet into the snowshoe thongs again he said, "You know, b'y, I never seen outside where you comes from. But I finds this pretty good —the country and the huntin' and all. I wouldn't want to go and live away. Sometimes I thinks, me, we'm happy here."

PART II
NEW LIFE

THE Indian camp ground across the river is deserted. In the long grass are a few old sealskin shoes, some bits of cloth and wire, and around the tent pickets, heaps of crisp dry shavings that curled from the Indians' crooked-knives as they fashioned canoe ribs, planking, snowshoe frames and paddles. Two or three worn-out kettles and some packages of clean-picked bones dangle on the bushes. Nearly a week ago the tribe broke camp and paddled away to that mysterious hunting ground back of Michikamau, where they are going to winter.

This is North West River, a Labrador village at the head of a deep 180-mile estuary, the Hamilton Inlet. On the wooded shore by the river mouth there is a Hudson's Bay Company post, a Grenfell Mission hospital and school, and the neat, low houses of some twenty-five trapper families. The men are housebuilders, tinsmiths, fishermen, boatbuilders, sailors, potato-farmers, and hunters all rolled into one. But most of all they are hunters. Soon they will be gone too, bound up the rivers "into the country" to the furring grounds hundreds of miles away. Until they come snowshoeing down the frozen rivers and lakes in January, the village, as though it were wartime, will be populated mostly by women and children and old men.

The summer indolence is gone, and in its place the energy that will last all winter. It's canoe-painting time and flourbag filling time. Every man must leave his family with three or four hundred turns of wood, sawed and split. By the saw engines and the sawhorses, the piles of wood-dust lie deep. By each house is a stack of clean-white, new-split wood.

Murdock is splitting wood near the path that is North West River's main stem. He shows me two birch chopping blocks he has worn out already today. The axe rises and falls and the split chunks fly, one from each hand, to the towering pile.

"Yes, b'y," he assures me, "it's the best life that ever was. I'm glad to go away now and I'll be almighty glad to come home again. I'm sick of so many people stewin' around and no fresh meat and so many kids. Off in the woods I've got nobody to bother about. I'm like the boss of the world. But after a while I'll get sick of the little tilts and the smell of silver-pine brush [balsam] and cookin' and skinnin' fur and walkin', and, oh, Lord, it'll seem wonderful fine to get home again." Murdock has been outside to the war, seen Paris and London, marched through Belgium, chummed with Scotchmen, and is a man to listen to. Like the few others who have ever been "outside" from here he'd like to go again some day for "a cruise" just to see the movies and the lights and all the incomprehensible things people do, but never to live.

As Murdock talks I pick up a spare axe and commence splitting too for the joy of seeing a straight-grained chunk part with a jump. A slow smile curls over his face. "I most alwus leaves a spare axe or two lyin' around because some-body's all the time stoppin' to have a chin. Most generally they picks up the axe and cleaves a few without thinking about it."

Each autumn Kay and I have seen the trappers go away,

16

laughing and shooting off guns as the loaded canoes swing into the river. Bright woolen sashes, sealskin boots, white cotton homemade coats, bronze faces with pipes stuck in them, paddles and caps waving; as picturesque a crew of northern woodsmen as ever lived. Each autumn we have wanted to go with them and see what their life is like off there in the bush.

Soon we shall get our wish. Tomorrow the first bunch of Height of Landers leaves and I hope we will not be too far behind to catch them. One of the trappers, a devil-may-care young Hercules named John Michelin, is taking Kay and me with him 350 miles up Grand River. We have known him for about a year. He says he is taking us just for company in the long, lonely months while he's tending his trap lines. But I think it is mainly because some people have told him he is a fool to try it. They say he'll never get us there and if he does he'll never get us down again.

John is among the men who go farthest up Grand River, almost to the watershed which is called the Height of Land, the vague border between Labrador and Canada. These men must leave early lest they get "froze up" on the lakes and ponds of the Big Portage.

Uncle Albert has told me of a trip of his when they went back of Nepishish toward Hopedale River and got froze up. The little chains of lakes were all skimmed over. It was in October. The ice would not bear them, but it was strong enough to tear the canvas almost off their canoes. They loaded their craft deep by the stern so they would ride up on the ice and break it down by their weight. This saved the canvas a little and they managed to make three or four miles a day.

It is bad to be caught by ice, for if it freezes solid you

must leave your canoe and make a sled. That means waiting for snow across the portages and leaving some of the grub; a man cannot haul anything like the weight he can paddle. Sometimes one must wait for days and days while the ice is too thin to bear one and too thick to paddle through.

The women are busy these days sewing for their lives, making duffel vamps and mitts, deerskin mitts and moccasins, finishing sealskin boots and patching faded shirts and trousers. Into a little cotton-duck bag go these things and the other suit of underwear, the flannel shirt, the shawl, the cap with the fur ears, that meagre stock that will stand between their men and the weather, keep them not dry, but not perishing in the sleeting late fall days; keep them not warm, but not freezing in the twenty and thirty-below winds of December. Some men never look in their clothes bag until they are way up the river and happen to want something out of it. The "old 'oman" knows.

Every man has something on his mind. Finyan is busy with rivets and tin, making a camp stove to replace the one that has been half rusted to pieces in his third tilt these four years; Henry wants a pipe coupling for the business end of his canoe pole; Fred forgot to get a bit of resin and some paint and fur nails from the Hudson's Bay Company store. Cecil wants a brinbag to jam some traps in and Arch is "bringing to" a trout net. Harvey is tying strings to the new tent his wife has just finished.

September 10.

THEY left this morning, nine of them. The H. B. C.'s motor boat takes them forty miles to Muskrat Falls, the first little portage. She was piled high with bags of flour, and snowshoes and guns were sticking out everywhere.

They had two canoes aboard and were towing three more. Every one was down on the wharf to see them off. As they drew off into the middle of the river, shotguns began to split the air, bang, bang—boom. The men on shore and the departing ones keep firing into the air until the boat is almost lost to sight. It is the custom, the ancient good-bye. All the women were there and not one cried. For four months their men will be away, and many times in danger. It is remarkable how seldom one is lost.

September 11.

OFF today ourselves in a big motor boat with John for engineer. Every one came to say good-bye to us too. Some wagging heads and a few old-timers who say we'll be back in about two weeks, having capsized our canoe in a rapid and lost all our grub. I sometimes wonder if they don't speak the truth. There are to be four of us in two canoes, John, his cousin Alvin, Kay and I. Of the four, John is the only one who knows Grand River, Alvin is only seventeen and not particularly strong. Kay scarcely knows how to paddle a canoe, and I am green as grass when it comes to rapids.

We left the wharf to the usual accompaniment of shotguns, and were scarcely clear before one of the canoes filled and swamped. I had tied her too short. Nothing happened to be in her except the paddles, but it seemed an ill omen. We hauled her aboard and slipped down the river past the abandoned Revillon Frères post, past the last houses. Bert was out on the beach in front of his house waving a shirt in one hand and a shotgun in the other. The Mealy Mountains were blue, tipped with faint white of the first snowfall, and the sun sparkled on the water as we rounded Point

Gibou and headed for Sandy Run and the mouth of Grand River.

A little after noon we were at Traverspine, where we spent the night. It is a narrow river flowing into Grand River, and near the mouth, perched on a high sand bank, are three houses. One belongs to John's father, Uncle Jo, and the other two to his half-brothers, Robert and Jim. A lonely place, but splendid for ducks and geese, partridges, rabbits, porcupine, bear, salmon, trout, and fur. That is why they live there. John and Alvin and I were all afternoon bringing home birch firewood in the motor boat from a pile cut a little way down the big river.

Uncle Jo is eighty years old, a queer old man with a bulbous nose. He can still cut and carry wood and hunt a little. On his seventy-fifth birthday he walked to North West River which is about twenty-two miles. Most every one stops somewhere in the sixteen-mile stretch between Mud Lake and North West River to boil the kettle, but he went right on.

His house here at Traverspine is of logs, about thirty-five years old, but still solid. Inside it is sheathed with perfectly matched tongue-and-groove boards. Nearly a year it took to cut the logs, haul them home with dogs in the spring, saw all the board with a whipsaw, plane it and tongue-and-groove plane it, build the house and what furniture it contained.

He had a large family of some twelve children and taught them all to read and write and figure. John has often told me how he used to forbid them to go hunting or fishing, or lick them with a strap if they couldn't do their sums. A few of them had occasional weeks or months with the itinerant

Methodist school teacher at Mud Lake and showed great promise. A wild crew of urchins they must have been, running barefoot in the summer, and even trying it in the winter. There were so many of them there were seldom enough boots or moccasins to go 'round in winter. Sometimes the boys used to race to the rabbit traps, a quarter of a mile from the house, barefoot. Each would take a flat board and scamper off through the snow. When his feet were paralyzed with cold he'd slap down the board in the snow and stand on it with one foot, rubbing and warming the other. Whoever made the fewest stops, of course, won the race.

The old man made skates for all of them—heavy barrel-hooping for blades, set in undercut blocks of wood shaped like a foot. They'd tie them on with rope or string or seal-skin or rags and swoop up the Traverspine River to the trout holes like a flock of swallows. In the early fall, just after the river froze, they'd sometimes get a dozen barrels of trout. Often they used them for dog feed. John can hardly believe it when I tell him that trout in the markets at home goes as high as ninety cents a pound.

It was returning from a day's trouting that John, at the age of eight, had the first of his miraculous escapes from drowning. Five of the children, none of them more than fifteen, were rollicking down the river on a komatik drawn by dogs one moonlight evening. The river was covered with new black ice. Slewing around a bend, the komatik went through and they all fell in. With the help of the dogs' traces the oldest boy crawled out on the ice, and lying flat on his stomach hauled the rest out, except John, whom no one could find. It was not far above the house, and the old man, hearing their shouts, came a-running with an axe and a long pole. All over the black ice they ran, looking down through for John. Finally some one spied the white woolen cap on his head drifting along. The old man ran ahead, cut a hole, and when the boy drifted by pulled him out. He didn't come to for an hour and a half.

By the time they were nine or ten the boys were all good hunters, keen for partridges and rabbits and signs of fur in winter and ducks and geese in the fall and spring. When they were too small to hold up a shotgun they went in pairs. One would let the barrel rest on his shoulder while the other stood behind, aimed, fired, and got knocked flat by the recoil. If it was winter they took a sled to haul the gun on, as it was too heavy to carry. While they were young Uncle Jo was busy scouting out the country and making new fur paths for his boys: Black Rock, The Long Path with eight tilts, Red River, Porcupine, Sand Banks, and three or four more, some close to home, some 150 miles away.

A fur path in these parts is handed down from father to son. It consists mainly of a hazily defined territory. When a man has blazed his trails and built his little cabins (tilts), each a day's walk apart, and set out his two or three hundred traps, that land is his to hunt, and no one else's. Sometimes he farms out his paths to another hunter. In that case the owner must provide a canoe, and stoves for the tilts. The hunter gives him one-third of each haul.

Picking out good fur ground is an art. There must be thick green woods for martens, brooks for mink and otter, lake shores and barrens for foxes. It means toiling through hundreds of miles of broken, unknown country, with always the problem of how to take enough grub. And then there is money for new traps and the work of carrying them in by canoe and on one's back.

John's half-brother, Robert, is going with us for a week to help us through the worst rapids. He won't say why, but I think it is out of gratitude to Kay, who spent three weeks here last spring when his children were dying of dysentery and pulled them all through somehow. Two winters ago Rob was guide for two Englishmen out here making maps for the Royal Geographic Society. They had some narrow escapes and would certainly have perished but for him. He always does a little trading with the Indians when they come out of the woods in winter, but he gives them more than he trades to them. If ever his wife says, "Rob, don't give them that kittle, we needs it," he's sure to give it away, so she has learned to keep silent. They say that when he went away to that mysterious war across the sea, in 1915, the Indians wept for him and always used to remember him in their singsong Catholic chants. He speaks the Montagnais Indian language fluently. When he returned from the war he was crippled, the muscles of one leg drawn up so that he could only walk on tiptoe. Doctors told him not to go back to Labrador, he could never snowshoe again, he could never be a trapper, for a trapper's main business is to walk. He told them to go to hell. Gradually he limbered the leg up until he scarcely limps now. He's done forty miles a day since. Some say he's never been the same since the war. The stories go that when he's drunk there's an inhuman light in his eye and he's been heard to say he'd as soon kill a man as a partridge. You should see him with his son, for whom he makes small sleds and toboggans. Robert practically

23

supports the Jim family, for Jim is a pale, tubercular shell, coughing all the time, and can't hunt.

Supper at the old man's house, and how he loves to talk! He's been a sailor in a schooner, been to St. Johns, Sydney, and Halifax, wintered, lumbering, in Nova Scotia. Winters long ago he used to do a big trading business, but he gave so much credit to people on the verge of starvation he generally lost money. He always used to raise lots of potatoes, and he's tried fox farming and keeping sheep and goats. Sooner or later the dogs always got out of the log stockade in which they were penned and killed them. He had a flock of tame geese one spring when some strange Indians coming down Grand River paddled around the point and shot them.

He loathes engines and has never learned to run his motor boat. When he goes from Traverspine to his salmon fishing place, ninety miles down the bay, he has the boys take off the propeller and sails down, with his old wife and an eight-year-old boy for crew. He came to North West River one spring where two of his sons have houses and families. They asked him in, but he put up his tent on the point and camped there for two weeks, saying he didn't want any kindness from anybody and anyway they had too many squalling kids.

Ghost stories are very real in this land of scattered, lonely homes and primitive fears. The Traverspine "gorilla" is one of the creepiest. About twenty years ago one of the little girls was playing in an open grassy clearing one autumn afternoon when she saw come out of the woods a huge hairy thing with low-hanging arms. It was about seven feet tall when it stood erect, but sometimes it dropped to all fours. Across the top of its head was a white mane. She said it grinned at her and she could see its white teeth. When it beckoned to her she ran screaming to the house. Its tracks were everywhere in the mud and sand, and later in the snow. They measured the tracks and cut out paper patterns of them which they still keep. It is a strange-looking foot, about twelve inches long, narrow at the heel and forking at the front into two broad, round-ended toes. Sometimes its print was so deep it looked to weigh 500 pounds. At other times the beast's mark looked no deeper than a man's track. They set bear traps for it but it would never go near them. It ripped the bark off trees and rooted up huge rotten logs as though it were looking for grubs. They organized hunts for it and the lumbermen who were then at Mud Lake came with their rifles and lay out all night by the paths watching, but with no success. A dozen people have told me they saw its track with their own eyes and it was unlike anything ever seen or heard of. One afternoon one of the children saw it peeping in the window. She yelled and old Mrs. Michelin grabbed a gun and ran for the door. She just saw the top of its head disappearing into a clump of willows. She fired where she saw the bushes moving and thinks she wounded it. She says too that it had a ruff of white across the top of its head. At night they used to bar the door with a stout birch beam and all sleep upstairs, taking guns and axes with them. The dogs knew it was there too, for the family would hear them growl and snarl when it approached. Often it must have driven them into the river, for they would be soaking wet in the morning. One night the dogs faced the thing and it lashed at them with a stick or club, which hit a corner of the house with such force it made the beams tremble. The old man and boys carried guns wherever they went, but never got a shot at it. For two winters it was there. They believe to this day it was one of the devil's agents or more likely "the old feller" himself.

Uncle Jo is very proud of his old smooth-bore muzzle-loader which he reaches down from the gun rack between the beams of the living-room ceiling. He explains that for a hunter in the country it has advantages over any modern weapon. You can use shot of any size, or bullet, so that in this one light gun you have everything you could need. Nowadays you always wish you had your rifle when you have your shotgun and vice versa, thereby losing a good many skins of fur. He admitted that on a blowy day at thirty below, loading was painful, sometimes even impossible.

September 12.

WE are camped on a bluff beside the portage path at Muskrat Falls. Kay and I were camped here just about a year ago, when we came up with a motor boat that brought a crew of trappers. It was our first taste of the life, the sweet, soft balsam in the tent, the trappers' camaraderie and jokes, the hard, simple life, "all brothers in the river," camp fires and the tall black spruces whispering in the dark. It broke our hearts to go back down the river with the motor boat, she to nursing in the Grenfell Mission hospital and I to teaching in the mission school. They were worthwhile jobs with many satisfactions, but we made up our minds next year when the canoes shoved off from above the falls we'd be along.

A stiff breeze of wind soaked us coming up from Travers-pine this afternoon, but it held the other boys here. The river above the falls is too broad and rough in a blow for deeply loaded canoes. When we came ashore here the boys had most all their stuff carried across. Fred Goudie was painting with a rag the canoe that he left here last spring. They helped us portage our stuff across in a friendly, matter-of-fact way.

Kay has a broad, bright woollen sash for a head strap. She made three trips, carrying each time a forty-nine pound bag of flour and some odd stuff such as snowshoes, guns, axes or sleeping bags. I am glad she is so strong. It will be invaluable to us on the Big Portage. This portaging seems to break one's neck at first, for most of the weight is on the upper part of the back and neck. The average man's load is two bags of flour and an odd pail of lard or so, but sometimes they carry three bags or even four on the level, "just for badness." Four bags is equivalent to a barrel. The head strap across the top of one's head supports the first bag, which goes lengthwise on one's back. It pulls back your head like a tight checkrein on a horse. The next bag goes crosswise on your neck, held there by the lower bag. This second bag pushes your head forward, so that the two bags are, or are supposed to be, in equilibrium.

I hoisted the middle thwart of the canoe onto my neck and carried it up the first steep bank to see if I could, and it wasn't as bad as I expected. Our canoes are both eighteen-foot Chestnuts, very strong and deep, excellent in rough water. They weigh one hundred pounds apiece. Robert brought his little one, which he will take as far as the rapids to come home in.

The situation between us and the other men is very odd. There is something in the air. We have known them all for over a year and I think they like us. But they are not as friendly as they used to be. They are afraid we are going to delay them. They travel fast and hard; this is their business, their livelihood, and we are only pleasure jaunting. They fear we will be frightened and awkward in the rapids and cost them many precious hours and days on this long swift struggle with the river, where there is no room for incompetence and a man has his hands full to exhaustion getting himself along. And here is a woman in our midst. Their code will not let them desert us, and their interests demand that they get along as fast as possible, lest the lakes on the portage freeze up. They are wondering, and obviously glad to see Robert along for awhile. Kay and I are wondering too and we resolve that we will go till we drop, and never murmur, and if we can't pick up the river ways fast enough, can't hold up our own end, we'll come back with Robert.

Just after sunset we left off portaging for a few minutes and went over to the rocks beside the fall. It's a mad chute, pretty, and frivolous, and mighty. Some visiting scientist's treatise says that it could be made to develop I don't know how many thousand horsepower, that it connects with 200 miles of navigable waterway, all forest bordered; in short, that it could easily be transformed from a merry, rainbow-sprayed flume to some dreary turner of dynamos and things, the accomplice of a wondrous sawmill that would devastate the country farther than the eye can reach, pollute the crystal waters, drive out the fish and game, and make day laborers of a unique race of coureurs des bois.

I'd rather recall another tale. It is told of the Grand Falls as well as Muskrat Falls. Once, long, long ago, two

Photograph by G. H. Watkins

MUSKRAT FALLS

Indian girls were fishing from their canoe on the river above. It was eveningtime and calm, a lulling, quiet time to soothe one softly. The spruce trees dip their pointed black pictures in the still water, where a first faint star lies mirrored. The fall sings far away, not so far away. A leaf upon a mirror, their canoe is drifting, motionless itself, but the mirror is moving. They look up from their dreaming and their paddles leap and their onyx eyes flash fire. But the merry mad flume has them in its grip, the mirror breaks in splinters, the leaf plunges and is drowned.

Since then the Indians never camp near the falls; they say they are haunted and at night the girl spirits moan. The two spirits are lying prostrate on the bottom, unable to rise to heaven or sink to hell, and on dark nights their cries float through the blackness of the trees louder than the rushing of the waters. An Indian would rather die any death than drowning. A drowned man's ghost lies uneasy and gets waterlogged like his bedfellows, the sodden stumps sunken in the riverbed.

September 13.

A CALM [caam] morning with fourteen of us in eight canoes strung out in a long line, paddling close in by the sandy shore to avoid the current. Early in the morning we got out our tracking lines. One end is tied to the forward thwart, a man takes the loop on the other end and walks along shore towing like a canal-boat mule. The other man stays in the stern and steers. Every now and then we change places. Alvin and I are a couple of monkeys, watching and imitating. Kay had to steer for John and had a bad time of it for awhile, either keeping too far out, so that it was much harder work for him, or keeping in too close, where the canoe would ground.

We all went ashore on a sandbar about eleven, made a fire and had bread and tea standing up in a cold, raw wind. I don't even know how to drink tea. I'm always putting my spoon down on a log or a stone and losing it. Every one else leaves his in his cup and holds it there with his thumb when he drinks, thus not losing any time hunting around for it.

The river is fifteen feet lower now than at its spring-flood level, and the steep sand banks are sometimes a hundred yards back from the present water. At three we boiled up again. It's wonderful how a cup of tea and a smoke and a rest picks you up. I like to see all the canoes drawn up on the beach and the blue smoke rising from two or three fires against the dark trees.

Arch Goudie, fifty years old, has been up and down Grand River the greatest number of times, so he's supposed to be boss, to say when we stop to boil the kettle and when and where we make camp and what time we get away in the morning. But Arch likes to go along easy and some of the others like to race, so John tells me Arch will probably get rousted out earlier in the morning than he likes and dragged on farther in the evening.

Camped on a high bank a long way back from the river in a cleared-out glade where the boys have often camped before. John and Henry raced up the bank, and John threw an axe and Henry his hat at the camp sites they wanted. It seems that whoever gets his hat or bandanna or any piece of his property on a site first, owns it for the night. There were

30

only four old tent places. John gave me his and cleared another.

It was almost bewildering—the speed with which they unloaded the canoes and piled the load on paddles far up from the water. The monkeys were not quite as quick. One man stands in the canoe and heaves flour bags, game bags, rifles, stoves, tents, blankets and kettles at the other as fast as he can throw them. Then the canoes are carried up and turned over, the load covered with the tarpaulin and weighted down with rocks or driftwood logs. If possible the canoes are tied on to something, as fall gales have often been known to blow a canoe away. Next it's cut sticks for pickets and tent poles, up with the tent, get brush for the floor and set up the little camp stove inside on a heap of sand or flat rocks. Then off along shore or into the woods for a small, straight dry spruce or juniper. When the firewood is chopped to stove length and split, the fire is soon lit and the tea and pork and beans on cooking. An old-timer in a good camping place can do all this in half an hour, and he'll lie in his tent, his head on a bag and his pipe in his mouth, joshing the young fellows for being so slow.

Robert showed me how to make a candlestick out of a split stick and a loop of birch bark. John is so busy telling us how bad Gull Island Rapid is going to be, Alvin and I have lost interest.

Went down to the river late for water. It seems to gurgle differently at night, slipping along so smooth; come from a thousand lakes on the Height of Land. The stars were small and dim behind wispy, creeping northern lights. Suddenly two beams of light swept the sky like a prelude to what was

31

coming. The wisps bunched up into a sea of golden radiance directly overhead and, moving like soft, yet swiftest, lightning the breaking sea of light flashed red and green and blue as it slipped into the form of a gigantic, open-petalled rose that burst in blinding light and was gone.

September 18.

WE are at the head of Mininipi Rapid and Robert is leaving us. I am sorry to see him go, but he has taught me a lot in these last four days of clawing our way up through Tom's Rapid, Flate's, Porcupine, Gull Island, the three Horseshoes, and Mininipi. He left his canoe at the foot of Porcupine and came in the bow with me. Alvin went with John, and Kay has walked the slanting shores of round, rolling rocks or knife-edged sliding shale for the past four days. One pair of new sealskin boots she has completely worn out, and her feet are so bruised she can hardly limp along. It's a good thing she can rest them up paddling with me in the next two days of slack water.

This last stretch has been all pole and track and wade, no paddling at all except when we crossed the river. Poling is the hardest to learn of all. Robert made me keep the stern all the way, but we zigzagged like a schooner tacking. Both men stand up in the canoe and push along on the side nearest the bank. The bow man is supposed to keep her off and the stern man to keep her in. The bow wants to shy off or on like a skittish horse. It isn't so bad if she swings in, but if she swings out you lose bottom with the pole, have to grab your paddle and give it to her for the shore. By this time you may have lost a quarter of a mile and there's nothing for it but to try again. If there are rocks behind when she swings off, the canoe may get broadside on the upper edge of one, and then she's done for. Rob told me he'd once seen a canoe turned inside out that way. She tipped down so the tide was running right into her, the rock forced the bottom right up through the gunnels, and the current, catching the two ends, folded them around the rock and broke her in half.

On the first stiff stretch of poling we got swept out into the middle of the river, but fortunately there was an island we could get behind, and so back to the main shore again. Several times the pole slipped and I nearly fell overboard. After this, if the canoe started to swing in a bad place, and the water was shoal enough for him to keep his feet, Robert would jump overboard and straighten her out, while I got a good grip with the pole; then jump in again and off we'd go. He used to be soaked all day and never seemed to mind. No matter what the day, cold or warm, rain or shine, he always wore an old waistcoat. There was never a day cold and wet enough to make him put on a coat, and never a day warm enough to make him take off the vest.

I have a picture of him in my mind one desolate cold afternoon in the rain. We were in the Horseshoes and he'd been all day on the line tracking me. The wet rocks were slippery and treacherous, but he ran over them like a goat, coiling up the line and giving it a magnificent heave over a boulder or a stump. The shore of the river is a series of coves and rocky juts shoved up by ice in the spring. He would stand at the end of these little rocky points and pull me up short, then dash around the shore of the cove above, letting out the slack as he ran. The canoe would drift back a little in spite of my paddling as hard as I could. Then with

33

the line far ahead, he'd pull me out around the point while I tried to ease her head straight into the current so she wouldn't take a dart out and yank him off his feet. John was once steering a canoe that darted out and yanked the man on the line six feet through the air. The loop slipped from around his shoulders and John ran down through the rapid in a canoe half full of water. The line was dragging on the bottom and he was afraid the loop would catch and capsize him so he cut it off at the gunnel with an axe.

If the point we were rounding happened to be a strong one, the bow would lift and the stern would settle as she took the up slant. Water flew over her and the steering paddle bent and vibrated. At the end of the quivering line I would see Robert drop to one knee, then crawl on hands and knees fighting for a foothold among the rocks. He never got "hung" in all the Horseshoes, though most every one else did. To get hung means that you can't take a step, can only hang on until some one comes along and gives you a hand.

At a rocky bend that rainy afternoon Robert stood on a boulder studying the river to figure out whether we'd better cross or try it on this side. The coiled line was in his hand, his sodden old felt hat in a thousand curls down on his ears, woollen breeches tucked in boots that shone with the wet, rain streaming down his thin, iron face, down over the eternal vest and flannel shirt. He looked so small and defiant in this desolate valley where the river has cut its way deep into enormous wooded hills. I was sitting in the canoe, rocked by the wash from the rapid, teeth chattering with the cold, watching him. He reminded me of some gallant, bedraggled old eagle who has lost a couple of tail feathers

ROBERT MICHELIN

Photographs by Varick Frissell

JOHN MICHELIN

in a fight—this cripple who could never go hunting again, this tender-hearted, flint-cruel man, this white-hot bar tempered to something fine. He came down off the boulder with a grin and said, "This river, she's a bitch."

Harvey Goudie and Ralph Blake are the best team on the pole and it's as good as a hockey game to watch them do a bad place. Both stand half crouched in the canoe, their poles swinging together like clockwork. Each throws his whole weight into the shove as though there were never any such thing as a pole slipping or breaking. The canoe surges ahead, never veering an inch, stops while the poles swing in unison, surges ahead again, as though by magic.

We stayed in camp last Sunday at a sandy beach beside Gull Island Rapid. Thundering white water day and night and the tent door framing a picture of open-jawed, ravenous waves. We took advantage of the warm day to spread out our wet beans and peas on a tarpaulin in the sun. Everything gets wet even though it is in canvas bags. Sugar is the worst, as it runs away and disappears, but we have our sugar bag painted. Flour isn't so bad, for it cakes up hard after a good soaking and the cake keeps the middle dry. You lose about one-eighth of the bag, as the cake is mouldy and sour. Flour bags will float, and more than one man has salvaged his flour after capsizing his canoe. Hicks Meisher picked up one of John's flour bags one fall fifty miles below the place where John swamped. John lost most everything, but the other four each gave him a little and he went on and stuck it out until Christmas with only a pound of tea, practically no sugar and short of grease, flour, and pork. He lived mostly on meat and fish, and used to steep his tea three times. Some of it he smoked, but it didn't taste very good.

35

Old John Montague was drowned at Gull Island many years ago. They came up in homemade wooden boats in those days, three men to a boat, two on the line and one steering. The boat was old and rotten. They had the line tied to the "rising," and old John was steering. The two on the line tore the rising right out of her and when the boat drifted back she shot out on an eddy into the maelstrom, turned bottom up and pitched old John out. He couldn't swim a stroke, but even if he had been able to it is doubtful if it would have helped him in the chaos of rushing water and boulders. The beach down by Porcupine where his body washed ashore is still haunted. Charlie Groves camped there once and had to pack up and get out of there in the middle of the night. Something that left no track was thumping his canoe and moaning, though it was a bright moonlight night. Dan Michelin camped on an island a good piece off one spring and heard groans all night. Alvin was with him, a boy then, and Dan told him it was only a horn owl, but he knew different.

We had to lighten for parts of Gull Island and Mininipi; that is, carry part of the load along shore so the canoe can be dragged over half-covered rocks close in. Every one's boots are generally full of water at such times from wading over their tops and slipping off rocks. Sealskin boots full of water are impossible to walk on and even if you empty them out they are slippery and treacherous for carrying loads over tumbling rocks. Rather than risk a fall with a hundred pounds on our necks, most of us carried in our stocking feet. Every one stops and helps every one else in places like this. Robert and John tied a pole and the line to the bow of each canoe. Then Rob went ahead to pull with the line and John waded along with the pole, pushing her out around boulders and pulling her in close where she would float. Where the water is more than knee deep it will sweep a man off his feet. We got our canoe jammed between two boulders, where we pushed and yanked and slipped for twenty minutes before we got her out. John says it looks cowardly to see a canoe going along with no one in her. But Rob replies, "She gits along, doesn't she?"

It is a science that is impossible to explain, this bucking the current and getting along by hook or crook. Different men have different methods. Some take chances and some play safe, and the careful ones get spilled as often as the "risky Jacks."

At the foot of Mininipi we were so soaked and cold we stretched a point and made early camp. We had had rain fo two days steady and were damn good and sick of it. I envied the fellows on the line who had a chance to work and get warmed up. Rob used to have me do all the steering, saying, "You've gotta learn; you might as well learn now." We got another drenching in the willows making camp.

When John and Robert got snugged away in their tent, with the fire going, John unrolled the little bearskin that he sleeps on, and Rob decided to dispense with the famous waistcoat. So he took it off and wrung it out, also everything else. The stove, as it grew dull red, poured off warmth that felt tremendously good. John and I decided it was a good idea, so we followed suit, and stark naked in the warmth we had a good game of draw poker for muskrats we never intended to win or to pay. Fred Goudie poked his head in, cleared out a place for himself and sat down. He and John are always kidding. John says Fred's hair looks like old rope

37

frayed out and that his face is blacker than the face on the Aunt Jemima pancake box, that being the only black face he has ever seen. Fred told me his grandmother was a full-blooded Cree Indian and he wouldn't care if she was a ring-tailed polar bear. He's one of the old-timers who can remember hard times, with the Indians burning his tilts and stealing his grub.

John told me it was here at Mininipi that he and Dan first met the Indian, Charlie Mark. He was a man of about thirty-five, alone with a dead wife, almost out of his head. The Indians had been portaging their stuff up over the steep trail that cuts off Mininipi bend. His wife had a baby on her back and a shotgun in her hand. Climbing over a windfall she fell and the shotgun went off, carrying away most of her right shoulder and missing the baby. The other Indians came running just in time to see her die. Either through superstition because they believed he was bad luck to them, or because they really thought so, they said Charlie Mark had shot her. They kicked him out of the tribe then and there, ostracized him forever, took the baby and went on. Dan and John found him there two days later, not knowing what to do. They buried the woman, much against Charlie's will, as these Indians are Catholics and will carry their putrifying dead for months to get them to a consecrated Catholic cemetery at North West River or the French shore on the Gulf of St. Lawrence. They told Charlie to buck up and come along with them, they had plenty of grub. Dan's place was two days farther on so they went up there and the three of them hunted around the river all the early fall. There was practically no fur. Charlie said he'd show them the way in southward toward the gulf to Nasquarro Lake, a hunting ground the Indians had always kept secret, a place where there were *meetcháy wabistan* (many martens). They made sleds and went in over some 150 miles of woods and streams and lakes with all the traps they could haul. They got more martens than they'd ever seen before. They've been back many times since and John says it is worth while to go all the way in there and out again for one haul, just five days with the traps set. He wants me to go in there with him for the spring hunt in February and March. I think Charlie Mark had a hand in John's education, taught him to speak Indian so well and gave him that uncanny sense he has for picking his way across unknown country simply by the look of the hills and valleys and watersheds, and never getting lost.

September 18.

ROBERT will have had a bad walk today over the rough rocks beside the rapids, big brooks to wade, and Bob's Brook to swim probably. Tomorrow he'll get to his canoe and be all right.

Everybody laughing and whistling this morning as we pulled down the tents, the air so full of cold and sunshine. Harvey Goudie set his trout net last night and we all had trout and whitefish for supper tonight, fried crisp brown. This has seemed like a day of rest after storm, this day in Slack Waters. The big, rolling hills are flecked with lovely, ragged patches of red and yellow birches that straggle up between endless spruces like little flames. All the hills are covered with blueberries and redberries. The famous berry banks are just above Mininipi, and when we went ashore to boil we picked nearly a quart. Tall yarns are a never-ending source of joy over the tin teacups. Arch demurely assured us this morning as we sat around the fire that when he lived down at Davis Inlet the berries were so thick that you couldn't step out of the house without rubber boots on or you'd get your feet soaked with jam, and that after a big breeze of wind in the fall when the berries were overripe, the brooks on the hillsides would rise a foot with juice.

Where the river runs shoal over sand bars or orange pebbles it doesn't look like ordinary water; in the slanting sunlight it has some super-clear, jewel-like quality, pure rippled joy, a roadway of it to travel on all day long. And it doesn't taste like water. It has a delicate, tasteless, crystal magic that is even better than champagne.

I told John that where I come from people pay for their drinking water, and it has a bad taste at that. At first he wouldn't believe me, and then he said, "What fools they must be. I wouldn't live in a place like that."

This morning as we packed the last bag and axe in the canoe and shoved off with paddles flashing it didn't seem possible that once mornings like this I was going to an office with a pain in my heart and a lump in my throat, going to do work I knew wasn't worth doing, alternately wracked by sorrow and indignation, for all the world like a recalcitrant schoolboy faced with the never-ending eternity of five hours in school. In the cold sunshine on the river it seemed ridiculous that I or any one could ever have been so sunk in despair. I think I never shall be again.

We could paddle or track today as we liked. Both were easy, and it didn't make much difference. For tracking there were miles and miles of sandy beaches, marked every now and then by the print of bear paws.

Alvin and John, heading the procession, shot a goose this afternoon. A number of offers were made to help them eat it. Harvey Goudie and Russell Groves have each a little hunting dog. This afternoon Harvey's "Tough" set up a big racket. Harvey can tell by his bark whether it's partridges or a porcupine. He said it was porcupine this time and sure enough it was. Porcupine, singed right down to the flesh and well stewed, are better eating than they look.

Tough is an ancient veteran who got his nickname from a very appropriate set of circumstances. Harvey was carrying the dog's mother in a gamebag on his back one cold winter day when Tough and his two sisters were born. By the time Harvey got to his tilt that evening the pups looked frozen stiff, so he pitched them out in the snow. After a while he heard one of them whine, so he brought the little fellow in and put him near the stove. It was Tough, and when he had thawed out he was immediately christened. A short-haired dog, Tough has a hard time living through each winter. He has to be allowed in the tilts at night in winter, since he can't bunk out in the snow like a husky or a long-haired dog. They curl their tails over their noses and sleep as peacefully as lambs. Tough hasn't any tail to reach even half way to his nose. He got it out over the flap of the bag on that eventful first day and it froze off. In a tilt or a tent Harvey says he is the greatest foot warmer than ever lived. He never eats anything he shouldn't and never knocks anything down. He can step around among a maze of plates, cups, kettles, and a wobbly candlestick without grazing a thing. Several times he's received scatterings of No. 3 shot when he wouldn't come back from partridges at a call. Before he learned that only a wolverene is clever enough to flick a porcupine upside down and rip its belly, he got enough quills in him to kill most dogs. On a cold winter day, crossing a wind-blown lake Tough will race way ahead out of sight. After a while, when Harvey gets across, there will be the dog, sitting behind a point or under the trees waiting "in the lun." He knows Harvey's several paths like a book and is handy guide in the short December days when it's too dark at four o'clock to see the blazes on the trees. Tough will trot along about three steps ahead and go straight for the tilt. Poor old fellow got his nose broken by a chunk of wood once when he tried to bite somebody and, in consequence, wheezes and snores like an old gentleman with asthma. He swam the river three or four times this week when we crossed and Harvey couldn't find him to take him aboard. One winter coming down Tough got lost or strayed too far away hunting. Harvey spent several hours calling and looking for him, then gave him up as done for. But Tough came 200 miles down the river by himself, hunting his living somehow and picking up partridge bones around the camping places. Some one found him in the Hope's lonely little house just below Muskrat Falls. Tough, who was used to stopping there on his way down the river, had jumped through a window and fallen asleep on a feather bed.

September 19.

THIS morning as we went by Jo Blake's cabin on a bank just below a big island, we went ashore and left some flour, baking powder, split peas, pork and tea, for coming down. This is his "house," his biggest cabin and headquarters by the main river. From here his paths go out in all directions and perhaps he isn't here more than three days in every ten. Jo won't be up for a couple of weeks yet, as he doesn't have to worry about the ponds on the portage, which freeze up long before the river. His house is on a high, steep sandbank, fully eighteen feet above the river, but at times of unusually high water in the spring when the river was dammed down below by ice and backed up, it has been possible to paddle right into the cabin in a canoe.

Alvin was with me today and we poled a place first time where a couple of the others got swept back twice. It was pure luck, but we almost burst with conceit, nevertheless. Kay steered it while John tracked her. She's getting handier with a paddle. John says she's as good as a man and better than some. She looks like a man in her boots and breeches, flannel shirt, canvas coat, and worn felt hat.

Mornings and evenings are getting pretty cold. There was ice on a water kettle this morning. We most always start off with woollen mittens on. They generally get wet, but even wrung out they are somehow better than nothing.

The next ordeal is going to be Upper Mouni's and the Devil's Hole. We have to cross the river twice just above some bad rapids and we have no spare paddle in case we break one. I've been meaning to make a birch one, but there is never time. If we get windbound on the big lake, Winnikapau, Fred Goudie says he'll make one for me, but we won't need one then.

Harvey and Ralph got two black ducks today. They played cards for them tonight and John and Alvin won them but gave them back. Most every evening there is a big game of "auction forty-five" or an odd form of casino. Generally the stakes are muskrat skins which are to be paid when

43

caught, if ever. This evening Arch said he didn't want to be boss any more. So they played to see who would be boss. Alvin won, and they all rolled on the ground shrieking with laughter. Harvey is twenty-four now and he's hardly missed a year up the river since he was ten. Fred, who is forty-five, has been up more than thirty times; counting his fall and spring trips, John has made twelve trips. Cecil Goudie is only seventeen, but has been up twice; Victor Goudie likewise. Russell Groves, nineteen, has made himself a new path in unknown country 300 miles from home, also Gordon Pottle, twenty-three. Henry Baikie, thirty-two, had been up the river before Alvin was born and Arch has lost count —all these men who know the river high water, low water, fall, winter or spring-breakup time, individual rocks, eddies, points, cliffs, better than the lines in their own palms— bossed by Alvin, who doesn't know what's around the next bend. They pretend to take it very seriously and ask him with exaggerated gravity just where he wants to camp tomorrow night.

We've camped in some lovely spots on bluffs and wooded islands, in grassy glades under huge old trees, beside brooks and on beaches. Some of the best times are in the evening when the tents are up, the fires alight, something cooking that smells good, and the blue smoke rising from every little stove pipe, curling up among the branches. The *chuck, chuck* of an axe sounds a little way off through the woods. Sunset reddens the lonely river to wine and fades away. Off there toward the dim west, over the brooding, ageless hills you could go for a thousand miles and not meet a single white man; probably not even a stray Indian family. No one has ever made the trip straight west across that inaccessible mid-

Photograph by Varick Frissell

ALL THESE MEN KNOW THE INDIVIDUAL ROCKS, EDDIES, POINTS AND CLIFFS BETTER THAN THE LINES IN THEIR OWN PALMS

dle wilderness, that Never Never Land from here to Hudson's Bay. Nothing has ever tarnished that bright coin of adventure.

We seem to be trembling on the brink of all that, here where the green hills are sharpening to black knife-edges that cut the sky. Now it's dark, and the candle-lit tents are luminous, ghost-white in the trees. Some one is yelling to John to bring over the cards, and somebody else is humming. A frying pan bangs on a tin stove. Pretty soon Harvey will wrap his calloused hands around a tiny mouth organ and a lovely Hungarian waltz will trip among the shadows, then "Irish Eyes, sure they'll steal your heart away," and "The Girl I Left Behind Me." Twenty years ago some Finnish lumberjacks brought that Hungarian waltz to this country and now it is part of the meagre inheritance. Beauty, the gypsy wanderer.

Some evenings we all sing and John will occasionally roar us a solo of "The Letter Edged in Black." Sometimes they get Katherine to sing "The Cheery Lights of Home" or "A Perfect Day" or "Believe Me if All Those Endearing Young Charms." When she gets through they want it over again. Alvin made her write the words on a piece of birch bark so he could learn them.

September 23.

SOME bad times since last I wrote. In our camp at Mouni's Island we had the ridge pole of the tent tied to a big fir with spikey dead branches all around its base. I went out of the tent last thing in the evening to get water from the river and rammed one in my eye. The first thing I thought of was an Indian I've seen, who lost his eye that very way.

However, I escaped with a cut eyelid and a closed eye for two days.

We left Mouni's Island before daylight, and Kay did herself proud that day. No one had ever seen Upper Mouni's and the Devil's Hole so bad before.

Alvin doesn't like the swift water much and is very excitable. It is quite natural, since he has had the tale of his brother's drowning, up above here, pounded into him so many times. He asked me to steer in the swift places, which was hard on him, for it was nearly all tracking, being too deep to wade or pole, and nearly all swift. He had a dreadful cold and I took the line in all the medium places to give him a spell. It seems sometimes as though the river is breathing, and between its mighty breaths you can get ahead; or as though the strength of the current comes in invisible surges, now strong, now a little weaker, now strong again. We got along somehow, but he used to get hung for minutes together on the crest of a rise. Sometimes he'd lie face down in the rocks, sobbing for breath and holding on. I felt sure he wouldn't be able to do it, and the rocks looked bad astern. Then he'd get up on his hands and knees and, fighting for every inch, creep painfully ahead. Now and then we'd come to a strong up-eddy below such a place. He'd get in while we swooped around the crescent of the cove. When we paddled across the river the first time, the boiling current hit the nose and twisted us almost straight downstream. We made the water fly, getting her straight for the other shore. We lost about a quarter of a mile and so did everybody else. It's hard to calculate the best angle for crossing in places like this. You're sure to lose ground however you go, and if you head upstream too much you take longer to cross and lose more than ever.

After the first boil-up we struck the toughest tracking we had ever seen, and got left almost out of sight. It wasn't until the afternoon that we caught up and heard that Kay had steered one of the toughest places in Grand River— a woman, impossible! In a place where a slip meant you lost your canoe and maybe your life. No one thought she could do it, except John, who just told her to jump in and have a try. She said she wasn't frightened a bit, and I believe it, for if she had been frightened she could never have done it. It takes catlike concentration, for the current tearing at the bow is constantly swinging it one way or the other. You lean on your paddle this way and that, tense as a spring, for if she swings off only three or four points you can't bring her back, she swings off more till the power of the current strikes her broadside and the man on the line can't hold her. Things happen quick in a rapid. That's the joy of it, I suppose.

Fred Goudie took me aside and told me honestly I shouldn't let John take such chances. It all seemed to be a little secret between her and John, and they didn't say anything in a way that shouted, "Oh, we do this every day for exercise." I didn't know what to say to Fred, so I said nothing. But I might have said somewhat thus: We are here. We knew what we were getting into. We've got to take our chances with the river like everybody else. John knows what he is doing. He knows she's got that iron something that never wavers in the pinches. It would be different with some one else. If she is growing strong and skilful I am glad. Should she stay at home forever washing dishes

47

and diapers? That is safe enough. Why should it be considered touching and beautiful when husbands coddle their wives into a state of whining incompetency? Why should wives teach their husbands to be careful? They should teach each other to dare, not to fear. For to dare is to grow. If this were some mere acquaintance, some boy whom I had never seen before, and might never see again, I would say this day had done him good. I would be glad with him that he had licked the rapid and grown stronger in quickness and self-proven courage. But because it is my wife that has steered the rapid, I am expected to be sorry. While we live we are going to try to live, when we're dead we'll think about it. We don't always live up to these high-flown principles, but today we have.

Above the Hole we passed two famous swift places, Baikie's Nose and Sweat Drops. The latter is so named for obvious reasons; the former is named for Tom Baikie, who was a tracker for one of the Hudson's Bay Company's big, flat, river boats that they used to bring up to the Big Hill every fall. The Company had posts way above here in those days, Fort Nascaupee on Lake Petitsikapau, a post on Michikamau and another at the head of Winnikapau, but they've been abandoned now for nearly sixty years. Fifteen men on the line tracked this boat. Some of them were Hudson's Bay Company servants and some were Montagnais and Nascaupee Indians whose families never left the interior. The trackers had to swim the big brooks that come into the river, and wade a lot of others waist deep. Their boots were so constantly full of water they often cut holes in them to let the water keep draining out. An Iroquois Indian named Louie steered the boat with an enormous stern oar and up forward was a man on a block and tackle so rigged that the tracking line's pull could instantly be switched from nearly amidships to the tip of the bow if she took a dart out. It must have been a great sight to see them all heaving on the line, and the boat right out in the middle of it. Tom Baikie was doing his share of the heaving when the line parted and he broke his nose on a rock.

After the boil-up it was decided in a council of war that when we got to the lower end of Winnikapau, if it was calm we would go on all night. At Winnikapau the river broadens out into a thirty-five-mile lake, walled in by mountains. The lake gets very rough in a breeze of wind, much too rough for a canoe loaded deep. Good landing places are scarce. It is windy so much of the time in the fall that it is not unusual to be held windbound on the lake for three or four days. Some five canoes in the last ten years have swamped on Winnikapau.

When we reached the two gaunt giants that stand like gateposts at the mouth of the lake, we fortified ourselves with more tea. And it was calm, flat as glass, not a ripple. We put on dry clothes, as we were mostly soaked from wading canoes at the upper end of the hole. A peaceful sunset lit the head of the lake; it was dark when we paddled out around Long Point. At eleven we were all freezing cold and went ashore to make a big fire and get warm. Then the seven canoes stole along again over the quiet lake like phantoms, only the glow of a pipe bowl and the endless *chunk plunk* of the paddles, trying to keep two ripples at the bow instead of one. I used to look at a star to keep headed right. It seemed as though we were conscious of the mountains, their monstrous weight, but could not see them. We paddled

49

as you would walk, without thinking about it at all. Only we wondered if we could hold out, for we were tired when we started. Our fingers got so cramped around the paddle we had to uncrook them with the other hand. A cramp knotted my arm, but went away again. Sometimes we nodded, fell half asleep, and woke up paddling. We thought we couldn't take another stroke, and hours later were still paddling. It grew darker, so that we lost the shore and all sense of progress. We had no idea that we were moving toward a goal where we would stop. No, we were simply enduring. Some day perhaps it would be over. At one o'clock Kay couldn't paddle any more. John and Alvin came alongside and she crawled aboard them and slept on the flour bags. I kept up alone for a few minuntes and then dropped far behind. After a while a little breeze came up astern. I put up the tarpaulin on a paddle which I held up with my feet. I washed my face in the cold water to keep awake. It was lovely, somehow, sailing along on a strange lake, alone at night, hardly knowing where I was going, hardly caring. By and by I saw a light. Some of them were stopped at somebody's tilt. It was all very confused. The wind was rising. Three canoes had gone on. Two were staying. John said we could go on. Kay came back with me, refreshed and strong. All the time it was getting rougher. We went out around one huge sheer cliff that looked 2,000 feet high in the darkness. Waves that gleamed white were slamming up against its base. Going around we shipped a lot of water, for the wind was just wrong and we had to take the seas broadside to get along. There looked like no place to get ashore, all sheer cliffs ahead. We were nearly half full and bailing all the time. John's canoe was to leeward of us and

Photograph by Varick Frissell

WINNIKAPAU—IT WAS CALM, FLAT AS GLASS

I yelled to him that we had to get ashore, we could never make it around the next cliff. Just inside of it there appeared to be a cove. Its shore was a rocky talus slope on an angle of forty-five degrees.

We jumped out to the waist in water and commenced heaving the load onto the rocks. One man couldn't hold a canoe off, the waves were rolling in so big. It seemed both canoes would surely be beaten to bits before we got them unloaded. Cans, bags, guns, stove, paddles, kettles, tents, axes, snowshoes, boots, lard, all hither and yon over the rocks in the dark. Some of them we never did find again. When we got the canoes carried up they weren't damaged much. It commenced to rain. Our bread was paste. Kay was making some more over an open fire when daylight started to show over the hills across the lake. John rolled up in his bearskin and slept by the fire in the rain, with a rock for a pillow. I got the tent up after a while on a slope like the side of a house. We slept for a couple of hours, when we heard a hail. The other two canoes were going by. The wind had dropped. John said we'd better go, it might blow again. So we pulled down the tent, threw our battered gear aboard again and paddled about three hours to the head of the lake. Every one was there, camped in a bight beside a brook, saluting the Sabbath air with snores. It wasn't long before we joined the chorus.

Monday morning a beautiful fair wind filled our tarpaulin sail like a balloon while we reclined and sped. Arch showed us the ruin of the Hudson's Bay post near Fox Island. A few bricks from the old oven, some rotten logs, and a grown-over path are about the only traces left.

WE gallop along so fast there is scarcely time for anything. The canoe is leaking from scrapes and cuts on rocks. Occasionally there is time to dry the canvas around the cut by taking a brand and blowing its heat on the bad spot. If it is dried this way, resin will stick on. But generally we slap on some butter or lard, which does well enough until it gets rubbed off. We put sticks in the bottom to lift the flour bags a few inches up out of the water, but even so everything is wet. The guns are getting rusty, and long ago everything small was lost and everything breakable broken.

We come to miles and miles of sandy beaches, where we race along with the tracking line. Then long stretches of scallops, where between each strong point a circular eddy makes an up-current near the bank. We sneak out from behind a point, pushing and paddling for dear life, and sometimes if we don't say a word we can sneak by before old lady Grand River knows we are trying to put one over on her. But sometimes the trees on shore commence to walk backward and it's get out the pole and dig. Paddle and pole and line, food and sleep, are all of life almost.

Alvin and I are together most of the time these days. We've taken the heavier load, but John does marvels with his pole while Kay does all she can with a paddle. Sometimes he throws us his line and one of us can track him 'round a point. But generally we are too far behind to help anybody. The most discouraging thing is to fall, by a series of minor mishaps and clumsinesses, so far behind that when we arrive at a boil-up place, starving for our mug-up, the rest are leaving.

Kay and I each got a partridge last evening. Fresh bear

tracks are everywhere in the sand. Fred Goudie was stalking one when Tough barked. He had a long running shot and missed. My stomach feels cheated yet at the proximity of unattainable bear steak.

Whenever I am tired or discouraged late in the afternoon, I think of the subway rush that is on now; Times Square and the people jammed against the platform bars, the clank of the chains as the guards unhook them and the wild mob fights its way into a car. Then I look around and feel better. No matter what any one says, men in the cities spend their lives and win their bread fighting other men. In primitive places they fight nature and are drawn to other men by the common battle. The difference in character and viewpoint between a hunter and a salesman is as fundamental and irreconcilable as though they lived on different planets.

To ascend this road of beauty, this silent, immaculate river, to see every day, every hour, some new spruce island by whose rocky shore the silver water croons, some bar piled high with white pebbles in the spring floods and plowed by the ice, some foam-crested rapid in the sunset, some quiet cove of birches at noon; to feel a part of it, to be a part of every sand bank and driftwood stump and shadow of mountain and ripple, costs something. It costs in back-breaking toil, in sweat and shivering cold, in hunger and wet, in aching, knotted muscles. The price is pain. The question is, have you grit enough to love it or must you hate it.

We had a big session with "Black Bartlemy's Treasure" this evening. It is a blood-and-thunder pirate yarn that Arch brought along. It seems I'm no marvel with a pole, but I've got the most book larnin', so they've elected me to read the hair-raiser aloud. We get in Harvey's new tent, because that's the biggest. I can have the candle anywhere I want. Generally Harvey is baking tomorrow's bread, a nightly chore with everybody. The tale unfolds to the accompaniment of a scraped frying pan and a flipped river cake. We read five chapters and disposed of nearly a dozen villains this evening. Tressady with the hook is more of a favorite than the heroine, I think. I'm hard put to it to explain just what a culverin looks like and how you fight with a cutlass and what a fair maiden really does when she languishes. We have tons of fun and break up swearing we won't any of us sleep a wink. Fred warns his tent mate that if he rolls against him in the night he'll slit him like a fish. There is no doubt about it, that fella Martin can swim just like a otter.

September 26.

WE are on top of the Big Hill portage tonight, looking back with respect and awe at that three-quarters of a mile of slippery, nearly vertical path down to the river. We have left the deep valley of the river and are up on the plateau. This is the beginning of the inner wilderness, a beginning that exacts the most painful toil. There is not a neck in camp that isn't stiff, not a leg that doesn't ache, not a man that will admit either. We crawled on our hands and knees, we cursed and sweat and never stopped.

This simple path is almost as great and true a monument to the pioneer spirit as a pioneer man. It rises 700 feet in a quarter of a mile and near the top it is so close to the vertical that there is real danger of falling back over, especially when carrying a canoe. Up this on some tortured back has come every one of the thousands of traps above the Big Hill, every tin stove, every Dutch oven, every bag of flour that ever nourished a hunter of this far country. Beyond this point every article of God's manufacture, or man's, undergoes a change in status. The value of merchandise is not calculated here by the currency of any nation on earth, but by weight and utility. A pound of tea is worth more than a diamond ring and ten pounds of flour is worth more than twenty pounds of gold. It took us the greater part of a day to transport our gear this terrible quarter of a mile.

To see an inverted canoe moving slowly up the hill on a stalk of two small legs is enough to make you believe there's nothing a man can't do. John did it by himself, and looked pretty sick when it was over. Alvin and I carried ours double and so did all the other men. John has more to carry because we are with him; perhaps two more loads than the other men every stage. It is hard to convey an idea of the additional suffering this simple statement means. But he never mentions it and goes to work as though he were glad of the chance to prove his superhuman strength, and I believe he is.

This is the first stage of the portage around the Grand Falls. It will take us about a week to make this semicircular series of carries between lakes, ponds, and brooks out around and back to the river again. The falls, which are nearly twice as high as Niagara, have never been seen by more than fifty white men and one white woman. According to A. P. Low, Canadian geologist and explorer, in his report of 1895, the falls are guarded above by five miles of wild rapids and below by the Bowdoin Canyon, a rock gorge more than eight miles long and between 500 and 600 feet deep; below this there are 12 miles more of rapids. The Big Hill portage, which leaves the river about 24 miles below the falls, represents roughly, at its top, the height of the falls and the rapids above and below them. We are on the same level as the upper river, as we start on the half-moon trail studded with jewels of water. This four-mile carry in to the first pond is the longest of the lot. After that the twenty-odd portages between water gradually diminish in length.

As though to disprove my theories of eternal brotherhood in the wilds, the boys have started competing in dead earnest. It's a race, with signs of bitterness already, to see which team will get its load up the hill and in to the pond first. Tonight we were carrying loads in the dark that would break a pack mule's back. It is something that has to do with their Labradorman's code that says, "I am not tired, I am not hungry, I am steel." I've seen them with their tongues hanging out, their knees trembling with exhaustion, and their stomachs rumbling so loud with emptiness that the appeals of that miserable organ for food were plainly audible to a bystander, and they'd say, "Hell, I aren't tired. Want to go on?" It was not a question, it was a challenge.

I saw Arch lose his temper today, a phenomenon I had hitherto believed impossible. Like most of us he had his butter tubs, lard pails, and "odd stuff" tied, by means of the tracking line and a tarpaulin, into a big bundle. With this and a flour bag he was toiling up the slope ahead of me this evening when a five-pound lard pail squeezed out of the bundle, rollicked down the hill, and bounced far off among the trees. He had taken four loads up the hill, and this was his last. He turned, with his load on his back and that peculiar peering-out-from-under-the-eyebrows expression that goes with a head strap. "Damn that kittle a lard," he said, between gritted teeth. "I ain't goin' back after it if I goes without grease for the rest of my life." Then the march went on.

We left some bags of grub in Edward Michelin's tilt at the foot of the Big Hill, so that by what we have eaten up and left along the river for going down, our load is reduced nearly one-third.

While we were making camp last night in the dark, Kay was limbing brush for the tent and cut her left thumb with the axe right to the bone. The rocks were spattered with blood. The cut goes right into the first joint and looks as though it might result in permanent stiffness. It bothers her all the time, night and day.

So far the portage is toil and bloody sweat; fine for the cultivation of a bullneck and very bad for the intellect.

September 30.

WE got into the Big Lake this afternoon and paddled seven blessed miles to our camping place beside a brook and waterfall that feeds the lake. Kay tries to paddle, but she shouldn't, as it tends to open her cut thumb. This lake seemed vaster than the ocean after some of the three-foot brooks and tiny puddles we've been in. A pool here below the cascade is swarming with whitefish, and we shot enough this evening to last us for two days. Whitefish sizzling over an open fire and the brook tinkling out music!

This is our fifth night on the portage and tomorrow we should get out to the river again. We are all twice as strong as when we started, and carry three of the forty-eight-pound flour bags regularly, on the level. Sometimes we carry four and John has once tried five. He showed me the moss-covered rock where he slipped with his load and fell four years ago and ruptured himself. That was quite a good joke, he assured me. When he carries the canoe he says that isn't heavy enough to keep his feet on the ground, so he gets it up on his shoulders and then has some one sling a flour bag across the top. Kay has been carrying seventy pounds regularly—a flour bag and a twenty-odd pound rice bag. She helps us even more materially by carrying the odd stuff that will not fit into any kind of a snug bundle, the guns and axes, the snowshoes, the lard pails and butter tubs, the tin oven and sleeping bags. When going along a slippery path with 150 pounds it is a calamity to have a lard pail, which was balanced on the top, fall off. If one is tired and kneels to pick it up, the straightening of one's knees again is a problem. We generally make stages of about a quarter of a mile and get everything to that point before carrying on to the next stage. To reach the spot, dump off one's load, and walk back light is the most exquisite pleasure.

For three days we kept up the bitter race, and at the end of that time Ralph and Harvey had pretty conclusively proved that they could leave us all if they wanted. At that point they were two ponds ahead of the rest of us. John would have been with them but for his various human and inhuman impedimenta. When everybody had proved to everybody else that he was a veritable elephant incarnate, we commenced to enjoy life again. The let-up was hastened by Arch's misfortune in straining his back so that he could hardly walk, not to mention carry anything. After that, whoever got his loads across first would go back and help Victor, Arch's beaming, imperturbable canoe-mate of the fat red cheeks.

Poor Arch had a touch of consumption some years ago, and it seemed as though it were returning. He coughed all one night in his tent. His face was ashen, his eyes had a hunted look, he couldn't paddle, he was worried sick, but he went on, saying he'd be all right in a few days. Sure enough, he seems to be nearly as good as ever today.

Many of the ponds we come to are so small it hardly seems worth while to put the stuff in and take it out again on the other side. The majority of them are of black, murky water which hides the countless sharp rocks lurking just under the surface to gore the canoes. Sometimes we go over one and the canvas screams as though it had been ripped from end to end. Fortunately the damage is never as great as it sounds. Because this is Fred Goudie's hunting ground, he knows the channels better than any one else. Somewhere in the back of his mind he carries a rough chart of all these invisible reefs. It's odd to see him zigzagging across a stretch of perfectly *bona fide* looking water, and on either side of him canoes shorn of their natural grace, heeled over in awkward attitudes on rocks.

Sometimes on boggy portage paths where we sank nearly to the knees we could feel with our feet a regular series of cross sticks under the mud. Arch told me they were old juniper sticks that Louie and his H. B. C. Indians put there long ago. He dug one up once. We found other signs of Louie at some of the reefs that bar the brooks. Rocks that must have taken two or three men to lift, had been pulled out of the barrier and piled one side to leave a little channel just big enough for a canoe to squeeze through. Sometimes it wasn't quite big enough, but by listing her down on one side right to the gunnel we could edge her through. At

59

half a dozen such reefs where there was no channel, we had to take everything out, lift the canoe two steps across and put everything in again. If only old Louie were here with us now he'd break a way through every reef. He had become a kind of legendary figure, like the French Canadian's beloved Paul Bunyan. No one else could manage Louie's big stern oar for the river boat, and he used to carry two barrels of flour and a canoe up the Big Hill, puffing meditatively at his pipe. In fifty years more Louie will be doing great things.

Even in sober reality this Indian must have been a remarkable man, of great value to the Hudson's Bay Company. For he was technician, foreman and slave driver in the tremendous yearly enterprise of supplying those most distant, most inaccessible posts on the shores of Michikamau and Lake Petitsikapau. Fort Nascaupee on Lake Petitsikapau, at the edge of the barren grounds, was situated almost in the center of the Labrador peninsula and one of the most difficult posts to reach that the Company ever maintained in this country. From North West River with heavy loads the trip must have taken nearly two months. It was largely because of the distance and the rapids and portages that Michikamau and Petitsikapau were abandoned in 1873. I can imagine with what joy Louie and his voyageurs were received each summer, for these posts were on permanent short rations and never free of the fear of starvation. The servants hunted by far the greater part of their living or went hungry. Perhaps it was they who started the Louie legend.

As we paddled up the lake this afternoon we could see a curiously shaped cloud, which Fred told me was vapor rising from the Grand Falls, nine miles away. Here in the tent, if I put my ear close to the ground, I can hear the mighty water thundering.

"HOME again," Fred Goudie yelled this evening as we beached the canoes in front of his house, back on the river again. He is the first of us to get to his hunting ground, and we will miss him when we go on tomorrow. It is no wonder he calls it home, he has spent so many months of his life here at this little log shack surrounded by stumps and piles of chips, broken sleds, remains of paddles, bones. I've seen lots of men in their homes at North West River, with plenty of chairs around, sit all evening on the floor with their backs to the wall. When I asked one of them why he did it he said he found it more comfortable, being used to sitting that way in his tilts away in the woods.

Fred has spent many springs here alone, waiting for open water to run his canoes down, the only man about the Big Hill. Two years ago he and Harvey hauled their canoes on sleds across the Big Lake the 25th of June. Thirty years ago when he made this place there was hardly another trapper about the Big Hill. On that first trip it took them ten days to find their way across the portage. Indians resented the encroachment of the North West River trapper, stole his traps and threatened to burn his tilts.

In one of those early years Fred and his brother Charlie were off to their traps down by the Grand Falls. When they returned they found the tilt cleaned out. Indians had taken three bags of flour and all the peas, beans, tea, sugar, and cartridges in the place. It looked like a desperate time for

Fred and Charlie. The two men rested for a few hours after their appalling discovery that the tilt was looted. Then they put on their snowshoes and swung off on the Indians' two-day-old track. Fred had a .44 rifle and Charlie a muzzle-loader, and they meant business. For two days and nights they chased the track, rarely stopping to boil some tea and doze by the fire for an hour or so. They had no sled, no tent, nor blanket, nothing to hinder them except a light game bag each, their guns, and one axe. Through valleys, across hills and lakes they kept up the hour-after-hour relentless pace, fearful lest a snow come and blot out the track they were following. In everything they read signs of the Indians' haste, camps far apart, few boil-up places, long snowshoe steps. On the second evening they came to a wooded glen where the Indians had made a cache to speed their flight. Nets, kettles, two stoves, a tent, but no food. The two men cut up the nets, burned the tent and smashed the kettles and stoves. Then they had to turn back, for they were nearly out of grub. Fred tells me he was glad when they turned back, for he would almost as soon starve as shoot a man, and he knows if they had seen the Indians they would have shot them. Early in the fall he had cached a few cartridges and a little flour on an island a mile from the house. The cache saved them. On the way down the river they ate, among other things, fox legs, jays, and tainted fish.

The country is very different here from that below the Big Hill. The trees are much smaller, mostly black or white spruce, with a few junipers. There is very little balsam or birch. They told me that up on the Height of Land there was almost as much water as land, and it certainly gives that impression. The river spreads out into dozens of channels among myriads of islands. The absence of prominent land-marks, and the many different ways of getting to the same place, make it very hard to find one's way.

The geese truly blackened the sky today, rising in companies of six and eight hundred from every island we passed. We all took different routes among the islands, cautiously stealing around every point with our guns ready and our mouths watering, but not one of us got a goose. Generally in large flocks they are wild, but these are exceptionally so. Their kronking filled the sky until dark, when we shook our fists at them and sat down to fish and tea.

October 3.

WAVES so high their curling crests broke at the level of the treetops—that's the way Louie's Rapid looked this morning as we paddled toward the lower end of its long white slant. The shimmering mirage or "loom" which hung islands in the sky and twisted them upside down, lifted the rapid up and stretched it out of all proportion. When we came nearer, the vision disappeared and left the rapid to its true form, which is bad enough.

For a light canoe that can be poled in and out among the boulders near the shore it is not a bad rapid, but for a heavy one that must keep out near the main whirl, it is nearly as bad as Gull Island. The other boys are all in single canoes now, having picked up old resin-smeared wrecks that they left on scaffolds by the lake shores last spring. Each man has to have a canoe for himself up here to hunt his place in the early fall. Alvin and I being the heaviest and the clumsiest, got broadside on a rock first thing. It was paralyzing to think that only two days from our goal we might get swamped. The current heeled her down until the water was almost coming in, and Alvin was screeching like a madman. We climbed out on the slippery boulder and jumped on the other gunnel to right her. Lying flat on the boulder, our combined strength was just enough to push her a quarter of an inch upstream broadside, but that quarter of an inch enabled us to slip her past the rock and swing her stern downstream. We drifted back, went ashore and carried more than half our gear to the head of the rapid, along the rocks and across a deep brook that soaked us. Another man got in with John and they poled it while Kay carried what they had taken out. Harvey and Ralph offered to pole our canoe through for us, but we'd have died first. With line and pole we got her up somehow, just as the last of the other canoes disappeared around a bend half a mile away. I try to think it is a compliment, their leaving us; they know we are competent enough not to drown ourselves. But I'm not sure even of that.

We found our ship had been cut on a rock and was leaking nearly as fast as we could bail. This necessitated unloading everything and smearing a mixture of butter and curses on the cut.

When we got to the boiling-up place every one had eaten and gone except John and Kay. As we crammed some bread and tea we hastily told of our prowess in the rapid. John grinned and said, "Uh."

At sunset on a quiet, long straight shore of sand we came to Victor's house, an old rotten cabin with the roof fallen in.

This is Saturday night and we are not going on tomorrow. Just finished Black Bartlemy and left Martin, marooned on an island, mourning his beloved. I am commissioned to send for the sequel as soon as ever we get down. What luxury to roll in one's bag and pull the soft wool up around one's face, knowing we do not have to leave at dawn tomorrow.

October 4.

Aroused by John yelling, "Hey, where's your .22, there's a couple of partridges back here," I gave it to him, and when he came back with the partridges I asked him why he didn't use his own.

"Well, ya see," he said, "if I shoots my own gun on Sunday I can't never kill nothin' with it any more and I got to trade with somebody else or buy a new one. But it won't hurt your one for you."

I had known for a long time that most people will not hunt on Sunday unless they are starving, and that many a trapper has let a Sabbath-promenading silver fox trot by unharmed, but this was a way of fooling the divinity that was news to me. John told me that Robert and lots of others found it the same with their guns. The summer he and Rob were guiding Varick Frissell up Grand River, Rob gave Frissell the choice of ceasing to hunt on Sundays or turning back—very friendly, but very firm. Scotch Presbyterian ancestors are certainly Scotch Presbyterian ancestors. Eskimo blood and influence are powerless before them. I tried with small success to explain that perhaps Sabbath observance is psychological and physiological as well as religious; that man needs a rest and a change from his regular bread-winning occupation one day a week; that perhaps it is all right for me to sew on Sunday, because that is the only day I ever do sew, whereas for a woman with a big family,

65

who is forced to sew late into every night, Sunday sewing would be wrong; that for a sportsman to hunt on Sunday for the fun of it may be all right, where for a trapper whose weekly business it is, it would be all wrong.

All afternoon we were picking redberries on some rolling, treeless hills across the river. Everywhere in the moss were tracks and signs of bear. I had John's Remington .35, but saw no fat, roly-poly bear sweetened by a diet of berries to use it on.

These redberries, or partridge berries, are a Labrador staple that takes the place of fruit and vegetables in many a home. September berry-picking time is the nearest thing to a vacation for Labrador families. They take a tent and stove, and pile into a rowboat bound for the berry banks somewhere. The flies are gone and the summer thunder showers. Days are cool and sunny, nights are cold. The birches are flaming and the millions of berries are firm and ripe. Somehow there is a holiday spirit about it that is not like other work. Fathers romp with their children and the little ones in faded overalls run laughing over the fields like zigzagging blue butterflies. Sometimes they take home two barrelsful. Over the winter the berries freeze and will keep until next summer if the family doesn't tuck away too much redberry pie and jam. In many homes redberries are the only confection, the only luxury.

October 5.

WE all stopped today to help Victor build a new house. Everybody cut and carried two or three wall logs to the site, while Harvey and Victor notched and fitted them. The walls rose up like magic and when evening came the ridgepole was in place and the gable ends up. Victor will have to chink it with moss and make a door, put on the "rifters," chink them and cover them with sheets of birch bark laid on like shingles to make the roof tight. Then he'll have to make his bunk against the back wall and fit the tiny panes of glass that were in the old tilt into his new window. His house will be about eight by nine inside.

I always think how marvellous it is that one of these men, with no tool but an axe, and no materials but those nature provides, can put up a snug, dry cabin so quickly. Eight spikes are a help to secure the first rafters which support the ridgepole and the gable ends, but they are not necessary. The doorway is seldom more than waist high, as it is a bother to hew out very many boards for the door, the tilt is weakened by cutting too many logs and too much cold comes in around a big door. If they have time, some men peel all the logs that go into their tilts. Bark holds moisture and makes the logs rot quicker. All corner notches are in the under side of each log, so they won't hold moisture. Some tilts last for fifty years. Some men's houses have floors of squared logs, but most have just brush on the hard-tramped ground. For nearly all of them the rafters are peeled and the inside walls chopped square. This makes the whole inside of new white wood and there is twice as much light as though it were of dark bark. Each one has its tin shoe box of a stove and its rickety stovepipe sticking through the roof.

Victor's traps take him down the river to Fred's and up the river as far as John's, so we'll see him once in a while. Perhaps after snow we will go with him on his path southward to Unknown Lake and there meet Harvey and Arch, who will show us the Unknown Falls.

October 6.

WE are "home" at John's cabin, high on a bank overlooking a four-mile island. We've done it.

October 11.

JIM GOUDIE and Walter Blake spent last night with us and went on in the morning toward the new paths they made last year, about seventy miles north. We thought we were all alone, just John and Kay and I, when toward evening we heard a stentorian "Hello!" from the river. They each have a canoe. Walter's is a small one that he left above the Big Hill last spring and picked up when they reached there a week ago. Jim is in the huge twenty-foot thing that brought them both that far. He has made a pair of spruce oars and sits in the middle, rowing hard to keep up with Walter. They were only a day behind us and used our camping places all the way up. Sometimes the ashes were warm, until Winnikapau, where they got windbound for three days.

Jim is another old-timer, Fred's and Arch's brother. He can build a boat or a canoe, fix clocks, watches, guns, make ovens and do anything with tin. I was trying to make some breadloaf baking pans for our small tin oven, and he showed me how to go about it. I told him how wild the geese are and he said he is sure they are among the cutest things alive. They can see better than a man with a good glass, hear better than a bear and smell better than a fox. I never knew geese could smell and he says most people don't know it either, but he has often been stalking them down the wind, when they smelled him and "fled away."

John was telling me a little this evening about the Indians' half-god whom they call the Man of the Woods. It is the Man of the Woods who sews up the caribou's eyes and makes the porcupine so pigeon-toed that you can scarcely tell by his track which way he was going. He puts out the fur and that's why some years there are no foxes and other years lots. He puts out the mink and marten, the ermine and otter, the beaver and lynx. Some years he doesn't distribute very many and some years none of one and plenty of another. He also has charge of partridges, rabbits, caribou, and fish. He seldom fails to provide plenty of fish, so they can be most depended on. Sometimes he pushes down trappers' tilts, too. They know there is such a being, for they have seen his track and he steps from hill to hill.

October 15.

THIS morning I woke up and looked at the roof and knew I was sick—fever, aching bones, hammering headache, and all the rest. I went out and tried to cut up wood, and made sure of it.

Lying in the tent all day to avoid the nauseating smell of muskrats that pervades the tilt, I got to thinking: "What a frail, miserable creature you are, you rover, you adventurer. What are you now but a querulous child, licked by a mere headache. The world is not so wide and free and doesn't stretch so endlesslee as it did yesterday. The world is warmth and a soft place to lie and a sip of water now and then. Suppose you were alone and it were winter and you couldn't cut wood and you were low on grub. Wouldn't that be thrilling, wouldn't that be adventurous. Is it any wonder some of them call it a dog's life?"

October 16.

BETTER today. John was hunting all day and came home with ten muskrat and three black ducks. The geese seem too wild to get anywhere near. Before he left he announced that the net which has been supplying us so bountifully with trout, landlocked salmon, and whitefish, was gone—torn up by an otter perhaps. When he returned he hooked it up at the outer mooring, snarled up on the bottom. And in it were an enormous pike and what he called a baby kukamish, each about three feet long and weighing around fifteen pounds. The "kukamish" seems to be a species of giant trout, and he says he has seen them six feet long. Uncle Jo told me he had seen one so big that the head made a meal for five men.

Had some Klim today and it tasted better than any fresh milk I've ever had. It seems almost miraculous to have milk here so far from cows.

The children in this country get on with surprisingly little milk. Perhaps that is one reason why their teeth are so bad. I remember Grandma Baikie telling me of one of her babies who couldn't digest mother's milk. So she fed it on pap of flour and water and sugar. They never had any nursing bottles in those days. She made one of sealskin and sewed it up watertight like a bootleg. For a nipple she used a doe caribou's teat.

October 17.

JOHN, the mighty hunter, is sick today and I am better; very superior though weak as boiled fish. I think Jim inadvertently brought us this touch of grippe, or whatever it is. Trappers away in winter are generally quite free from such ailments. Though they are cold and wet a good part of the time, they practically never get a cold while they are away in the country. But when they return to the villages they all regularly come down with heavy colds.

It was a whiff of the elemental to hear John say this morning, "Cut up some wood, b'y, get a good stack in here. Tomorrow I may not be able to get out the door and you may want to go hunting rats. Pile it right up to the roof." That is the first thought when a trapper gets sick, wood to keep the fire going. And though it is not really winter yet and only goes below freezing at night, it was instinctively John's first thought. I imagine a good many men have perished because they were too weak to cut up wood; their sickness would not have killed them, but they froze to death.

It reminds me of the story of John Pardy's brother. He used to fur the path that cuts in over the hills from Grand Lake, near Cotter's Point, some twelve miles from North West River. On one of his rounds he was a week overdue, so John went looking for him. He found his brother frozen stiff in a tent on the brow of a hill overlooking the lake. He had evidently been ill when he camped, for the trail-in showed that his last camp was but a short distance out from the previous one. However much wood he had been able to cut up he had burned, then all the sticks he had been able to crawl around to and pull down near the tent. And at last he burned the brush he was lying on.

Mrs. Bert Blake once told me another tale of life that ebbed low as the embers died from red to gray. She is a frontierswoman. When she married Bert he hadn't a canoe, or a boat, a net, gun, house, dish, or trap to his name. Gradually they won these things living in a log house at the mouth of the Nascaupee River, forty miles from the head of the bay. There were just two houses there, Bert's and a similar house belonging to one of the Michelins and his brood. One winter when both of the fathers were way up the Nascaupee at Seal Lake on their trap lines and the two women with their small children were holding the fort at the river mouth, a sudden scourge of virulent dysentery swooped down on them. It is very contagious, often fatal to children and not uncommon in this country. One by one the children fell sick, and lapsed, through sheer weakness, into a coma. The women were busy day and night trying to save their children. Then Mrs. Michelin took it. She kept up for a day with a high fever, then collapsed in her bed and couldn't rise. Mrs. Bert had no time now for those beaded moccasins she makes more skilfully even than an Indian woman, the bright-colored mitts and caps and all the clothes for her family. She was trying to take care of both houses, carrying water from the river, cooking, washing, trying to get the children to take a little bread and redberry jam or a few spoonfuls of partridge soup. One of the Michelin children, who had been in a delirium for two days, died on the day that Mrs. Bert felt the fever and ache creeping over her. The men had left plenty of wood sawed and split, in piles about fifty feet from each house. She carried as many armfuls as she could into each house and collapsed. Mrs. Michelin could just manage to crawl from her bed to the stove to put in a chunk of wood now and then, and Mrs. Bert likewise. Mrs. Bert told me that as she lay in her bed that night listening to the children's moaning, she realized it would be touch and go whether the men would come home and find them all dead or not. Neither Bert nor Joshua Michelin were expected

72

home for two weeks. Unless one of the women recovered or some one passed along soon, they were done for.

This went on for two days, with neither woman able to do much for her own children. Neither one could stand; they could only crawl, and then but a few feet at a time. They put on just enough wood to keep the fires going low. Soon the bread would be gone and some one must cook something, soon the water buckets would be empty and they must melt snow from around the door. The thought of crawling to the woodpile made Mrs. Bert tremble, for she did not know whether she would ever get back again. Mrs. Michelin in her cabin might be dead for all she knew.

Late one gray afternoon, with a light snow falling, a faint, blurred sound echoed from the river, "HellOO! HellOO!" She crept painfully to the doorway and lay there with her elbows in the snow watching three white shapes come round the bend in single file, bent forward, arms swinging with that peculiar rolling gait that goes with snowshoes and hauling a sled.

They were three trappers from up Nascaupee River, bound for home and North West River, three hungry, dirty hunters with frost-bitten faces and icicles in their scanty beards. They didn't find her lying half in the snow, weeping—not she. They found her sitting on the floor just inside the door, with her back to the wall and an apology on her lips for not having the kittle on.

Next morning in the starlight the youngest hunter was swinging down the river and out onto Grand Lake. The other two stayed to play nurse. He made the forty miles to North West River in ten hours, and two days later the Mission's hospital team pulled into the two little houses on the

73

river bank, with a nurse who had snowshoed the last fifteen miles through deep new snow while the dogs followed, to their bellies in snow, just able to haul the empty komatik and keep up with the driver and the nurse breaking trail. Three Michelin children died.

October 18.

WE are getting the house fixed up very cosy. I have put a new wooden latch on the door and plugged up the open chinks where squirrels had the moss pulled out. Our little tin oven is very much worth the trouble of bringing it. On occasions we have baked rice pudding, baked stuffed duck and partridge, baked beans, and best of all, beautiful white or whole wheat "rose bread." After soggy old bannock, yeast bread tastes like cake. We don't have all those things at once. We go very light on our food, as we don't know how it is going to last. When we have partridges, which are our mainstay that we never get tired of, we generally stew them with a little salt pork and a little rice. This makes a fine soup, a little of which we try to save for breakfast. The soup is also fine sauce for bread and saves on the butter or lard.

Whenever we have luck with partridges we eat all the meat we want and don't eat much else. With a meat supper we often go without our tea as we would rather save it and the accompanying sugar for some time when we have no meat. We live like Indians in every way we can, for they know best. We never waste a crumb of food, for in the woods some natural superstition whispers, "If you waste today, the gods are watching and you will starve tomorrow."

I have made a new bed for Kay. The tilt is crowded with

74

three of us in it and all our endless belongings, so it had to be something that could be put out of the way in the daytime. It is a stretcher made out of dry spruce poles and an old canvas tarpaulin. The poles bend and the canvas stretches, and altogether it is very comfortable. The inside pole is fixed to the wall and the ends of the outside pole are fitted into notches, one in the edge of John's broad, hewn-board bunk and the other in an upright stick nailed to the opposite end-wall. In the daytime the ends of the outside pole come out of the notches and we fold the whole thing up against the wall. I sleep on the broad bunk, head to feet with John. We have filled two brinbags with dry grass for mattresses and are going to save all the partridge and duck feathers after this to make a featherbed.

October 20.

JOHN tied a handkerchief tight around his aching head this morning and said he was going off for the day to set some otter traps and hunt. I went along. It was a cold, blowy morning with squalls of sleet now and then. Paddling across some of the big open stretches it was rough enough so that we shipped water. We will all be glad when freeze-up comes and we can walk everywhere and there is no wetness, only dry snow and ice. A canoe this time of year is the coldest affair that was ever invented. You sit cramped up with your aching hands hooked around the paddle and your feet in water, for all the canoes above the Big Hill are leaky. Boots are old and they soak dampness.

In the course of a long day's rambling across islands and up channels, almost to Eagle Cliff River, we shot seven muskrat and three partridges and set traps on two otter rubs.

75

A rub is a smooth, worn shoot-the-chutes down the side of a bank where the otters play, running up and sliding down like children. John says that otters make regular rounds, travelling roughly in a big circle. If you see them here today, you can depend upon it they will be back here again in two weeks' time. We set the traps right on the rubs, covering them up with grass and dry leaf dust very carefully. They were without the usual bait of rotten fish, as otters are so cute, bait more often than not frightens them away. The trap chain was fixed to one end of a pole whose other end was lashed with salmon twine to a tree. This would allow the otter considerable leeway to thrash around and give him nothing solid to pull against. So savage and strong is an otter that if the short trap chain is firmly fixed he will break his foot off and get away. For otters one needs double-spring traps, because they often bite the one spring of a single-spring trap, release the pressure on the jaws, and escape.

John looked like a pirate chief with his scrubby beard and ragged coat and the red bandanna knotted tight over his forehead. Every now and again he'd stop to tie it tighter, as he said that stopped the headache. We have a big bet on. Whoever has the longest "whisker" when we get back to North West River can pull ten hairs out of the other's chin.

John's beastly Spartanism ruffled me some as we were paddling home in the sleet. He saw me shivering and asked me if I was cold. I answered a little tartly that I was not a damn bit colder than he was. Home down a little place I call Ripple Rapid and through a lagoon which opens up at the house. A candle in the window and a fire in the stove. John says he's glad we're here and I believe him.

Kay had some partridge stew and new bread for us. After

supper a long smoke of good old plug tobacco, with the wind roaring 'round the tilt and the waves breaking on the shore. I don't wonder Indian women love their pipes. Kay is half tempted to cultivate the vice. A pipe in the woods takes the place of dessert and satisfies the craving for sweets.

October 21.

THE river is late in freezing up and the fur in getting prime. John doesn't set any more traps. He has already caught three "stage" minks; that is, the inside of the pelt is blueish black instead of almost white, as it should be when they have their winter coats. Kay shot a pure black muskrat yesterday and two partridges. She is a better shot with the .22 than either John or me. She is making a pet of a little ermine that lives in the rocks by the shore near the tilt. He pops his head up from a crevice like a little bird, and will let you come ever so close if you don't blink your eyes. The minute you wink he is gone.

I've been all day at wood, cutting long, slender, dead spruces on an island to the west and bringing them home in the canoe. There's a little dry wood a hundred yards or so back of the tilt, but we are saving that for after ice. There are also two good trees quite "handy." Often when everything close around has been cut, you will see a couple of dry, firewood trees still standing beside the tilt. They are there in case of sickness. Most trappers girdle a good many trees around their tilts each year. With the bark cut off all around, they die, and in three years make excellent firewood. No one ever cuts a tree bigger than nine inches in diameter at the butt if he can help it. They are so much harder to chop up and split.

Our net continues to give us more fish than we can eat.

John is saving some for bait. We dread the time when it will have to be "soured" over the stove.

I often think of Dillon Wallace's and Hubbard's trip from North West River in 1903, when Hubbard starved to death; of "The Lure of the Labrador Wild," and how different that tale might have been if they had had a good trout net and a native guide.

FOUND a broken Indian flat sled in the bushes to use as a pattern, and I am going to make one. We've got to have a sled for tripping around as soon as freeze-up comes. On it Kay and I will lash our tent and stove, sleeping bags, grub, kettle, axe, and gun, then ho for Unknown Lake.

A toboggan sled is a bit of pure art very much like a canoe, useful, strong, graceful. Indians invented both, and white man has never discovered anything to equal either for travelling overland in this country. If an Indian breaks his sled or canoe almost anywhere in this part of Labrador, with his axe and crooked-knife he can build another. Perhaps they took ten thousand years to evolve. In their lovely curves are the cries of ten thousand starving ones who cannot transport food or themselves; in their sharpened slenderness is the laughter in ten thousand tents where there is plenty meat. Half the beauty of a sled or canoe is its stark, essential efficiency.

Strength grows with the use of either. Running long steep rapids in his light canoe, hauling his load through hundreds of miles of white wilderness, an Indian boy learns courage and endurance. There's pride in Indian workmanship, for a life depends on these "primitive" implements; a cranky canoe swamps, and an ill-made sled breaks in the rough ice where time may be pressing.

For strength, both the canoe and sled depend on suppleness; on give, on weakness, if you like. A canoe on a rock bends or it would smash, a sled in rough ice bends nearly double over the sharp edge of an upturned ice pan. Originally there was never a nail in either one. Joints were lashed together with caribou hide, allowing the whole contrivance to "work" in time of strain, as well as bend.

With a canoe one man can transport a 900-pound load. It will stand rough water that would fill a heavy flat-bottomed rowboat. It will stand battering on rocks that would smash a rigid craft. If a hole is cut, it can be quickly patched with bark or gum. Light, it can go in three inches of water and it moves against a current much easier than a boat. It makes a shelter for a hunter without a tent. Unlike a rowboat, a hunter can propel it without a sound. In a fair wind he can sail. Its simple beauty is unsurpassed by anything that man ever made. You can carry it across miles of land, launch it, and it will carry you.

When I remember that Indians never change their underclothes, I remember also that they invented canoes.

There is one man at least who has a feeling for a canoe, and they say he is half crazy. He has a canoe way up Kenamu River, where he hunts. He is a funny old fellow and every one claims that he goes into his cabin in the country and sleeps away the winter like a hibernating bear. For six years this canoe has been up there on a scaffold and for six years she has not been in the water. One day Douglas Best said to him, "Your canoe is no good to you. Will you sell her? I would use her."

"No," said the man, "I won't sell her."

"I'll give you ten dollars," said Douglas. "What good is she to you, cracking up in the sun all summer here?"

"Well," answered the man with a feeling for a canoe, "I'm a-goin' to keep her fer the good she's done me. An' some year I'm goin' to put 'er in the river and I'm goin' to shove 'er off into the tide and let 'er go wherever she wants to, fer the good she's done me."

"And I hopes I'm down around the next bend when you does it," said Douglas, convinced that here was proof of something he had suspected for a long time.

This morning Kay and I scudded across to the long island facing the tilt, in a gale of wind. I spent all day hacking at a big juniper tree and she hunting partridges. Heavy wind all day. My dream of a lean toboggan, springy as a panther, with a beautiful curled-up nose and a long tapering stern, an Indian hunter's sled that will fit in a snowshoe track, light as a feather over frozen lakes and through the green wilderness, is fading to a presentiment of a cross-grained, awkward-looking botch that runs like a log.

October 24.

Most of the day at the juniper and finally brought home two boards for my sled. At two o'clock I was very hungry and sat down to eat a small loaf of bread I had brought. Suddenly the sky grew dull and thick, the strong wind freshened, and a blizzard from the north whirled down like some riotous dance. It was a black, smothering cloud of snow that erased the landscape in an instant. I ran down to the beach to make sure the canoe would not be blown away, for that is a calamity I fear. I had driven a picket in the half-frozen sand, turned the canoe over and tied her to the stake. The rope was stretched tight and the canoe had moved several feet. But for the stake she would certainly have been blown away. In the canoe I had brought what I thought was an empty ten-pound butter tub to sit on. It proved to be full of butter, which was a comforting thought in case I had to stay there a couple of days. I retired to the woods again, built a big fire and stretched out under a fir tree for a meal of bread and butter and a smoke. I don't know when I've ever had so much butter with my bread. It was cosy there and I wondered how long the snowstorm would last, for I could never cross the half-mile of water in that wind.

In an hour the snow suddenly stopped and the sky cleared. I put my two precious pieces of juniper aboard, loaded the canoe slightly down by the head with rocks, and started across in a side-on gale. The wind blew me nearly a mile down along shore in the course of the crossing. I pulled the canoe up among the willows, tied her on and walked up to the tilt.

Somehow the wind was fresh and the earth fair under its thin blanket of snow. Enchanted winter coming again. The white-capped waves tinkle in and out amongst the broken ice by the shore. Rocks in the coves have a round shelf of ice about them. They look like hats, a snow-covered crown and a crystal brim, cocky hats, sober hats, panamas, derbies, felts, and dunce caps. I have a hat myself, a shaggy maroon wool tam-o' shanter. It's a swashbuckling, villainous, lovely thing and when I throw it in the snow it is like a big bright flower. Frost gets into the red wool fuzz and forms white gossamer lace. At the cabin, in the warmth, the lace runs apart into silver beads.

Kay had partridge pie cooked and we ate in candle light

81

in the five-o'clock dark. A beautiful, lonely day and I love my life, every minute of it.

It is clear tonight, the stars are bright and the wind has died. One solitary north light bow arches across the glittering sky. The still water catches it up and makes a huge dim oval; the day is complete.

October 26.

OFF in the canoe this morning just after the stars had paled. A sunshiney morning iridescent with frost and ice, everywhere ice making. Shelley should be here with the frost in his long hair, writing with a pencil in his mittens and a piece of birch bark on his knee:

> "I love all that thou lovest,
>   Spirit of Delight!
> The fresh Earth in new leaves dressed,
>   And the starry night;
> Autumn evening, and the morn
> When the golden mists are born.
>
> I love snow, and all the forms
>   Of the radiant frost;
> I love waves, and winds, and storms,
>   Everything almost
> Which is Nature's, and may be
> Untainted by man's misery."

We ran through fields of crinkly new ice, plains of drifting loveliness set with jewel-like etchings in silver and black, designs of exquisite delicacy bending over the ripples that curled from our bow, sounding as we cut them a song of glass chimes in the breeze. In all the maze of million-lined tracery one design appears over and over again. It is a curve-tipped leaf, a tiny thing no bigger than my hand, a tiny thing no artist ever will or could draw, acres of them, made last night, melted this noon, in Nature's devil-may-care way that says, "That's nothing. If you live to be a million I'll take your breath away every day you keep your eyes open."

No one to feel this ice symphony but Kay and me, and maybe Shelley, gliding through the water. I often think the same of the sun sinking behind the islands. The rippled water smooths to glass and the spruces melt to black—all northern, all cold, all lonely. The air grows cold and still. A horn owl calls from a point across the water and the rapid, far away, whispers, like wind in the tree tops. A million times this has happened and a million times it will happen again with not a soul to watch its peaceful change.

Yet millions watch the movies. How can it be that men love the real world so little, and love the sham they have built so much? It does not matter, and there is no use thinking about it. I am glad they stay in the movies and do not come here.

As we paddled along, on the watch for ducks, we came around the point of an island, from the shadow into the bright sun. The point was fringed with willows, as all points are hereabouts. But these willows were iced, a blue, blinding tangle of silver network gleaming. Just inside the point lay a frozen cove on whose snow-covered surface the frost sparkled. It was as though the Man of the Woods had come down from his hilltops and bowled gigantic handfuls of diamonds across the cove, then gone away and left them winking there just for fun.

When we shot a teal and two black ducks, one of which got away, we came down to earth for a few minutes, but not for long.

Near Norrie's Point we came on a letter from a company of geese—just their footprints in the frozen mud and now-hard ice. It was a farewell message, for they have all gone south in their swift trailing V, led by a canny old gander. We've seen them going and heard their good-bye as they flew. A week ago there were hundreds of them about the channels. We scared them up everywhere we paddled. They always spotted us first and fled away in a long, ragged line, kronking derisively. There is no sound under heaven quite so derisive as a goose's kronk. A few days ago ice started forming on their shallow feeding grounds where the goose grass grows. Then we saw them overhead, in V's, for the first time. For that is the sign; when they get in formation they are bound south.

The message in the ice and mud was typical of geese, for they were laughing at us when they wrote it, I know. We have never shot a single goose since we arrived, though we have spent days hunting them, creeping on our stomachs through marshes and tangles of willows. I like them just the same. They'll be wild and free till doomsday and after. And they are incurable romantics. Other lands, other seas, other lakes and forests and rivers; a winter is long enough in one place, or a summer in another. There are so many dawns and beauties between the inner Arctic Circle and the bayous of Louisiana; a raucous, harmonic, lovely call at evening and the swift whirr of wings, we're on our way to see them all. Why is it that the call of a wild goose does such things to people, makes their eyes fill with tears or their hearts beat like hammers, makes them clench their fists or sigh and sing, or lie in the grass and kick? Well, that's why.

At home they are reading the inky morning paper now. Our morning paper is smudged with mud. It says:

WE GEESE HAVE GONE SOUTH AND WE THUMB OUR NOSE AT YOU THAT YOU NEVER CLAPPED ONE OF US INTO YOUR OLD STEW POT. SOMEDAY YOU MAY SEE A GOOSE BEFORE HE SEES YOU, BUT IT IS DOUBTFUL.

DISRESPECTFULLY YOURS, MR PINFEATHERS LEADER-GANDER, DR. OF AERONAUTICS AND EXPERT SMELLER OF HUMANS

KAY and I were muskrat hunting all day yesterday in our leaky canoe, a gray day, ice making everywhere. It was sleeting and nearly dark when we came down the lagoon to the house. We were singing "The Cheery Lights of Home" and keeping time with our icy paddles. Dim and melancholy everything looked through the half dark and slanting sleet.

We'd been getting quick shots at swimming muskrats and it was for this reason that I had my .22 pistol loaded. There was so much water in the bottom of the canoe, I had pushed the Colt in the big pocket in the front of my shooting coat as the only place to keep it dry. As we came ashore and I leaned over to pull the canoe up, I must have cocked the protruding hammer with my cuff. The gun fell out of my pocket and clattered on the rocks. I heard its bark and felt a sharp blow, as though some one had struck my right thigh with a mallet. Its force moved my foot fully ten inches.

Kay told me to sit down, so I sat down, not knowing what else to do. It seemed impossible I could have been such a fool as to shoot myself off here. John came running from the tilt. He was convinced I was shot through the head.

Being able to walk to the tilt seemed encouraging, and when Kay had a look at it we discovered a hole on the inside of the thigh, just above the knee, and another on the outside about eight inches higher. The bullet must have missed the bone by about half an inch. The underwear and trouser leg appeared to have been cut, rather than carried on in, so we put iodine on entrance and exit and hoped for the best.

By the time we had finished supper my leg was drawn

up tight and paining. I couldn't help recalling tales of chopped-off septic toes and fingers. John said he would finish my sled and haul me down as soon as the river froze. I said I would not have it.

Stupidly enough, I felt cozy and safe in the strong little cabin, and I felt that renascent, complete change of viewpoint that comes of an experience one feels might have been fatal. It seemed much cozier to be alive than dead, and I realized, as I have several times before, that I didn't want to die yet awhile. I wondered what I would do if it went septic.

Kay was pretending to sleep, but John lay on his bunk, head to the candle, reading a paper-bound copy of "Dick Merriwell's Return."

"John," I said, "do you believe in Heaven, honest true?" He laid down the book and unwrinkled his brow. Apparently this was easier than Dick Merriwell.

"Yes, I guess," he said. "I believes Heaven must be a real place because the Bible says you shouldn't work on Sunday and that's true, so Heaven must be a real place."

He gave me example after example of men who, by trapping on Sunday, had lost their luck and even ruined the path for anybody else. Generally the spell, however, was lifted from the path about three years after the heretic left it. He told me of Job Mackenzie, who went on a path that had previously yielded $2,000 worth of fur in a winter. Job trapped Sundays the same as any other day. He cursed and blasphemed as a regular thing, and when his sled kept turning over in the rough ice he swore himself almost into a fit, shaking his fist at the sky and daring God to come ahead down and fight him. On the third year in that path he didn't get forty dollars' worth of fur, though it wasn't a bad year for other people. The same way with Willie Pottle. He is as hard a worker as any. But he traps Sunday, and he makes a small hunt.

It's a question of doubt what is permissible on Sunday. Nowadays many believe it is all right to track a fox that has got away with a trap on his foot, or that it is not wrong to kill an animal found alive in a trap. You must not take it out, though. Some believe it is all right to skin and scrape and spread fur on Sundays, but Harvey spoiled his luck one year that way. The old folks had no doubt that all these things were wrong.

All the most successful hunters take no chances—though a few are not as strict when they are alone as in the presence of another. John sets himself up as no paragon. He admits often shooting partridges on Sunday—with some one else's gun. One of the very best hunters won't even chop up wood on Sunday. No matter how late he makes camp on Saturday night, he always chops up enough wood to last over Sunday and Sunday night. The majority would be close to starvation before they would rend the Sabbath calm to shoot a partridge.

"What about Indians?" I said. "They hunt and fish and even dance on Sunday, and they're good hunters, when they want to be."

"Oh, them," he replied. "They don't count."

The old, Scotch, fear-of-God Christianity and an even older fear of nature blend in these men. I am conscious of the latter myself sometimes. When night comes down, a lowering night with rising wind, one feels that some power is watching. A good many misadventures can befall one, the slightest slip, the slightest carelessness may mean trouble and serious trouble. Merely to lose a mitten, to put an axe down flat in the snow when it is getting dark, to fall through bad ice, to forget a match safe, to leave a poorly silvered, "verdi-greasy" spoon in a kettle of stew, may lead to a serious situation. It is easy to lose one's way when travelling after dark, and there is the ever-present danger of the axe. The axe is a most indispensable tool, serving as saw, hammer, plane, wedge, anvil, blazer of trails, brush cutter, ice tester and a thousand other things. But it is also a dangerous friend where there is wood to be cut for the night and it's dark and the fingers that grip the helve are stiff in a pair of icy mitts. There is not a man in North West River who hasn't a scar on foot or leg where the bright-bladed friend bit him.

The fall gales can hurl a canoe sixty feet in the air, they've been known to blow Goose Bay nearly dry. Sailing the Inlet in a thirteen-foot boat, and paddling the big lakes in canoe, a man gets acquainted with the wind's strength. And in winter there are the sudden blizzards that tear up age-old spruces whose roots leave a hole big enough to build a house in, that pile the snow in twenty-foot drifts and drop the mercury forty degrees in half an hour.

Perhaps it is wrong to say Labradormen are afraid. They're not, they're merely respectful. They understand old Dame Nature, read her warnings, know she's kind and at the same time merciless. Indians feel the same and so do I, now I am here. Nature is almighty and so is God. It is well to be on the good side of them both. If Sunday observance will placate the jealous Old Testament God and give us the New Testament God, we'll gladly observe Sunday. And whenever we speak of any future plans we'll say, "God willing," or "if I lives."

The Old Testament God is the God of a people at the

mercy of nature. When one is living in a civilized community where a storm is merely something interesting to be watched out of curiosity, or more often ignored, it is easy enough to scrap the whole business.

I knew I wouldn't be able to sleep much, so I tried to keep John yarning as long as possible. Just to cheer me up, he told me about the time they hauled Willie Montague down the river on a sled.

Willie's partner found him stretched out on the ice by the water hole one evening in December. He was almost completely paralyzed, could only move his fingers and mumble a little. It must have been a stroke.

Several days after, John and Harvey and Bill Baikie and Juddy Blake came along, bound for home, racing as usual, trying to do 250 miles with sleds in ten days. One look at Willie and they gave up all thought of that. With a blanket and a sleeping bag under him, they put him on the biggest toboggan, and with him, one man's load. Willie's shoulders stuck out on either side and made her run harder than ever. It was a terrific load for one man to haul. They took half-hour turns, at the end of which they were dripping wet and weak in the knees. Whenever they boiled the kettle, they'd all have to get together, pushing and pulling, to drag him up the bank close to the fire. His shoulders would catch on the willows and they'd see him trying to swear. Even this solace was denied him.

One afternoon at a boil-up place, they had Willie's sled on a bed of brush near the fire to try to warm him up a little. The sled had to be on boughs to keep it from getting wet and iced-up in the thawed snow beside the fire. If the bottom got rough with ice, all of them together couldn't budge it.

They were all a little way off, chopping more wood, cutting a water hole or getting brush. Gradually the fire melted the snow out from under Willie. The sled began to cant. In another moment he would have been tipped helpless into the blaze. Bill saw him, dropped his armful of brush and pulled him away just in time. It was one of the blessings of the trip that he appeared to feel neither heat, cold, nor pain.

Farther on down, the river had dammed itself with slob, backed up and burst, and then frozen lightly in an impassable chaos of rough ice. It was the worst winter for rough ice on Grand River that any one could remember. They had to haul up over the steep hills beside the river and try to progress through country cut up with ravines and thickly wooded. The first day of this, they slaved for nine hours and when one of them went out to the river in the evening, walking light, to see how far they had come, he found they were but half a mile below the place where they took in. Going down hills was as bad as going up. They could not keep Willie's sled from capsizing sometimes, and slewing sideways against trees. The poor man's shoulders were nearly worn out.

It took them a week to cover a distance they might have done in half a day on good ice on the river. And when they finally came out on Gull Island Lake they had still a long way to go. Often they thought it was useless, that they would only be hauling a corpse by the time they reached home. But Willie lived through it somehow and arrived at North West River with his back raw from the cross bars of the bending, twisting sled.

It is just another vague tale, with most of the dramatic details forgotten or never noticed, but any one who has hauled a sled day after day knows how they slaved to get him home; and all for nothing, for the hospital burned to the ground that winter, and Willie with it.

Every one gets tired of talking sooner or later. We had pinched the light out long before and talked in the dark, as we have none too many candles. A little after midnight John's voice trailed off and left me to watch the firelight from a hole in the stove, flickering on the logs.

October 31.

TODAY it is very cold and raw. There is just enough snow to make the land desolate, not enough to cover its shivering surface. John says he guesses the river is never going to freeze. Some years it is fast early in October and the fur is all prime before the middle of the month. He is busy setting all his traps now, putting out some new ones in a big bight up by Cross Island, where Alvin is, about twenty miles away.

My leg is better, I think. It is not swelling much around the holes and I guess it will be all right. Kay was hunting partridges three or four miles down along shore this afternoon and got nothing.

While I was alone, a jay strutted right into the doorway and looked around as much as to say, "This is not such a bad place you've got in here, my man." Every day they get more brazen. Even throwing chips at them does not frighten them away. It is considered bad luck to shoot them, or we might, they are such a nuisance. We had a fair-sized piece of pork out on the roof in the cool, covered with a bit of tin, when along came two whiskey-jacks, pushed away the tin and pecked the pork to ribbons.

Now they are after our big bag of pork out on the scaffold where we keep our main supplies. We only have about a week's stock in the tilt and the rest of the flour, beans, rice, pork, tea, sugar, cartridges, butter and candles stays on the scaffold, covered with a tarpaulin. This is a precautionary measure. If the tilt should burn down when we are away, we would still have our food. Most trappers also keep their fur on the scaffold. Ours is made of cross poles lashed about ten feet off the ground between a clump of three trees. This will be none too high when the snow comes deep. Meanwhile we reach the top by a rickety ladder.

November 1.

THE moon has two enormous circles around it tonight, swinging up above the trees. John says that means snow. And we can hear the hushed, sibilant murmur of Eagle Cliff rapid, like a sea conch held almost to your ear. Its faraway whisper only comes to us on nights before snow.

Reading a paper-bound copy of *Aucassin and Nicolette* this afternoon. How charming it is, like the music of a brook. And how long ago it is already since the first jongleur told the chanson, and how long it will be before the last reader puts it down with a sigh. Only the simple and beautiful lasts. All ugliness vanishes finally.

November 2.

RAIN last night that turned to wet snow. And now the trees are tufted deep with branch-bending, heavy whiteness. Every now and then outside, a lump of snow slips off a branch and the limb flies up as though it were glad to be relieved of the weight. The whole tree seems

93

to shake itself and say, "There!" like an old maid smoothing her dress.

Kay has always thought snow on the trees very pretty, and it impresses her more, I suppose, because she comes from Australia, where she never knew snow as a child. One day late last fall at North West River, when the trees were heavy with snow, she remarked how beautiful they were to a grizzled old veteran named Fred Rich. He laughed and said, "Yes, and I wonder how beautiful you'd think they was if you had to cut and carry all day in the woods."

With every tree the first axe blow brings down a shower of snow. And often with a big log on one's shoulder, carrying it to the pile, the end of the log will knock a tree or a branch and a ten-pound lump of snow will break on the wood-cutter's head. Gradually the snow seeps into his mitts at the wrists and gets them soaking, finds its way into his pockets and under his collar, until a slow cold stream crawls down his back.

Whenever Fred sees her he always says, "And do ye still find the snow on the trees beautiful?" and she always answers, "Yes."

If only all wood-cutters could always answer "Yes."

November 3.

THIS is the fifth day since the shooting and though I can get around pretty spry with a crutch, I sometimes feel like a prisoner when I see John going off to his traps and Kay to her partridge hunting and snares.

But there is plenty I can do here. I am the woman now. I wash the three plates and the three cups and spoons and knives, and sometimes bake bannock or fry grease cakes.

Three in the big frying pan do us for a day. I can pluck and cook partridges, get the meals, sew and sweep the floor with our balsam broom and a goose wing. It is good to be able to do something. I am going to carve a birch spoon.

What good fun we have at supper-time, with the candle flickering in the trap-spring candlestick and John home, bubbling over with laughter and telling us about the places he's been today and what he saw and how many muskrats he's got now, and each day a new cove that is fast for the winter; and Kay telling us about the partridge she missed and the ones she got, and how she was almost lost somewhere or other.

November 4.

THE frost was not melted from the long brown grass this morning when we heard women and children's voices on the river. For a second we were almost afraid. Then the others ran down to the water and I limped, and we all yelled, "Helloo."

Back across the water came "Bo jou" and children's laughter as pretty as thin broken ice washing in and out among the rocks. There were three canoes, all one big family of Indians. The prow of the foremost touched the pebbles and the man advanced, a tall man with little feet in minutely plaited sealskin moccasins. His long legs were wrapped around with rags and salmon twine. Worn, cloth breeches, a very dirty white coat, and a pair of knitted mittens covered the rest of him. The straight black hair under his mouse-colored, ancient felt hat was well down over his ears and collar. He leaned on his long-bladed Indian paddle, his straight, lean body bent and his wrinkled face laughing from embarrassment. Then, wiping his hand on his coat, he held it out to John, saying, "Bo jou, Puckutushand," for he had seen this one before. Then he shook hands with me, half looking at me from under his eyebrows, but with Kay he would not, for she was only a woman.

With him were a little girl and his woman, whom you would have thought to be fifty-five years old, had she not dug down among the bags amidships and unearthed a pair of sparkling shoe-button eyes belonging to a one-year-old baby.

As soon as the eldest son's canoe grounded, he advanced and shook hands, too, a good-looking fellow about twenty, with a round, Chinese-looking face. With him were his French-Canadian wife, a little Indian hunting dog and Poone, a pert, plump little brother in a red cap.

The last canoe was paddled by three children. Two of them were boys about twelve and fourteen, and the third a pretty girl around fifteen. In the middle of their load sat a mongrel hauling dog, his nose tied up tight with a *babische* thong.

All three canoes were small. Indians never make them longer than seventeen feet, and generally fifteen or sixteen, to be more suitable on the portages. And they floated light. The whole family hadn't as much of a load as two white trappers would require for the hunt till January. The Indians were cold from sitting cramped in their canoes. John was dancing for joy on the stones. "I love Indians," he said to me. "Come up, come up, and have some tea," he repeated to them.

As we scrambled up the slippery bank, the old man

96

pointed to the tilt and said, "Cheena meetchwop, your house, 'ee sez."

Whenever Indians try to talk English they always inter-lard the conversation with that curious " 'ee sez." I think it comes from the use of interpreters. They have noticed that when an interpreter turns from an Indian to a white man, he always precedes his remarks with " 'ee sez," and fre-quently repeats it as he goes along. They haven't any idea what the expression means. They think it is some strange but customary way of beginning an English conversation and filling up the pauses in that absurd tongue. And when they speak English there are many pauses to be filled.

The kettle was soon boiling and they wanted to run and get their grub bags, but we, in an enthusiasm of hospitality, wouldn't let them. We scraped together three cups, two deep dishes and two little kettles for them to drink their tea from; the baby sipped from its mother's cup. The family was ranged all round the walls, on the bunk, on the floor, on boxes and a lard pail. John was conversing with the men sixteen to the dozen. Occasionally he vouchsafed me a word or two, but I could only make out the general drift of the talk. The two women gravitated toward Kay, asking her over and over again by signs and stray words how she came to be here. They had never seen a white woman in the coun-try at freeze-up time, and I suppose they wondered if she was going to live like an Indian always after this.

"Toganish squish," they called her from John's informa-tion, and their name for me was "mishnaygan napio," or teacher man.

Kay was buttering big slices of bread for the children, but they were very shy and hid away if anyone looked at them or tried to talk to them. They would not eat until their mother told them it was all right, and then how lovingly they dug into the *kushiwash* [sugar] for their tea. All but Poone. He began to shake his hands and cry with rage. Very gently, as always, his mother crooned, "Naneen, Poone," and the girl untied the little boy's long sleeves which were bound up at the ends with twine, in lieu of mittens. Poone was the only one of the children who wasn't shy. His bright eyes danced under his red wool cap and he laughed and fingered everything he could reach.

We said we were sorry we had no meat for them, but they answered that it made no difference, for, while camped five miles above us on an island they had killed a beaver. They knew we were here but we did not know they were anywhere near. They asked Kay if she liked beaver meat, and she, thinking they asked her if she had ever tasted it, said no. So we missed a "scoff" of beaver.

For half an hour John and the two men talked of signs of fur and what a late fall it was. The foxes would not take bait this year, the old man said, but next year they would be plenty. (They come and go in six- or seven-year cycles. For a year or two there are lots of them. They are fat and well fed and not afraid to cross a man's track or go after the bait in a trap. Then the mice, their principal food, commence to get scarce. The last year the foxes start to fight and eat each other. The next year there are none, not even the track of one. No one knows where they go. Gradually they start coming back again, but for the first few years they are lean and too cautious to go anywhere near a trap or a man's track. When they are starving hungry they will not go after the bait in a trap. When they are rolling in fat

98

they will walk right into the jaws.) The father, who calls himself Mathieu André, said there was much sign of muskrat, mink and marten, also weasel. Soon there will be plenty ptarmigan with the big snow-storms. In two risings and settings of the sun the river will freeze.

The family is going twenty-five miles farther down the river to fur for a month or two in the vicinity of Fred Goudie's. Fred will not like this much, but Indians fur anywhere they please, saying the country is theirs anyway. Generally, however, they prefer an isolated region where fur and game are sure to be more plentiful.

The Indians never get as much fur as the whites or halfwhites, for, even though they know the country and the ways of the animals infinitely better, they do not trap as intensively and haven't as many deadfalls or traps. They always bring so little food with them they have to spend more than half their time hunting meat.

Mrs. Mathieu dragged her long skirts down to the canoe and showed Kay a French Catholic calendar on which were printed for every day in the year the names of five saints. With this she showed the names of nearly all her children and indicated that she intended to name a new one in about a month, and one for her daughter-in-law in January. The girl is not a real Inu and they may not be able to travel for a week or more after she gives birth. They intend to come out at North West River for more food late in January.

I could not keep my eyes off Terese, a little girl about eight. For amongst her black-haired, swarthy brothers and sisters, she alone had blue eyes and brown hair. Her elder sister, Naneen, is so lithe and dark and beautiful she needs an eagle feather in her hair; she is the stuff legends are made of. But Terese is a lone marguerite in a field of clover. She made me think of a fair-haired child captured from the forts of the pale faces, or a Nordic infant kidnapped by gypsies. She, with her flower face and small hands, was more shy even than the rest and would not speak to me. I wonder where and how the white strain entered. Perhaps an English boy in the teepees on the shore of James Bay, perhaps far down the Mississippi, or beyond the Lake of the Woods, or an English girl captured from Deerfield.

Two winters ago this family camped on Lobstick Lake and it was there John met them and they christened him, Puckutushand. They always have their own name for whites they know. This one means something funny and scurrilous, I think. When John visited them on Sundays the woman sewed buttons on for him and mended his trousers. He traded them flour and cartridges for meat and moccasins. Now he wants Mathieu to make him a sled, for the old man is a good hand at that.

Mathieu is unwilling at first, but at last he says he will for flour, much flour, for he has many mouths to feed. He goes to the scaffold and says, "Look, you are but three and have five bags of flour. With me are ten and we have only three."

John is willing to give him most anything he wants, but consults me, as we have agreed all the food here is to be ours jointly and while there is anything to eat we will share it equally, no matter that I paid for more of it at North West River and he paid for more of it on the portage. And I am not pleased to give the Indians much flour, for we cannot spare it. And I feel the air grow tense.

We agree to give him half a bag, but John is not content, and neither is the Indian. "If he wished to have more flour, he could have brought more, as we did, and started from the

Gulf earlier to allow for the slower travel with heavier loads. Every year the Indians do this; shall we starve because it is their custom?"

But Mathieu will not make a sled for half a bag of flour. Well, we give him four double handfuls of beans and five of peas, one hundred .22 cartridges, six shotgun shells, a little sugar, and he consents.

The old woman shows us by putting her hands to her stomach how hungry the children will be this winter. She begs us for a pair of sealskin boots and demonstrates again and again how cold and wet the little ones' feet will be. So we give her an old pair of boots and a big piece of sealskin to patch many pairs with, and we do not think the family quite as quaint as before.

If our hearts are hardened against them it is because they do this same thing every year. Moreover they can live off the country, finding porcupine and beaver, rabbit and partridge, caribou, fish and bear better than we know how. Every winter they come out to the trading posts and they have been *sham sheevan* [very hungry]. And sometimes the strong men are staggering with weakness and must hasten back with food to their women and children who are keeping themselves alive on squirrels and mice and jays a week or two weeks back on the trail, where they dropped with hunger. And every year a family or two comes down Grand River and all down its length eats up the precious flour in the tilts, and their dogs smell out the lard that is buried in the snow against them. And always they say they were starving, and a starving man will fight or steal for his food and they could not help it. And the next year they do the same and the next and the next.

John knows this and still he would give them more. I

know it, and I would give them less. I am glad he is a sunny, carefree one, and not surly and one to nurse a grudge. It is so easy in the woods to fight over food or little things, for a little thing as small as a match means the difference between life and death sometimes.

But now it is all arranged; the man will make a straight-grained juniper sled, so long, and so wide, with the bars lashed on with *babische* and will leave it at Fred Goudie's house. It is like sunshine after a shower, now the bargaining is done. The smiles come out and they are all, from the oldest to the youngest, happy children of the forest again, and not evil, threatening beggars.

The woman must needs take us to the canoe and unwrap her private store of treasures all done up in clean white rags inside a blanket. To John and me she gives a big, round soda biscuit each, and a small pack of pipe tobacco. There is more tobacco there too, though, oddly enough, none of the family smokes. In most Indian families everybody smokes the two or three pipes the family possesses and when a little girl of twelve wants a smoke, she reaches the pipe out of her mother's mouth and plants it in her own.

But this old lady is a canny one. She knows that trappers when they get out of tobacco will trade flour or anything else for it. A trapper has been known to trade a forty-dollar marten for a thirty-cent plug of tobacco.

To Kay she insists upon giving a small, white canvas bag, stitched all over with bright-colored tapes in the form of a star. Then, after a moment's hesitation, she decides she will entrust to her presents for Shwasheem's wife and her sister Pen-am-ee, who will come to North West River in January. They are, a tattered snapshot taken on the French shore, a string of imitation-pearl rosary beads, and an Indian woman's cap. This latter is a work of art made from red and black triangles whose points come together at the crown. The material costs twenty cents an inch at the post. The close-fitting band, which is about two inches broad, is solid wampum made of red and blue and gray beads—the work of many weeks.

Child-like, the woman has to see where Kay is going to put these gifts for safekeeping on the long journey down. They are carefully wrapped in a clean towel, and stowed in Kay's "progbag" with her tooth brush, sewing bag, bandannas, pencil and paper, comb and three favorite little paper books. A progbag is to a trapper what a dittybox is to a sailor. In it he carries a few matches, a few candles and cartridges, a spare pair of sox, his pencil, an awl and crooked-knife, a snowshoe needle, sewing materials, deerskin and sealskin patches and other cherished encumbrances. The Indian woman recognizes this as the appropriate place and nods her approval.

Now Poone's cuffs must be tied up again and the flour put aboard. In the old man's canoe there is a pair of snowshoes no bigger than salad plates. Swiftly they step into their canoes, kneel and sit back on their feet. White men cannot sit that way all day. The paddles grind with a push on the pebbles, they hold their hands up and softly call, "Miami," and are gone.

They will have covered more than fifteen hundred miles before they get back to their "home" at Seven Islands, on the north shore of the Gulf of St. Lawrence where they spend summers. And the men, with their hunting, will have done twice that.

At Fred's they'll put their canoes up on scaffolds, for the river will be frozen when they get there. At the end of a month or two they'll start for North West River, hunting as they go. They'll trade their fur, then back again by way of Michikamau, hauling big loads. Toward May they'll be getting back here again to their canoes before the ice breaks up. It is bad to be caught by an early spring far from one's canoe. Or perhaps they'll get here early, make runnered sledges and haul their canoes over the watershed before the ice breaks up. Then down to Seven Islands on a fair tide.

These Montagnais have changed their ways a little since the days when they had no stoves, no canvas, no nails, no steel traps, no matches nor rifles, but not as much as one would think. The depletion of the caribou has changed them more than the coming of the whites. I think this is the last stand, and they don't intend to change any more.

In summer the men do practically nothing to avert the hardships of the coming winter. Perhaps they make a couple of extra pairs of snowshoes to sell, but these are never as good as the snowshoes they make for themselves. They could salmon-fish, or make canoes to sell, as the trappers have asked them many times, but they will not.

They dangle their legs and say the white men and half-breeds are fools to live in the big houses that they must work on all summer and spend so much time providing firewood for. And in the fall when they start into the woods again, as often as not they camp within forty miles and eat up half their grub so they will not have so much to carry. And that winter they are *sham sheevan* again. They are children,

GRAND RIVER—SLACK WATER

Photographs by Varick Frissell   GRAND RIVER—TIDE

careless of the morrow and forever scornful of the whites. One cannot but admire them in a way. It takes a certain kind of courage to forget tomorrow. They would rather die than change, and they are dying, I am afraid.

So many days necessarily spent in the tilt have made me pretty well acquainted with its interior. But I don't feel any particular antipathy to these walls; logs are better scenery in the long run than plaster. I can close my eyes and see every split in them, cracked by the heat when they were green. They are convenient places to stick knives, or fish hooks, or odd nails or wooden pegs to hang clothes on.

John always sticks his fork in one split and hangs his cartridge bag on the fork. I used to keep my sheath knife in a split over the bunk, until one night, groping for the matches in the dark, I knocked it down and it cut my nose. Everybody thought that very funny, including me.

Under the bunk are two small wooden boxes full of clothes, cans of baking powder, soap and muskrat skins. We use them for chairs and the bunk for a table. On the bunk in the daytime we keep the sleeping gear, a clothes bag and the partially used flour bag that we lighten every day.

In the front end of my room is the low door, with its seal-skin hinges, a wooden latch and latch-string. The window is a little square hole cut out of the upper half of one log and the under half of the adjoining one. The seam between glass and wood is caulked all around with rags.

Against the east wall is Kay's stretcher bed, and on the other side is the stove and a place to pile wood behind the door. The stove, which rests on two big, flat rocks, is a rusty thing half crushed in in the middle. This is from the time when a wolverene got into the tilt about five years ago and jumped on it from the rafters.

The bunk against the back wall has been somewhat chewed by porcupines, but I don't think bears have ever lived in here as they have in some tilts. Squirrels like the place pretty well, and are forever pulling the moss out of the chinks.

There is a hole in one of the base logs where two mice come in every night to do a dance in the middle of the floor and chew holes in the flour bag if it is not hung up. Two continue to come, no more, no less, though I have shot three with the light rifle. One sneaked in the hole this afternoon and looked around. I decided if Kay and John could hunt away all day, I'd hunt at home. Hunting begins at home as truly as charity. I was trying to get him on the run, and following him through the sights. Just as he scrambled over our best frying pan, I let go and took a piece out of the side of it.

Hunters all hate mice, for they ruin thousands of dollars worth of fur every year. Some years they are very plentiful, and this is one of them. As soon as an animal dies in a trap and gets snowed-over a little, the mice tunnel through the snow and chew the hair off whichever side of the pelt is nearest the ground. They don't eat anything, and they don't use the hair to line their nests, as some people would like to believe. They simply leave it lying on the snow. Some say they are sent by the Lord to plague trappers, just as partridges were created solely to feed hunters in winter. Whatever the reason, they are a pest, and it is because of the mice that men with 150 and 200-mile trap lines to cover get lean as ramrods.

The mice are also a menace to flour. Generally, if it is to be left any length of time, it is hung up from the sticks overhead. Mice run down the string, cut it and let the bag fall. Then they waste the flour at their leisure. Oddly enough, they seldom touch a clean, dry flour bag. What they want is the caked, soured dough. But since all bags that have come this far have become wet and caked, this knowledge is small help to a trapper. A mouse ran across Kay's pillow one night, and that is the greatest menace of all.

I've described the ground floor of our home, but forgot to mention the second storey. Overhead, in the peak of the roof, there are three spruce poles running from end to end. On these we store boxes and bags and pans and fur boards. They also provide a convenient rack for drying fur when it is being stretched on the boards.

Of the boards up in our attic, nearly every one has writing on it. Fur boards are a hunter's correspondence cards. Many of the notes are impossible to decipher. Two of them are as follows:

We come here the night from Cross Iland snowin and rimy and hard hawlin. No strange news with us and not mutch furr. Home agen. Come on boy. Henry Baikie and Henry Best Dec 23 1925

Dec. 12 1927 Here tonite I got a mink at Clifty island and a marten in the south bite. 20 minks now how many you no lies. I saw fox sign all over Norries. I took 2 candels and you can have them back when I gets donn burnin them. See you 2 weeks Sunday here no strange news with me and not much fur. H. G.

P. S. here is ½ fig of stimu for your nose warmer. Got lonesome for her yet.

I CAN get down to the river for water now and can chop wood some. Pretty soon I'll be almost as useful as a five-year-old child. I made a holster for my pistol today out of a boot leg and a piece of a flour bag. It is a chef d'œuvre of the seamstress' art, cunningly wrought with stitches an inch long.

I also tapped a boot, and the sealskin patch is waterproof, sewn on with the stitches hidden, so they won't wear out. It is the first time I have ever examined the inside of a seal-skin boot closely, and I don't think anyone could help being impressed. I wonder how many thousand years ago Eskimos perfected this remarkable device. To fit right, they have to be cut out with the utmost skill. The bottoms are made of an old "harp" whose skin is thick, and the legs of a thin-skinned "jar." Every seam is sewn three times with sinew from a caribou's back, which is twice as strong as any thread of equal size. And with all the work the women in this country do, they still have time to make boots for the family.

This Labrador woman is a remarkable person, worthy of more notice than she gets. And though she does more work than it would seem possible for one human being to accomplish, she is still a person, not simply a drudge. In most households the woman has to carry her water from the shore in buckets, she has constantly to stoke the big wood stove, and carry in the split wood from outside. She does all the washing, and more than half the time she has to put on her snowshoes to get out to the clothesline. She mixes and kneads and bakes her own bread (and it's twice as good as bought bread). Almost all the foods she cooks take time to prepare.

Frequently there is no lard, and pork must be rendered instead, salt fish must be soaked, coarse salt must be pounded up with an axe for use in bread. She has to clean fresh fish, and pluck and clean ducks, partridges or geese, and save the feathers. Rabbits must be skinned and porcupine butchered.

When her husband is away she feeds the dogs and takes a little time now and again to hunt partridges around close or go to her rabbit snares. But that is pleasure. As the children grow up they help her very materially.

She picks berries and makes jam and pies, she fills and cleans the lamps and scrubs the wooden floor. Every day she sweeps out its many cracks and fissures. Saturday nights she scrubs the children, and it is almost as heavy work carrying out the waste water as carrying in the fresh. In the spring she is busy for days on end cleaning sealskins, a dirty, smelly job of shaving the hair off one side and scraping the fat and vellum off the other. All year long she is making boots, and then there are all the other clothes.

Now that trading schooners come every spring to the inlet, she does not make as many clothes as she used to. But she does knit sweaters and sox and mitts and make fur-hooded parkas, duffel wool mitts and vamps, caribouskin mitts and moccasins, in addition to patching and repatching the bought flannel shirts, woollen underwear, woollen trousers, overalls. Her needlework also includes the manufacture of canvas flour bags, game-bags, leggings, tents, gun coats, cartridge bags, a sail for the small boat and a feather-bed now and then. If she lets the children go barefoot and half ragged all summer, it is hardly any wonder. It probably does them good. In her spare time she often helps to knit trout nets or salmon nets, though this is regularly the man's job. Ten and twenty years ago the families all used to migrate up and down the bay to hunting, sealing or fishing grounds two or three times a year. This was rough on the whole family, especially the women. Many families still do it, but they have motor boats now instead of skiffs.

In addition to these things and in spite of the fact that here is a dearth of milk, eggs, fruit and vegetables, she almost invariably bears many children. With washing the dishes thrown in for good measure, it sounds like a nightmare. And it has been in times past. Nevertheless, it has also made some remarkable personalities such as ease does not produce. And mostly this trapper's wife is very happy. And always she is an indispensible partner with her man in the business of living.

November 7.

LAST night the river froze, all but a narrow channel down the middle. If the wind would ever cease and let the water quiet down, that would soon catch over too. The open lane is crowded with gray, amorphous masses of slob, slowly drifting, ready to jell. The water looks viscous, as though at any minute if the waves flattened out it might wrinkle once, and lo, be stiff.

John's spare suit of woollen "insides" got caught in the ice last night. Among trappers there are two different schools of thought on the essential subject of washing underwear. It hardly assumes the importance of a schism, and never prevents a convert of one faction from drinking tea with an upholder of dubious doctrines. Nevertheless, the difference of opinion, with its consequent conduct, has a certain indefinable significance, and a true believer seldom goes over to the ritual of the opposing camp, preserving throughout his lifetime a naïve loyalty to a soapless cause.

Briefly, some trappers prefer to turn their nether garments inside out and pull them down over the top of a bushy little tree. There, like inverted scarecrows, with limp arms and legs, they remain for a month or more in the sun, rain, frost, snow and wind. At the end of this time, when the other suit develops an irritating tendency to stiffen into a coat of armor, the quintuple processes of a natural laundry return the wash as white as snow and as soft as velvet. As with other laundries, there are sometimes casualties among the ranks of the buttons, for the jays, thinking they have blundered upon a civilized luxury, namely the cuttlefish of their pampered cousin the canary, have been known to pounce upon the lustrous pearls with the vigor of lumberjacks pouncing upon rum.

John is a faithful believer in the other school, whose members turn their backs upon such an uncouth display of intimacies and bury their grimey treasures beneath the waters of the river. There, in the shallow water they respectfully lay them, murmuring the words as though it were a chant, "Damn botheration anyway." Rocks are piled on to mark the sacred spot and anchor the corpse. Then the devotees solemnly come away. The fish do not constitute the menace to buttons that the whiskey-jacks do in the Five Star Open Air Laundry. But there are dangers, as you shall see.

In a zealous attempt to secure absolute perfection, John left his insides in the river too long. He spent half the morning at the shore with his axe, chopping. I've never seen him so happy or heard such guffaws as when he brought up for exhibition the resultant stiff conglomerate of mud, pebbles, ice and wool.

November 8.

I WALKED three miles this afternoon hunting partridges and looking at some rabbit traps we have set among the willows. Got one white partridge and one rabbit in a trap baited with tobacco. The appealing thing was alive, with its big pink eyes beseeching. I stunned him quick with an axe handle.

A rabbit with a limp, raw leg, and a ptarmigan nestled in the snow, his little black eyes already glazed, his neck hanging limp, beak on a snowy breast, the beautiful black-tipped wings folded for always, snow spattered scarlet with blood— how cruel it all is. But it can't be helped. It's we or they, and it doesn't do to think of such things. When one is hungry for meat, it is easy enough to kill. And I don't suppose it is any worse to do one's own killing here than to have someone else do it for you, as is the custom at home.

If only the living grace of wild creatures were not so beautiful; the long hops of the rabbit with his floppy ears and the white, button tail that somehow shows against the pure white of the rest of him; the partridge and the mark of his black-tipped wings printed in the snow as though in marble, where he pitched for the last time.

For even their tracks have beauty, the records of wild creatures' lives, heedlessly written in the whiteness. It seems a magic revelation that a mere human should be privileged to see the shadows of their play, their desires, their fears and even their thoughts. It makes me think of days when I might have surprised a band of fairies in a wood by any brook, ferrying themselves across on chips and curl-prowed oak leaves. After a spell of moonlight nights and a fresh new snow I've come on a glade in the thick spruce where the rabbits have danced. You can see it with your own eyes written there, though it seems shameful to pry so.

And the partridge tracks along the shores among the willows, prints of wide little feet, strutting pouter breasted, tangled ribbons on the writing tablet of the earth. Here they pitched, see where their wings brushed the snow; here they were feeding, see the willow bark on the snow; there the old cock ran out onto the ice to have a look at me creeping close through the willows; here they fled away where the ribbon of footprints ends with a short run. Sometimes one sees a few feathers straying over the snow in the wind. It signifies that a hawk has struck true or a fox has leapt on a bird asleep in the snow.

The open channel in the river has been jamming all day with slob and thin pans of ice broken in the rapids above us. Slower and slower the cluttered mass moves down the center of the river, grinding the edges of the solid ice and itself. Tonight it will solidify.

My leg is stiff and makes me afraid of falling. But it is going to be all right. I am so thankful and glad. I stand in the bright, sunlit snow and hold up my arms to the blue winter sky and say, "Thank you, God," though I don't know why. I didn't blame him for the hurt.

Yesterday the channel of miniature rough ice was fast. We poked it with poles and they went through. But this morning we all went across. John swung off toward Forget Me Not Bight, his gamebag on his back and his gun and axe in his hand, trotting over the ice till he disappeared.

Who should lope up over the bank this afternoon but Tough. He strolled into the tilt as though he belonged there, but he came out pretty quick, barking and looking over his shoulder. He is mortally afraid of bears, and it is John's cubskin that bothers him.

Victor was not far behind, back bent under a heavy load. He came up the path, fatter and jollier than ever, his cheeks all red, and frost in the down on his chin. Slung on his back was a black, shiney otter. He was proud and had to tell us all about it, how he came around the corner of the island and saw something black by the bank where his trap was. But he thought it couldn't be a otter because there was no open water close by, but it was, and he must have got in a week ago when there was water right to the bank.

We gave him tea right away and he sat down on a box by the stove and took off one boot. He'd been through the ice with one leg and was wet half way up the thigh. Thin films of ice dropped from his ragged trousers to the floor. He exhibited with much pride his patched, darned knees, and a rip in the side of one leg, skewered together with a willow twig. He said that was proof he had been working hard. Hunters always wear out their knees kneeling to bait and set traps, and if they aren't ripped a little here and there that shows they have been sleeping all the time.

It was a great event to see him. He confessed that when

we first started up the river he was "too shamed of us" to eat where we were, but when he saw we chewed our bones the same as anybody else he felt better about it.

If Victor only knew how the struggle up the river stripped me of my manners and even my decencies, how I forgot to brush my teeth and neglected to wash my hands, and was too tired to care; how I didn't pluck partridges absolutely clean and secretly gloried in the fact that the feathers were lost in the gravy, how I inadvertently cooked a spruce partridge with the crop in and knowingly tried to eat it, I would be as shamed of myself as I ought to be.

But that is the way in the bush. At first glance the newcomer is appalled by the grossness of life in the raw, seeing it for the first time in its whole reality. He hadn't realized there was blood and entrails in the business of preparing food, and that there was so much dirt and sweat connected with humans.

But soon he gets swept up in the hard, fast rush of the trail which strips him bare. The change is so overwhelming for him that he becomes dirtier and more careless than the old-timer. The old rivermen always wash their hands before they mix bread, and leave off smoking their pipes lest ashes fall in the dough. Greenhorns are horrified at the sight of those horny hands in the common bread, but as often as not, forget to wash their own when it is their turn to mix. It is the same with washing clothes and preparing meat and all the rest. When they first start out they are unnecessarily fastidious. At the end of a month they are dirtier than the dirtiest, shocking the hunters who formerly shocked them.

Rob Michelin guided some men from outside on a trip to Hopedale one winter. When they first started, they couldn't possibly eat partridge stew without a knife, fork, plate and spoon. They would not pick up a bone. They were loath to wipe the gravy off their plates with bread. Sometimes they'd put a slice of bread in the gravy, then manipulate it with knife and fork, disdaining vulgar fingers.

On the way back they ran very short, they were starving. At this point they were a shocking spectacle to Robert. They required neither knife, plate, spoon nor fork to eat meat. They dove into the pot with their hands and after they had gnawed the last shreds from the bones, they cracked them with axes and sucked out the marrow. Who can blame them? You or I would do the same. Nevertheless, Robert thought it was funny. For the strength and will power of a seasoned hunter restrain him even in time of hunger, and his manners, in the presence of another, are not much different whether he is starving or well fed.

John came in about six and he was also wet. We put on five partridges, two of which Victor had in his gamebag already plucked. Lots of rice and pork in the stew, and a piece of chocolate all around afterwards. Kay had just baked, and Victor said the rose bread was the best thing he ever ate. John and Victor "dried the pot," splitting the last partridge.

These simple meals in the log house, I don't ever expect to forget them. We are not greedy, but we are hungry with a great, soul-filling, tooth-wetting hunger that starts in the toes and ends just under the hat. Sitting cross-legged on the floor, John gets Kay's and my gizzards, as we don't like them. He'll trade a neck for a gizzard any time. Tough is behind the stove, wheezing. What a feed of bones he is going to get. He's already had the feet, heads, ends of wings and entrails.

Blue smoke fills the tilt, contentment fills the heart. And I should be the last to deny credit where credit is due: food fills the stomach. This is the time for a little gossip.

Victor has been down to Fred Goudie's. Fred was sick just after Jim and Walter passed by, and so was Victor. Old Mathieu and his gang are camped near Fred and not getting a cordial reception. Fred is making a sled for Victor and another one for himself. The Indians set two traps right beside two of Fred's. Uncle Fred struck them up and told Mathieu he could at least set them on the other side of the cove. And if he sets any more so close, Fred is going to smash them. Oh, Uncle Fred's a great old fellow, he's got 'n scared. Fred's sickness done him a world of good. Since he got well he hasn't felt so good in twenty-five years. He says he's good for twenty years more in the river, which will make him close to eighty.

Now that the lakes are frozen, Victor is going in to the end of his south path to look for Harvey. The latter was going to build his new cabin right at the end of the path, on the shore of Unknown Lake, if he could find the place by the new all-water route.

"How much fur you got, b'y?" says Victor.

"Oh," says John, "I got—oh—'bout twenty martens, thirty minks, forty weasels, 139 muskrats, two crosses and a red. How much you?"

"Well, about the same, p'r'aps a little more. I had some pretty good luck with a family of mountain cats in over the north heels."

Then they looked at each other and grinned. They've

each got about nine mink, a marten and twenty weasel. John has 100 muskrat, but no otter. There is always rivalry between the boys in the river as to who made the best hunt, and they seldom tell the truth about their catch. John confessed to me that whenever he makes a good hunt he tells every one except Rob (to whom he tells the truth) that it was the worst year he ever knew. And whenever he has a bad year, he claims he has made his everlasting fortune.

But Victor must get to work. While we are washing the dishes and John is skinning a mink, he whets his jack-knife on his boot and, with the otter head between his knees, skins the pelt back from the jaws. Then he strings the animal up by the teeth from the poles overhead, and as the long, powerful body hangs there, the beautiful black tail brushes the floor. It is six feet from tip to tip. He slits the forelegs from the knees down, and the hindlegs all their length. Then it's nick and pull, nick and pull, rolling the pelt back all the way to the tail, taking special care with the eyes, ears and legs. When only the tail remains to be skinned, he wraps the pelt twice around its base and twists it tight, then with a terrific heave, peels the brush off its bone.

What an ugly thing the skinned carcass is, hanging there, dripping blood. When the fur is off, all carcasses look thinner than they should. The mouth has a perpetual grin, all the ribs show like the timbers of a rotting schooner and the whole thing is a ghastly red.

But it is false to be sentimental about it. This appears to be the way the world is ordered. And when you realize how few comforts these people have and how hard they work for these skins that will buy necessities, and remember the long trip up and the journey home, the first scouting out of the wilderness, the hungry days, the eternal walking, the wet and cold, the countless empty traps and the skill it takes to catch anything, it doesn't seem so horrible that this otter had to die. Only don't look at the carcass.

Otters live on fish, and trappers often see them on the edge of the ice, enjoying a meal. If they are close to the water they have to be shot square through the heart or brain or they will slip in and lose themselves under the ice. More than half that are shot, lose themselves with their last, convulsive wriggle. They can go up the strongest rapid, under water, pulling themselves from rock to rock along the bottom. And in very strong current they pop their heads above the surface and look about, not drifting back an inch. They do not see very well, but they hear and smell with amazing keenness. If they are cornered they will jump for a man's throat, and they'll kill a husky dog in no time. They have a curious method of locomotion over the ice, long jumps and a slide on the belly. If it is slippery they can easily outrun a man, but sometimes they are caught out on the middle of a lake far from water on a day of soft or sticky snow. Then trappers run them down. Henry Baikie caught a crippled one by the tail once, but it curled its muscular back till the jaws were within slashing distance of his wrist and he was glad to let it go. The meat is fishy and makes a person sick.

While the boys go out for a breath of air and a look at the weather, Kay slips into her sleeping bag. They take off their caps and boots and we draw lots to see who will sleep on the floor. We roll up in our blankets and John douts the candle.

119

The fire is crackling and the aurora is across the frosty window.

About two minutes after it has been dark, John says, in an anxiously polite voice, "All hands ready?"

It is an old joke with us. Two springs ago, John was deer hunting on the Mealy Mountains with Byron Chaulk and Graham Blake. One night in their tent, when all three were rolled in their blankets, John asked, "All hands ready?" with finger and thumb poised above the flame.

"No," Byron answered.

So he waited for several minutes, though no one moved. "You ready now?" he asked, smelling a rat.

"No," said Byron, "I wants to turn over." And they all went into fits of laughter.

Since then he puts the light out and asks about it afterwards.

These are the strong, silent men of the North.

November 12.

KAY and I walked fifteen miles today, up around the otter rub island to the mouth of Eagle Cliff River. We saw lots of mink sign, and set four traps up along the river. There is still an open channel down the middle, and the ice by the shores under the snow is bad. This is the prettiest place around here, and the fact that it is not on any map makes it so much the better.

In a bight full of willows we shot ten white partridges. They were very tame, and after every shot they only flew a short distance before pitching again. One that we shot flew two hundred feet straight up into the air. Then he crumpled, stone dead, and hurtled down end over end like a wrecked plane. When we ran to pick him up, we found he had a bullet hole through the middle of his body. There are few men that die as game as that. If we weren't hardened savages, we couldn't eat that one.

November 14.

I FOUND an old pair of rusty skate irons in the tilt today. Rob brought them up years ago. I filed an edge on them, hammered them into two blocks of white birch and burned holes through the wood for thongs. Tonight it was bright starlight, and John and I went out for a skate. By the ripple rapid, water has flowed over the snow and made a smooth rink where we circled and swooped by turns. At last there is something I can do as well as John. We tried to write our names, but couldn't read them by the longest stretch of imagination. All about us lay the silent forest, frowning at our levity. The skates rang on the frosty ice and the black water chuckled where it slid under the ice.

I should like to travel a 500-mile trip on skates sometime. What fun it would be, and what curious thoughts it would bring. It is man's closest approach to the life of a bird, I think, much closer than riding in a plane.

November 15.

I HAVE been for a walk alone today and am still out. It is so good to be able to walk again and walk as far as I want. I've been up to Paddle Rapid. It is named for Bert Blake, who broke his paddle coming down through and steered the last half with a pole. The way leads past big bights that stretch away two miles or more on either side, all whiteness and solitude and free, free distance. The long white spaces make you no more rational, no more cynically wise than a child who feels and dreams and wonders. Then the big white plains break up into dozens of narrow channels, full of mystery where there is danger and the ice is thin, with swift water singing underneath. I set two traps, but they don't count. I set them so hard a mink will have to dance on the pan if he wants to get caught.

On either side, on the shores of the islands are huge spruces that make it dark and like a lonely passage to somewhere. Here and there on a point a giant tree is blackened where John or somebody had a fire against the base, years ago. Then the passage leads out to wide places again and the rapid; open white water swinging down around a bend and splitting on either side of an island.

And now it is sunset time and I am sitting on the side of a high, round island, cushioned by spruce branches laid in the snow, scribbling this with a two-inch pencil. It is very cold on the hands, but I don't know whether I shall ever go away from here.

The sky is a huge, blue axe blade, ground round by a little boy who is not a good hand at grinding axes. And the spruce tops on the sunset side aren't green, but russet, the color of apple time at home and cider sipped in a dry, rustling cornfield. A faint breeze stirs the russet needles, saying, "Sh-h-h, we're not going to do any thrashing about or screeching tonight. Go to sleep, you silly things."

A hillside has advantages, such as sliding down, but it is best of all for lying on. Business men should be required to lie on a hillside for twenty minutes every week and look at the sky. I have a vision of hundreds of miles of hillsides deep in business men, no talking or smoking cigars allowed. By and by there wouldn't be any more business men.

I don't even have to sit up to see the sun plunge into a bath of gold-streaked flame and splash scarlet soap bubbles all round the sky. The lanes of orange snow between the trees have dulled and all that red-gold color loops the western sky. Purple has crept over the ice and swallowed the shadow fingers that were pointing me home.

It will soon be zero, now the sun is drowned and it's time to fly over the frozen plain through the crisp twilight to a square of light between two logs. Come on, you lazy fellow, pick up your eternal companions, the gun with the cracked stock and the slender-stalked lily of steel that bites trees. Get along. One must be running to see properly the first pinpoint star prick the blue roof.

I feel as I felt once on a sunny afternoon in Maine, wandering the salt marshes in a canoe, trying to shoot a blue heron with an air rifle, but not trying very hard, he was so pretty. Sidney Lanier's lines never come to me except at times like this; sometimes the mood disappears for months, and once in the city it was a year and a half.

The tide's at full: the marsh with flooded streams
Glimmers, a limpid labyrinth of dreams.
Each winding creek in grave entrancement lies
A rhapsody of morning-stars. The skies
Shine scant with one forked galaxy,—
The marsh brags ten: looped on his breast they lie.

Oh, what if a sound should be made!
Oh, what if a bound should be laid
To this bow-and-string tension of beauty and silence a-spring,—
To the bend of beauty the bow, or the hold of silence the string!

I fear me, I fear me yon dome of diaphanous gleam
Will break as a bubble o'er-blown in a dream,—
Yon dome of too-tenuous tissues of space and of night,
Over-weighted with stars, over-freighted with light,
Over-sated with beauty and silence, will seem
  But a bubble that broke in a dream,
If a bound of degree to this grace be laid,
  Or a sound or a motion made.

I came home and started to cut up wood. My left foot was on the log. The axe glanced along the log and came up under my left toes. My foot was cold and it didn't feel like much. I went inside to have a look at it. The boot sole was cut from side to side and the wool vamp and both socks. My big toe almost made me sick. It is cut half off.

And now I'll be chained up again like a dog in a kennel. I don't mind the cut, I don't mind being laid up, I don't mind anything, only that nature is hostile, always waiting to bite. My silver urn bubbling over with beauty has jumped off the table and fetched me a crack behind the ear.

Three times reality has turned her too-hard, too-real face on me. First, the stick in the eye, then the shot, now the cut: a sudden, unreasoning swoop of pain like a grim voice from the depths of a clammy cavern saying, "You are too happy. You are too free." Perhaps it is not so much a swoop of pain as a sudden, overpowering helplessness before an annihilating force. You glory in nature. She turns and cripples you. Then it is hard to keep on glorying.

Each time the warning came, it was only my own stupidity that spoke. Yet each time it forces me to think, "Pain is the ultimate reality, not beauty." And I am cautious for a little while and spend all my time watching her and taking care. I'd rather be dead than live that way. But it knocks the props out from under one. Honestly, not for myself, but for the world and everything in it.

A WEEK gone, and my mind is all right, if my foot is not. It is simply that I must learn to be more efficient in the woods. My axe technique is bad. It is no wonder I cut myself. My mishaps have only been due to my own ignorance. It is nature's way of teaching one or warning one. Whether teaching or warning it matters little. It is her way of making one a somebody in either case. I will learn. Some day she will do for us all. Meanwhile she delights us. It is enough.

It is snowing and rough. Kay and I have been in all day while the snow piles up outside and the river is hidden. She has been telling me of the strange people she has met, nursing in Australian cities and on sheep ranches and in Paris and here, and of the women she has known who had their babies alone in isolated homes. I think doctors and nurses should write most of the books. They see people, not as they think they are, or say they are, or would like to be, but as they *are* deep down under, in the middle of the night. They help humanity, not in a sentimental way, but starkly, truly. It is their business and their way of life, and so they have the attitude necessary for great creations. Shams do not deceive them long, they are forever ferreting out the truth. And they understand how curious and fascinating life is in its uttermost realities.

ONE remembers odd things living here, away from ten thousand extraneous stimuli. There is one scene that comes to my mind over and over again. It is a windy evening on the Jersey commuters' ferry boat. New York stands wreathed in fathomless purple enchantment. All the city's ugliness is softened and blurred to beauty. Downtown, with its towers and hints of canyons is a fairy Camelot hung halfway to the sky, mysterious in the twilight and jewelled with golden lights.

On the upper deck as far toward the bow as they can get, one or two souls are watching the spray as it hisses up over the round, soup-plate bow and wets the front tires of the trucks in the gangway below. Pressed against the iron chain and gateway that form the forward rail of the deck, they have set their backs to the city and to their fellow passengers who sit inside where it's snug and warm, buried in their newspapers. An occasional man who is proud of his vigor or ashamed of his fat, pounds his way round and round the deck, head ducked on the windward side, taking an evening constitutional. But they pay no attention to him either.

If there are two or three of these comfortless ones pressed against the rail, they get as far away from each other as possible. The icy wind tears at their pitifully useless hats and flapping coats, their senseless trousers or bothersome skirts. It seems to say, "These are not the clothes for you, my children, change them for oilskins, or for parkas, or breeches and boots." But they are lost in dreams though they are shivering.

If ever there is a tramp, rusty-sided, sliding down the

river to the sea or coming in, they look at it more closely than they do at a liner. Perhaps they fancy they are in the fore chains of a ship that is butting her way through ice floes; perhaps they see, opening up ahead, some deep-shadowed African river mouth. Their eyes are staring, and some of them see nothing.

Whether they see blankness or strange harbors, they stand, never moving except to lean against the gusts, until the boat noses into the slip at Jersey City. Then they are lost in the thousands swarming aboard the long rows of suburban trains.

I always wish I had intruded upon them, those people of the wind, and touched them on the shoulder and said, "You too?" I wonder what they would have said. *Go to hell*, probably.

They say . . . What say they? . . . Let them say what they will. So decided a strong old Persian long ago, and he was right. Let them say what they will.

But it is fun to be weak sometimes and bicker with the people who say things. They say it is time wasted to live in the wilderness like this. They say other people are staying at home, soberly at work, getting ahead. Where will I be when I am old? Well, where will they be when they are old?

They say, "You are a fool. You go away and freeze yourself so that it feels good to get warm. You deliberately get yourself in a situation where you are starving, so that it will feel good to have plenty to eat again."

And suppose I do, I do it for a very good reason. I want to become inured to hard times that I may really know what nature is. For she does not give up her secrets easily. Unless one is hardy and can enjoy, though he is hungry and cold, he cannot know her.

Truly man must suffer. It is an old doctrine but few believe it. We must hit ourselves on the heads with hammers because it feels so good when we stop. Yes, truly we must. We are so constructed. If we don't, we get soft and bored; we are shoved off onto one tiny island of experience where we go round and round forever.

For me and thousands like me, it is necessary to learn that meals are not three inevitable formalities per day, clothes a bother and a house a real estate venture with a certain amount of frontage. It keeps one out of touch with the world to have too much food, too many clothes, too many ways of transportation, too much house.

What was a pair of socks to me in the old days but another possession, something to find room for in a drawer. How differently I look at them now. I've never really seen them before. How deliciously warm and soft they are. How many, many painstaking stitches they contain. I wonder who raised the sheep, who dipped them, who sheared them, who carded and spun the wool. They'll keep my feet warm, actually keep them from freezing. Why, that's what they're for!

It is good to learn that a house is, in reality, a place to return to when your clothes commence to stiffen with ice. It's a place where you can sleep without having rain drip on you or snow drift down your neck. It's a place where you don't have to cook your food on a stick; there are so many utensils you can either boil it or fry it or bake it, whichever you like. In a house you can keep warm without getting smoke in your eyes and burning your clothes full of cinder holes.

This life, and the half-life I used to live are so different I can hardly believe I am the same being. You know what it is like to wake up on a sunny spring morning when the apple blossom scent is coming in the window so strong and sweet it pries your eyelids open? That first few seconds of consciousness when you are glad you woke up, because it's too good to miss? There is nothing hanging over you, nothing you are afraid of, nothing you hate. You can run out in the sunshine, stretch your arms up to the sky and roll stark naked in the dewy grass. There's no one within 500,000 miles. There are no neighbors to watch you through the window, saying, as they ring for the patrol wagon, "What a shame. I always said he was a little funny."

In this golden first few seconds there is no thought that you must shave and your last razor blade is dull and it is late and you will miss the train. There's only an instant of freedom and truth. Well, weeks and weeks go by up here, just like that.

This uncivilized life is worth while for a civilized person as a sharpener of the senses, if nothing else. We can smell wood smoke half a mile away. Our sense of taste is remarkably sharp. "Food's got no taste after you been down home awhile," John says. We seldom have all we want to eat, but our simple meals seem like banquets. When we sit down on the floor to partridge stew, we can distinguish between the rich oiliness of cubes of salt pork, and the partridge's own fat. Every kernel of rice tastes good. Our weekly dish of prunes or apricots is an event. The smell of a tree or the willows, the air or the taste of water, we are conscious and glad of everything. Everything is true and simple and good to the core. This is the absolute antithesis of being bored. How do we pay for it? By work of a certain kind, work which makes us stronger and keener still.

THINGS are so valuable here where we can't buy anything, but must use what we have. We wouldn't dream of throwing away a nail, or an old piece of wire or an old boot. As likely as not we'll need the wire for a kettle handle. Partridge tail feathers make excellent pipe cleaners, and John made an ornate candlestick of an old tin plate.

The men often use an expression, "You can't stick an old trapper," for they are proud of their slap-dash ingenuity. Some of their tricks make a joke of situations that might otherwise be desperate.

The sap of spruce or balsam is excellent for a cut. It seems to have disinfectant qualities. It sticks tighter than surgeons' tape, keeps the dirt out, and in the case of a large cut, holds the edges together like stitches. It is not bad for chewing gum and is good for small cuts in canoes. For big rips in the canvas a birch bark patch stuck on with sap keeps her "tight as a cup," or "dry as a bottle."

For a "rising" or infected wound, many swear by a hot poultice of the white pulp just inside the bark of a juniper tree [tamarack, larch].

Birch bark makes a good torch, and of course, the finest tinder. Indians make birch-rind kettles and boil water in them. It also makes a serviceable plate, and to clean it you have only to peel off one of its dozen or more layers and it is a new plate of a new, pastel shade. There is nothing so good for roofing tilts or wrapping up fish when there are flies around.

Old sealskin bootlegs with very little sewing can be transformed into waterproof mitts, cartridge bags and bait bags. Long strips cut round and round make strong strings for mending snowshoes. If there is no skin for patching a hole in a sealskin boot, pork rind will do. If one's boots are old and get damp inside, grass in the bottom will keep one's feet warm and dry.

If you burn your deerskin moccasin, or lose it, a duffel vamp will last on snowshoes for a day's walk, or a moccasin patched with a piece of eight-ounce, flour-bag duck will go for two days on soft snow.

Trappers seldom have a pencil handy, but they always have a cartridge. A sharpened cartridge serves as a useful pencil for a quick note on a blazed tree, or an impromptu map.

If stockings have a big hole in the heel they just turn them over and let the hole come on the top of the instep. If the toes are out they tie up the end with a piece of line. If the whole foot is worn out they cut it off, tie up the bottom of the leg and put it on again. In roomy, soft moccasins, well-fitting sox are not a necessity. Pieces of rabbit fur sometimes save frostbitten toes. Rabbit skins also make good mitts, but they do not wear.

Smooth rocks are useful whetstones. Fred Goudie, who loves stretching things, says he's picked them up around the Devil's Hole, smooth on one side and rough on the other, set in a block of wood and already oiled.

In winter, when it is rimey going for a toboggan, a hairy sealskin tied across the bottom makes her run like greased lightning.

John broke his axe handle one morning, and in three minutes it was fixed. The stump of the old handle was jammed in the eye of the head. He shot that out with his Remington, pounded in a piece of an old canoe pole for a new handle, hammered in the empty shell for a wedge and was off.

It is nothing to make a stove pipe of baking powder cans fitted together, bottom to top, with the bottoms cut out. Anyone can mend old stoves with pieces of lard pails riveted on by means of filed-off nails, using an axe and a rock for hammer and anvil. Trappers always carry a file to sharpen the axe with. The pointed, handle-end of the file serves as an awl.

Any kind of animal fat, from porcupine, duck, rabbit, muskrat or bear, is good for greasing guns, and won't gum and jam them in cold weather the way bought gun oil does.

John has the crowning tale of ingenuity. One fall in November when he went in on his path for the first trip, he found his old second tilt with part of the gable end and a good many of the rafters fallen in. He had no tent. It was cold and snowing. He went to the brook, chopped a hole and brought up kettle after kettle of water. As he lifted each log into its place, he cemented it there with water that froze almost as soon as it touched. He vows it stood till spring, and boasts it isn't everybody that can stick a tilt together with ice. Nevertheless he always slept under the bunk lest the roof tumble in.

MY poor abandoned sled boards have leaned disconsolately against the roof, calling to me these many days. Today I could not resist them any longer.

First the axe and Indian crooked-knife must be sharpened to razor edges with file and whetstone and loving care. With these I smoothed one side of each board as flat as possible. Then, with a little block plane which Robert pressed upon me just as we were leaving Traverspine, I shaved them both. It is like scrubbing a floor, down on one's knees, rocking back and forth, and for soap suds, heaps of curled orange shavings, graceful as flowers and fragrant as honey. The clean new wood glistens with smoothness, and against one's cheek it feels like satin. How sad it would be to buy everything!

It is very cold on the fingers, even working with mittens, and sometimes I take the boards in the tilt and work on the floor beside the stove, letting the ends stick out the door. Toward evening both pieces are a smooth, uniform quarter-inch thick, shaped narrow at the head for parting the snow, a little wider just forward of the middle where the main weight goes, and tapering away to a frictionless stern that will bend like a whip in the hollows and send her leaping up little banks. I am ready for the bending, with first a prayer to the patron saint of carpenters, whoever he may be. This is the crucial moment, for my boards are too short to allow any bungling. The wise old hands start with boards fourteen or fifteen feet long, so that if they crack in the bending, there is still room to saw off a foot or so and try again.

Two humble genii assist in the operation, namely a pair

of trousers and a pot of boiling water. Wrapped around the board at the point of bend, the breeches hold in the steam and help soften the naturally pliant wood. When it is soft, the wood must be worked, and sprung and bent both ways. Very slowly, very carefully one is bent up into a beautiful, oval curve, then the other. I lash them fast to dry so, and the lashings sing like mandolin strings.

After supper, I had to go out and caress them twice before I could go to bed.

John is always picking up strange and utterly outlandish words from us. He gives them whatever meaning amuses him at the moment. There is none of our servile kowtowing to dictionary, grammar, punctuation, spelling or etiquette rules here. Lots of people have two or three different ways of spelling their own names, according to the weather or how their rheumatism happens to be. I imagine it resembles the spirit of brave old Elizabethan days when the queen swore if she felt like swearing.

The latest word is "medical," which means remarkably good, or unusually desirable or something of the sort. We have medical mugups, otters and candlesticks. Tonight he told me, "Sure enough, that's a medical sled all right—to a certain extent."

Someone once told him that a feather on a liner's rail would list her down on that side, *to a certain extent*. It made him ripping mad that anyone could say such foolishness. Now it is a synonym for anything so patently absurd that a person can hardly talk about it without collapsing of mirth.

We have picked up some odd words from him, too, such as *cripsy*, which means brittle, *slink* which means thin, and *boxy,* which is used only of wood, and means the dark, tough wood that grows in the bend of a crooked tree. Boxy wood is the only hardwood in this country.

November 25.

WOKE up this morning with a feeling something good was going to happen to me and I couldn't remember what. It was like a birthday morning when I was a kid. And then I remembered, "This is the day for finishing the sled."

Tonight it is finished with seven curious-shaped cross bars lashed with thongs to join the two boards. John claims old Mathieu will make him a better *tabanask* than that, but I don't believe it.

At sunset Kay crunched in, with her gun over her shoulder and eight partridges, tied with line, slung from the barrel. Every day she goes hunting, and for weeks she has kept us in meat. So far, she has shot over 200 partridges, and many's the night we would have supped on bread and tea but for her. It does a person's heart good to see her walk and hunt and shoot. She knows the sound of hollow ice or the look of snow that is "hung up." She can manage her snowshoes up and down banks and over windfalls as though they were nothing. She has learned to kick them off and on without the use of hands as the Labradormen do. At a glance she knows a likely spot for partridges, and has learned a variety of ways of setting rabbit snares. She can put up a tent or light a fire in no time, and she knows the look of the sky, the taste of the air and the feel of a breeze that threatens snow. She is taking care of me now, not I of her. She carries a matchsafe, a gun and an axe with her wherever she goes, and they are more serviceable than a thousand worries.

Alvin came yesterday to say hello, and this morning Kay and John went off with him to try to find a new route up Eagle Cliff River to Eagle Cliff tilt, which is on an island in Sandgirt Lake. Next day they will go with him down beside White Rapid and Goose Rapid to Cross Island, and the third day home.

So I am alone tonight with only the crackling fire for company, and everything is different and more intense, as though solitude had polished familiar objects to richer colors and given my endlessly tumbling thoughts new edges. I think I have a pretty good idea what the back side of the moon must look like.

I am lying on the dear old hewn bunk, and under my hand are its smooth timbers, worn shiney by many sittings and lyings. I feel like Daniel Boone or Kit Carson, or somebody who amounted to something. I wonder what kind of a person Daniel Boone would have been if he had been a floorwalker in a department store all his life. I never want anything softer or more elegant to lie on than a hewn bunk with a few skins thrown over it. Purer air and harder work make up for box springs. I never want to go away from here, even to the village down the river, and neither does Kay. What will you do way up there in a tiny cabin half the winter? they asked. And think of the monotony and discomfort and dirt.

I've heard it said that the country makes men and the city uses them, and I know it is so. I think all great men have known the land or sea, have sat in at the secret, odd hour conferences of storm and terror and peace; have understood and longed and been awed. And in my mind there is a huge difference between men who did big, spectacular things, and men who were great in themselves. Probably some of the greatest men who ever lived have never been heard of, never had one line written about them. They were of the earth and returned to the earth and their bodies fertilized good wheat. And a thousand Napoleons, streaking the sky with blood, cannot equal one of them.

November 29.

KAY and John came home today, and they had a rough time. John forgot the flour the day they went away, and when they got to Eagle Cliff tilt, long after dark, after being lost for a couple of hours, they had a third of a partridge and a piece of bread the size of a match-box, each, for supper. It's a good thing Kay is handy with the racquets or she would have dropped on the way. Alvin nearly gave out before they got there.

The tilt was very old, and the chinks wide open. They had no blankets and the stove wouldn't draw. The roof leaked as soon as they lit the fire, and snow water dripped down on them all night.

For breakfast they had tea, and late that afternoon when they got to Cross Island where there was plenty of food they baked up six pounds of flour before they were satisfied.

Today it was "blowin and driftin" all the way down, and John froze his chin a little coming across Forget Me Not. Coming through the narrow channels where the water races underneath, the ice sounded hollow and Kay hung back. All

137

of a sudden with a crash a big piece went from under John's feet. He was right beside the shore. Like lightning he threw his axe onto the rocks and jumped after it just as the pan sank. "When you bust through the ice," he says, "alwus heave your axe. If you don't you'll lose it, and you needs it if you gets out."

December 7.

A week ago John and I left for Unknown Lake (Ossokmanuan). Against the tilt I had piled a big stack of split wood for Kay, and she had four partridges in reserve. On the scaffold we put my tent and stove with some clothing and the reserves of food. My main worry for her, beside a visit from some hungry Indians, was lest the tilt catch fire some day when she should be away hunting.

She stood in the doorway and waved her cap as we went down the bank. I thought as I waded through the deep new snow and the sled slipped down behind me, bumping my legs at each step, that it was plucky of her to tell me to go. Three of us couldn't go, as that meant too much load for the sled and John was in a hurry. But I could have stayed, and I discovered later that ethically I should have. The last thing we saw was blue smoke drifting up from the funnel, and then trees shut out the cabin.

The sled ran hard and it was not good walking. It is always rimey after a new batch of snow before it has settled or the wind has hardened it. About every twenty minutes we had to turn the sled bottom up and scrape off the thin coating of rime that made her stick.

Lashed tight to the sled inside the canvas wrapper we had a small aluminum boiler for tea and a larger one for meat, a handleless frying pan and a tin bowl for mixing dough. These nest together and go in the curl of the nose; back of these a half bag of flour, and on top of the kettles and flour our two grub bags each of which contain a cup, fork, spoon, little bags of salt, sugar, tea, a quarter of a pound of baking powder, a small can of butter and a loaf of bread. The load was completed by half a pound of pork, half a pound of beans, fifteen traps, John's funny old tent, his blanket, my small sleeping bag and a gamebag containing candles, matches, cartridges and four sox. Outside the wrapper the gun was tied to the crisscrossing lashline. If John's tilts were any good we would have dispensed with sleeping gear and the tent, left the sled behind and carried what we needed. We each carried an axe, and we each had a big square scarf or shawl tied around the neck. We did not take dickies, and the shawl was to do us in place of a hood when it blew.

The rest of our equipment, such as snowshoes, double mitts of caribouskin and wool, moccasins the same, canvas leggings, sweater, canvas coat, cap with fur ears, match safe, tobacco, pipe, bandanna, was on us.

When we left the river and plunged into the woods southwest, John was ahead breaking trail and I came behind with the sled; then up a little hill and through the thick trees for about two miles, stopping at a trap now and again. We couldn't see John's old track, but we could feel it. Whenever we got off it, we sank about six inches deeper. We came to a narrow, crooked lake with islands and points that stuck across nearly to the other side. The snow was blown hard by the wind and our snowshoes rattled on the crust. About three-quarters of the way up the lake we turned off into the woods again.

So far we had passed but two blazes and those were so old you could scarcely tell whether they were overgrown natural scars or marks of man. A fur path is, of course, not a path at all. It is a trap line. Once in a while there is a trap, half or completely buried in snow, every mile or two there is a broken-off stub; in other respects the "path" is just like the rest of the forest, unless there are blazes. Many trappers mark each trap with a three-cornered blaze, and their path with single blazes that can be seen from one to the other. Some of John's traps are marked, but most are not, and parts of the path are hardly marked at all. I suppose there are nearly 250 traps on that path all the way in to Unknown Lake. John has a picture of each one's location in his mind's eye, can start at the first and describe the surroundings and distinguishing features of every one, right to the last. What does he care about blazes. Every time he goes in on the path he changes the location of ten or twenty or thirty traps and never blazes one of them.

We had not been gone two hours before I had to call a halt. "John," I said, "I'll go back, if you say. My toe is paining me with the strain of hauling. If I haul much more, I know it's going to split open again. There is no reason why you should haul my stuff. You are in a hurry."

"No, boy," he said, "give me the sled now and you go ahead. You'll be all right in a day or so."

I didn't want to go back, but I should have. I could walk all right, but the strain of hauling, leaning forward and pushing on my toe at every step was too much for the new-healed cut. I carried the gun and went ahead, and after we boiled I carried the two grub bags in the gamebag. Carrying didn't bother me and, of course, the lighter a sled is the easier she runs.

I used to look back at the sled gliding over the snow, bending and rippling over the hummocks like a live thing. It really has a very graceful curl. I wouldn't trade it for one ten times as good that some one else made. It makes a polished track in the snowshoe trail, with a little seam in the middle, where the two boards come together.

Sometimes we'd stop, leave the sled and go off one side a quarter of a mile or so to an open brook where there would be an otter trap set in the water on stones, or a mink trap close by the bank. In one such place we had a mink. He was caught by the hind foot, and he'd worked his head and shoulders down in under the pan and frozen that way, coiled up in the trap. John tried to get him out, but was afraid of breaking him in half, so we took along the trap and all to thaw it out in the evening. It was a beautiful black one, but the mice had shaved the tiniest little patch on the under side. *Su-ish, su-ish, su-ish,* hour after hour through the snow, over little hills and through groves of huge birches, down into little valleys full of half-covered boulders, and willows that sting one's cold face, across lakes where we could run, and between trees so close together we had to kick up our snowshoes on edge to get through.

Toward noon John's track petered out and he had to tell me which way to go, where the blazes were few. This was as far as he had been this fall, for the lakes were late freezing up. From here on we stopped about every fifteen minutes to dig out a trap, bait it, set it and fix the trap house if necessary. Mink traps are in little houses against the base of a big tree. The sides of the house are of split rotten logs, held up by stakes. The roof is of brush to keep the snow out. Bait goes in the back of the house and the trap in the entrance. Whenever it seemed an especially likely place and there was mink sign close by, John rubbed the stakes at the entrance with beaver castor, which has a strange, heavy-sweet scent that all animals find alluring.

We came to a ridge which runs like a backbone east and west across the land. We climbed a tree and looked back. There were miles and miles of spruce tops, and then on the river a glimpse of Lobstick Lake and Sandgirt Lake and, down below, Flour Lake. The woods here in winter are not desolate like the woods of northern New Jersey. All the hills are clothed with green and the forests are not bare and black and shivering. And in the snow is the open book of tracks, the record of life and means of life, instead of emptiness and death and old stone walls.

As we were skirting a small, half-open brook John began to laugh. "Ho ho, look where somebody got fooled." He pointed, and I saw where a rabbit had tried to jump from the far shore to a round, icy rock in midstream and thence to our bank. The marks of his feet were on the rock where he had landed and slipped in; then the record of his scramble to get up on the ice, the drops of water from his fur, and his jumps away into the woods.

In the greenwoods, far from lakes and brooks, marten traps replaced mink traps. They are set about four feet from the ground, in notches chopped into stumps or trees. A flat, pointed slab is driven between the bark and the wood of the tree, to close up the notch except for a small opening where Mr. Wabistan enters. The trap spring protrudes out through the back door, and through this a stick is passed, so the marten cannot reach up and pull the trap out the front door. Without the stick, they will often spill the trap out and enjoy the bait at their leisure.

Nevertheless, even though marten are the lightning terror of the woods to rabbits and squirrels and mice, they are not as canny as most of the other fur bearers. Other fur animals are nearly as plentiful as always along Grand River, but marten are getting scarcer. They don't travel as much as other animals, and where they happen to live near a trap line they get caught one after another until the family is exterminated. This means considerable potential loss to the race. Other animals are on the move, except in the bitterest weather and when the snow is deep and soft. One may be caught and the rest of the brood go on to wilderness where man never troubles them.

At the edge of a marsh we shot two spruce partridges and plucked them on the spot. Once they have frozen it is twice as hard to get the feathers off. It is very cold on the hands, but the bird, though dead, is still warm and you can warm your hand against his breast as you pluck.

In a thick clump of trees we came on a huge spruce, squared down and written on in scarcely legible pencil letters, "I came here the day. Dan Groves Dec. 20, 1905," and underneath, "Here today March 6 1922, Robert Michelin." Dan was killed in the war, along with thousands of other men from the mountains and deserts and jungles of the earth for whom the insane conflagration had no cause, no aim, no meaning whatsoever. I like to think this is where his spirit rests; not in France, but here under this lonely giant tree, here in the woods he first explored, here in the life he understood. The spreading green branches curve down their tips to shield him. What did he know of or care for the war? This is his tombstone.

It was bright moonlight when we halted in a glade where

a rusty tin stove hung on a stump. There was no water handy, but we decided to camp. We tramped a place for the tent, and John cut two "macoms" and a ridgepole and pickets while I cut brush. The tent was soon up and I set up the stove on legs and fixed the brush floor and lit the fire while John was cutting up wood. We drove pickets along the walls inside to hold them out, then banked them outside with snow.

I suppose it was about fifteen or twenty below. To unlash the sled, to tie the tent strings, to get out a candle and light the fire all require that you take off your mitts.

The stove was soon roaring and we put on the kettles full of snow. Snow from down under is icier and contains more water than the top snow. A kettle full of this under-snow gives only a quarter of a kettle of water. The quickest way is to let this quarter kettleful get boiling hot before putting in more snow. However you do it, it takes about four times as long to get tea and start the partridges, as if you have water.

With the snowshoes hung up, the axes stuck up in the snow, the sled brushed off and stood on end against a tree, sleeping gear and grub in the tent and plenty of wood piled within reach, we crawled in and closed the door tight. John commenced to sing:

> Give me a tent and kittle,
> Snowshoes and axe and gun;
> Send me up in Grand River,
> Steering by star and sun,
> And you'll see me in finest fettle
> Return when my hunt is done,
> And, you'll see me in a big black kettle
> Roll home before my hunt is begun.

We coiled around the snapping, roaring stove like a couple of snakes. We spread out the bag and blanket and sat on them; then took off our moccasins all stiff with frost inside.

John's tent is a ragged old thing that he swears he's going to use for five years more. It has been used a great deal for a wrapper on a sled, where rough ice and thick trees have ripped it. In summer it serves as a sail for a skiff. We stuffed up the holes with our coats and caps and mitts and the little *meetchwop* began to get hot. How we lay back and stretched and drank the heat into our bodies like thirsty men drinking and bathing in cool water!

While we were eating supper he demonstrated a use for every hole in the tent. On either side there was one for each man to throw his partridge bones through. In the front a big one gaped. "That's for shovin' out the flour bag when we'm done bakin'. And in the roof there's twenty-three. Many's the time I've counted them, unless a couple more have got burned. They are for havin' a look what the weather's doin' when you wakes up."

After supper I mixed up and baked four river cakes while John skinned some weasels and the half-thawed mink. The smell of a mink is almost as sharp and unpleasant as the smell of a skunk. While we were smoking our pipes John must needs tell me a verse:

> Oh, tobacco is a filthy weed,
> And from the Devil doth proceed.
> It robs the pockets
> And soils the clothes,
> And makes a chimney
> Out of the nose.

I tapped and weighed in my hand the last sweet-smelling brown cake to see if it was done, then stretched out in my

145

bag. John says my baking always gives him heartburn, but bannock gives everybody heartburn, so I am not chastened by the announcement. Through a hole I could see the moon sailing over us and the forest and the world. A sharp silver disk, and John still talking when I dropped off.

John boasts that Harvey Montague is the only person who can "freeze him out." He can certainly out-freeze me, for I had to make on a fire three times in the night. The last time it was near dawn. He was chattering when I opened the stove door to put in some shavings and splits, and in another minute he'd have had to do it himself I think.

It was colder than ever when we pulled down the tent, lashed up and went off. We had to take the stove on the sled, so I carried some traps and the grub bags in the sack. Swish, swish through the woods again, the sun sparkling through the trees no higher off the snow than a man's head.

Two or three miles down a long slant brought us to the burnt woods. It was a ghastly looking sight, a desolate barren, cut up with hills and little lakes, sprinkled with small, black poles, leaning and pitiful. It looked like a bad place to be caught in a snowstorm. We were two hours and a half crossing to the greenwoods on the other side, and never a mark did I see all the way across. There was nothing to go by except the hills, and they were uniform, round and bare.

The first time he hunted this path, John found his way across here by himself and picked up the path on the other side. He had to, there was no one to show him.

In a cove of the last lake on the barrens we found a beaver house. In front of the dome of snow, heaps of willow browse were sticking through the ice. Indians have a way of driving stakes like a fence all around the house on the water side.

Then when they chop through the top of the house the beaver can't get away. We didn't want to take the time for this, so we tried another scheme.

I went off to the green hillside after two long, forked birch sticks, while John chopped two holes in the ice and got the traps ready. The ends of the chains were fastened to two poles that were laid flat on the ice, and the traps were set and lashed in the birch crotches. Then one birch stick was lowered into each hole until the bottom of the stick was in the mud and the crotch and trap were about six inches under water. The hole was filled with snow and the job was done. The theory is that a beaver much prefers birch to willow. He chews the bottom of the stick and works on up till he puts his fore paw in the crotch trying to eat the top.

It was a cold job, and when we were done, we lit a fire as much for our hands as to boil the kettle.

Toward afternoon we wound down a long narrow lake where there were fox traps in burrows in the bank, and caribou sign by the shores. At the far end a steep hill barred our way. The snow was more than waist deep and we slipped and floundered, trying to get the sled up. While I held it from behind, John would climb up a few steps and get a good grip on the hauling line. Then he hauled her up short while I pushed. Then over again, and so we progressed, foot by foot, panting and sweating in the cold, filling our mitts full of snow and falling on our faces in the powdery nothingness.

When we came to the first tilt it was so tumbled in and covered with snow I couldn't see it. Five or six miles more and across a big lake, we camped. We hadn't come very far, but the beaver house delayed us, and fixing traps every quarter mile takes time.

When we were snugged away I asked John how he thought Kay would be getting on all by herself. "I dunno," he said, "Bein' alone in the woods fer the first time is alwus somethin'."

My conscience hurt me for leaving her, although she said she wished it. "We want to know what Labrador life is really like," she said. "Well, plenty of women have been alone for months."

"I minds," remarked John, "the first time I went in the path alone. I was fourteen. We was livin' Traverspine them days of course. I wanted like the devil to go to the fair to North West River that year. I wanted to step up with a girl and do the Lancers, an' buy a basket 'n' all that, least I thought I did. The old man said I could go if I'd go in Black Rock fer 'n. Maa made a big bakin' of new bread so's I wouldn't have to bake for three or four nights.

"The old man come up along the river with me to where the path takes in 'n' then I swung off with my sled an' never looked back, makin' the snow fly an' feelin' pretty big. I had a good little pair of snowshoes and the sled was light, 'cause the tilts was all good so's I didn't need no tent n'r stove. I'd been in that path twenty times or more with the old man an' I knowed I couldn't miss the way. It's four tilts distance in.

"Well, I got four weasels and a mink that day and along toward sunset I starts gittin' jumpy. I come to the first tilt, buried right to the eyes, with nothin' but the peak of the gable end stickin' out of the snow. The tilt's right slap in the middle of the big trees. If it'd been by a lake 't wouldn't been so bad. All the stumps commenced to look like crooked black ghostes just standin' all around and waitin' fer me to turn my back.

"Whilest I was diggin' out the door, two children got to talkin' to each other, and then to moanin'. It were two trees rubbin' together, and you know what wunnerful noises they makes sometimes. I laughed and laughed, but the more I laughed the scareder I got. When I was done cuttin' up wood I was scared to make a noise, almost. Lord Harry, I was glad to crawl inside an' light the candle. It was little good in there. I took in my gun and axe an' I wouldn't of come out again fer a barr'l of apples. While supper was cookin' I hung up the weasels and the mink to thaw, and when I was done eatin', I skinned 'em and put 'em in a bag to leave fer comin' out. I left a little flour in the kittle under the bunk too, like the old man does.

"I had two big sticks cut just for it, 'n' I jammed them against the door. Every time I'd hear the trees crackin' with the frost I'd think it were the Old Feller out there a-crackin' his tail. I remembered all the damnedest yarns I ever heered, and the shivers was goin' up my back, an' when I thought about blowin' out the candle I commenced to cry. I tried to pray 'n' all I could think about was how Charlie Groves shot two wolves right in the door of his tilt.

"I'd sneaked a piece of Rob's plug before I left, 'n' I took a little chew off that. It made me sick an' then I weren't so scared. I couldn't think about goin' to sleep in the dark, so I put the candle on the bottom of a fryin' pan fer when it burned down, an' I tried to git to sleep.

"I waked up early, boiled the kittle an' scraped the grease off the fryin' pan so's the old man wouldn't ask me next

149

round what I done that fer. I lashed up the sled and legged it. Lord Harry how I did drive 'er. It was two hours before daylight, but a kind of a bright night you know. I didn't find the morning-dark so bad. I passed a lot of traps in the dark, but I didn't care about that. I was only thinkin' about night comin'. I wanted to git to the next tilt 'fore sunset.

"I only boiled up once and then I wouldn't take time to break off brush to sit on, or cut green sticks for the fire. I just made a fire on top of a rotten stump and stuck my feet deep in the snow so's they wouldn't git wet, and had my mugup standin' like that. I boiled and was gone in twenty minutes.

"I saw a big company of partridges but I'd only stop long enough to shoot one fer supper. The old man always used to kill all he could get and hang 'em up fer comin' out, in case it snowed heavy or somethin'. But I couldn't bother with that.

"I got to the second tilt an hour before dark and was all fixed away an' the door barred when it come on dark. A 'arn owl give me the creeps that night an' I had a worse time of it than the night before. I got to thinkin' what would I do when I'd burned up all my candles, an' every time I went to sleep I'd have some strange dream and wake up sweatin'.

"In the morning I turned around and beat 'er fer back. I back tracked all morning, an' when I boiled the kittle, the sun was shinin' so bright I got to thinkin'. An' I thinks, I got to be a man now if I'm ever goin' to be one. And look at Jess Poole and Peter Naklik. They'm scared to go alone even now. An' look at how everybody laughs at them an' they can't never be good hunters, but always got to take some little boy 'r somebody off with 'em. So I gits out the piece of plug and cuts off a few pieces an' rubs 'em up fine. Then I took a piece of paper my candles was wrapped up in an' I rolls a cigarette and lights it with a brand like I seen Rob do. I layed back on the brush by the fire and smoked it right to the lips, just like I was a man and didn't care how late I was, gettin' back to the second tilt.

"That night wasn't so awful bad an' the next night at the third tilt was a little better. I left my sled at the third tilt and went in to the fourth tilt and back the same day. It was blowin' and driftin' somethin' wunnerful on the lakes, and my shawl was all raggedy. I began to take care how I fixed the traps too, cause the fur was runnin' pretty good. I was drivin' 'er some I tell you b'y. I wanted to make up for the day I lost and git home.

"Saturday I was tryin' to make two tilts' distance again, on the track comin' back. I lost a lot of time chasin' a fresh otter track up a little brook, and when it come on dark I was caught half ways between the second tilt and the first. It come on to snow at sundown and I was scared of the big marsh if I went on. I decided I'd have to barricade out. So I picked a good spot in a gully under some big silver pines, and dug right down to the ground fer the fire. I was tired, and didn't dig right to the ground for a place fer me to lie on, just put down a lot of brush on the snow. Then I cut some poles and stuck 'em in the snow in back, slantways almost out over the fire and lashed a bar across the top; a kind of a lean-to you know, covered with brush and banked up with snow.

"There was a lot of dead junipers around and I spotted a couple of good ones before it got too dark. I had to cut up lots of wood and then I put on a partridge.

"After supper I got in my sleepin' bag. I couldn't git to

sleep for a long time, the wind was bafflin' around so much. Finally I dropped off, an' sure enough of course the snow melted out from under me.

"When you barricade out, you got to dig to the ground a big enough hole fer yourself and the fire. Well, the snow caved in on the side nearest the fire, and rolled me right into it. I woke up full of smoke and sparks an' the bag was all afire. I was so scared I got caught all up in it and burnt one hand a little gittin' out. The bag was no good anyway and I was that mad I threw what was left of it in the fire and watched it burn. The Indians say when you burn yourself you got to burn out the pain, just like you got to put on snow when you gits froze. So I held my fist near the fire 's long as ever I could, and in the morning it was better."

"Oh, John," I said, "what rot."

"Gospel truth, and I swore I'd never sleep in a cursed old bag again an' I never have. Give me a blanket any day. Same weight, same size, you can roll up tight in it and get two doubles 'round you 'stead of one. An' you can git out of it quick too.

"Well Sunday was a hellish day. I went on to the first tilt, but I couldn't fix the traps on account of Sunday, so I had to go back next morning. I saw one live weasel in a trap and I made up my mind it was all right to kill him, but I didn't take him out. The snow was deep, right to the knees, and hard haulin'. Sunday afternoon I spent roarin' out hymns. Lord, boy, you don't know how I can yell when I'm alone in the woods. I heered the echo comin' off a hill twenty miles away once, no lie.

"Tuesday, goin' down the river I met the old man comin' up the river to have a look fer me. He was mad about the bag, but I made a pretty good haul and he was glad a' that. He asked me how I got on in the nights and I says, 'Oh, fine.'"

"Did you have a good time at the fair?"

"Oh, I didn't go! I wanted to go right back in the path again, and I did, the next week. But the old man came along too, an' that spoiled it and I wished I'd gone to the fair. An' he smelled the candle wax burnin' on the bottom of the pans and I had a bad time of it then. That time in Black Rock is the last time I ever turned back from anywheres."

Next day I could haul all right, and I took my turn regularly with the sled from then on. On the side of a ridge we came on crisscrossing chains of oval holes in the snow. There was a crust here and we made a terrific noise as we walked. "Caribou," said John, "one day old. They aren't far."

We followed the track and saw where they had pawed the snow away with their hoofs to get at the white caribou moss. We left the sled, and taking only the big rifle, followed in their track. Our snowshoes were slung over our shoulders and we stepped in their steps so we wouldn't break the crunching crust.

The steps were pretty long, and we almost had to jump some of them. The snow at the bottom of each hole was frozen hard, but at the top of the next ridge we saw where they had bedded down for the night, and after that the snow in each step was soft—today's track, a stag and two does, John whispered. It was bad going for them. On the forward edge of a hole now and then we'd see hairs shaved from their legs, and once, a little blood.

The trees were very thick, and though we took infinite pains to be quiet, they must have heard us before we saw them; for soon the meandering tracks converged in one, and the steps grew longer and longer till we could see they had started to gallop. We put on our snowshoes and drove 'er, thinking perhaps we could run them down in the deep snow and crust. At intervals we could see where the head one had jumped aside and fallen in behind to get a rest on the track. The stag went ahead for longer stretches than the does, but he took his turn behind, nevertheless. This is exactly what the trappers do, when a party of them are hauling sleds in bad going.

For two hours we legged it after them, bursting through branches and running down hills. Then they got out on a windswept marsh where the going was better, and thence to a lake where their jumps were about ten feet long. It commenced to snow and we decided the chase was no go.

"Which way is the sled?" said John, laughing in his Russian whisker. I took a chance and pointed, but my guess was nearly a quarter wrong. He led the way in a straight line to the sled, paying no attention to the wandering way we had come. It was two o'clock when we got there, and we hadn't had anything to eat since seven. While we boiled, he told me that Indians have chased "deer" for two days and nights, trying to run them down. Cases have been known where they were starving, their strength was failing them, and if they didn't catch the deer they died. He told me Arch and Fred killed two deer one spring going down the river. They hauled a heavy load of meat nearly 200 miles to get it down to their families, and when they got home they found the warm sun had spoiled it all.

We crossed a wide lake and camped early in a glade beside a brook. In the evening we got to telling orthographical stories. John told one about old Aunt Caroline. The Methodist minister was visiting at their house for a couple of days as it was bad going and his dogs were limping. One afternoon the wood box got low and Aunt Caroline went out to the pile for an armful. On her way in she met the minister and he said, "Well, what have you got there?"

" 'ood," said Aunt Caroline.

"What?" asked the minister.

" 'ood," the old lady repeated.

"How do you spell it?"

"Sometimes I spells it in my apron, Sir, and sometimes I spells it in my arms."

I told one about school teaching last year. A little black-haired fellow about nine years old was telling a story he'd made up about a seal hunt. In it he mentioned the word "oonock." It is an Eskimo implement, used for harpooning seals.

It was a new word to me, and I said, "What is that word? How do you spell it?"

The boy's black eyes snapped and he stamped his foot as he almost shouted, "You *don't* spell it, you dart *seals* with it."

Unknown Lake, how I've dreamed about it, a mystery even to the trappers. Ossokmanuan the Indians call it and the inaccurate maps give little idea of its size or shape; a huge inland sea, unexplored, like its name, unknown.

On the fourth morning, after crossing several ridges we caught sight of it through the trees, an enormous expanse of crooked whiteness studded with high islands like shapes of dark animals crouching. Standing tiptoe on our snowshoes we could not make out any limits to the lake.

I've never been happier than that morning on the hill. I thought to myself, "This is the place in the world where I would like most to be, and I am here." People say it is no use poking off to far corners, that you are still you and you see but yourself through your own eyes. Well, they lie, poor things. I am a thousand different persons, and today I am the freest, strongest, happiest of them all. I can feel the charm of a city park, that oasis of green amid the stone, but it is not like this and why pretend it is. Why be satisfied with half a loaf, with half-beauty, with half-honesty, with half-life. This moment is worth months of pain and fatigue and hunger mixed with the tight cramp of cold. This moment is worth twice what it cost. I should like to die in a place like this. I'd die five years sooner to be allowed to die here alone without benefit of clergy, for the clergy is no more necessary to my religion than ships are to the sea.

What fun it would be to build a cabin on the lake and live here for years and years, just Kay and I. And in the spring the ducks would come, and in summer the grass and wild bluebells, and our canoe would creep in and out of every bay and cove. And the world could go its way and we would go ours in our own hidden world deep in the wilderness. We would not know of wars, or increased taxes or inauguration addresses or who was the world's heavyweight champion or how many were murdered yesterday and it would be good not to know, and not to be forced to know. And after years and years, we'd come out and say hello to everybody that thought we were dead, and refuse with icy hauteur to give exclusive stories to the *Times*.

A pleasant dream, but one that little suits this country. In summer there would be the flies, and no time to raise grain. In winter we should have to be nomads travelling hundreds of miles after food. The Indians haven't much detachment, much thought of beauty when they look at nature. We with our empty stomachs would have less, for we could not live as well as Indians. Where would we get twine for nets, knives, cartridges, guns, canvas, matches? When we died at an early age, we would have the dissatisfaction of knowing that we had been kept alive even so long by products of the civilization we despise.

We swung out onto the lake in the shadow of a five-hundred-foot cliff and headed across. Our snowshoes clattered on the hard crust. We took them off, slung them over our shoulders and trotted a half mile in and out among islands to an immense one that stood across our way. We had left the sled and tent at our third camp, and brought only the light gamebag.

Snowshoes on, and up the long slope through the trees. It took us an hour and a half to cross that island, and there were almost no signs of fur. So we went, travelling very fast, over an island, then a mile or more of ice, then more land, and on and on.

John had never been so far before. We wanted to cross if we could. But toward sunset we stood on the top of a mountainous little island whose shadow was creeping farther and farther over the ice, and the high slope of the shore to the south still looked twenty miles away.

157

I looked in every direction with sadness, thinking I might never see this endless lake again. Then we turned back, following the serpentine trench in the snow, setting our feet in the patterns they had made before.

Endlessly, endlessly we walked till my legs reminded me of the gleaming arms in a steamer's engine room that never stop for weeks on end. Four snowshoe prints behind John I kept step, watching the webs drag and stop, drag and stop, the moccasin heel rise and fall, rise and fall, never letting the distance widen. When one is tired, one keeps step. This is the time when every faculty of brain and muscle combines to save energy. The rhythm of the man ahead draws you on, if you keep step. You glide over the snow, leaning forward, making your back and arms help your tired legs, pulling yourself a step or two up hills by grasping little trees.

When you are fresh in the morning it is all very well to gambol about like a puppy, one side of the trail and then the other, looking at tracks or a brook or getting a moment's view from a rise, a stop to light your pipe or adjust your snowshoe thong. You can run a little to catch up and any one knows you are lagging for the fun of it.

But in the evening on a long trail when darkness is wringing the last warmth out of daylight, when your legs ache and the sum total of a thousand small pains sighs for rest, then it's time to keep step and hold a steady pace. Soon the time is coming when you can't run to catch up, and if you drop behind you'll stay behind, and drop farther behind and every one will know that you are weak.

Swing, swing, swish, swish, ducking under low limbs, squeezing between close trees, stepping over buried logs. Sometimes I lose a step and make it up again, sometimes I reach out to clutch up the space that is lengthening.

By and by the four steps grow to five, and six and seven, and I cannot close them up. The trail is plain, it doesn't matter if I fall behind, but it is a matter of pride. For a time I lose fifty yards or so on every island in the deep snow with the racquets on, and then make it up trotting on the ice where my moccasins tap tap and the racquets clatter on my shoulder. The moonlight is getting brighter and we go on.

Labradormen seldom ask if one is tired. They know that if a man is tired he drops behind. Why mouth words about it? If it is snowing or blowing or the trail is faint, they will keep an eye out for him. If not, they decide he will come along when he can. They travel almost to the limit of their own endurance. Another must too. They do not baby themselves and they are kind enough not to baby anybody else. It is hard, it is torture, but it is not so cruel as smothering a naturally weak person with comforts and producing in the end a lump of absolute helplessness. After months or years they would force you to be as hardy as they are, which is the best of all.

I hear the chop of an axe a little way through the trees. We are going to boil up. The sweet oriental scent of tea and the feel of bread between my teeth sweeps over me like a dizziness.

The fire leaps at the base of a big spruce and we whisk the snow from our moccasins and leggings as we sink before it like worshippers. We sit on our mitts to keep the warmth in them; our moccasins are put aside so the frost in them will not melt. The heat soaks into our bare hands and stocking feet like a miracle-sent blessing. Who can describe the feelings of such a moment, the sensation of leanness, a flat stomach and a body that one is glad to own, stripped to essentials, filled, despite fatigue with latent strength that is

159

rising through legs and torso and arms like a pleasant vapor. The slightest movement, even of a toe, brings a comfortable ache that one repeats over and over again for the sheer pleasure of it. There is no sound but the crackling of the fire.

The kettle, hanging on a bending, blackened stick, starts to sing, and then to jump. For a minute we pay no attention to it. We are not hungry somehow. At first it is a definite effort to drink the tea, and butter and bite the half-thawed river cake. We only do it because we know we should. But then we taste the taste of the tea, ah how warm and good, and the bread, and then we eat like starving animals—which we are.

A pipe lit with a brand tastes much better than a pipe lit with a match. I wouldn't believe it at first, but now I know it is so. There is something about the wood smoke that mellows tobacco. And it is pleasant to keep up an old custom that reaches back so far to the days when matches were a curiosity, to the time of flint and steel, and long before that.

The fire is dying and the moon is rising. Moccasins on, and we are marching again. At first there is a slight stiffness, but soon it works off. Soon again my clothes and the axe in my hand and the snowshoes on my feet become innate parts of my body, like my fingers, and I am unconscious of them.

Every tree was a dark green pyramid drawn up beside an aisle of pure white satin. At the edge of the marsh each pyramid had a blue counterpart sleeping at its feet. It was ten o'clock when we saw the peak of the tent. The silent encampment with its maze of tracks seemed like an uncanny discovery. We had been driving toward it so many hours, and now we had reached it, it wasn't the place at all. Frozen moonlight caught between trees, sinister, fragile, ready to splinter. Orchid, meringue, crystal, rapier-like, is winter moonlight. Up-side-down, exotic. Nervous purple, not like summer moonlight. Cold gleams from a polished scimitar so beautiful you don't care if it slays you. And the strangest thing of all was a tin stove inside the tent. It had a rasping, saw-edge door that shrieked, and smashed the moonlight jagged.

Down at the brook by the frozen water hole, an otter had been playing, not an hour gone.

When we got in the tent and sat wriggling our bare toes, John confessed something to me. It was out of a clear blue sky. He said he went away when he was sixteen on a very long furring trip to Michikamau with his elder brother Stewart. Stewart has a name for being the best snowshoe walker in the bay, which is somewhat like being the best coal shoveller in Newcastle. He used to leave John way behind every day and have the camp all up and the kettle boiled when John dragged in at evening. Like a born trapper boy John thought of the pain and the hideous weariness of the extra long, extra fast days as inevitable and to be simply endured. What he could not stand was the blow to his pride. To be left behind, to be physically inferior, that he could not bear.

"But I slung to 'un," he told me, "step fer step, and when I couldn't do that I tuck off my snowshoes and run on the lakes to kitch up jus' like you. An' bymby he couldn't leave me. I was good fer it, 'n' when it come to makin' camp I was right there to do my part cuttin' up wood 'n' that."

I froze John out that night, for even the cold couldn't wake me.

In the morning we had to bake before we started. The flat round cakes didn't taste golden brown and fragrant. They seemed sour and heavy, and the most noticeable flavor was the cream of tartar in the baking powder. The two partridges our first night had been the only meat we'd tasted. We only had enough peas and pork for one meal, and we ate them for supper the second night. Breakfast made our eighth consecutive meal of bread and tea. We were hungry all the time, but whenever we ate a little bread it stuck in our throats and lay like a lump of lead in our stomachs.

It was very cold when we lashed up, and blowing hard from the north. Whenever we crossed a marsh, the trees at its edge were tossing as though in pain. At every step clouds of snow like splashes whirled away to leeward. It was like walking in running water. All the surface was moving, a thin, white granular flood, a whispering plain of white streamers on the march. The wind searched out every cranny in our clothing with white-hot irons. It crept under the mitts we held to our faces, down our necks, into our wrists and through button holes.

When we came out of the woods onto the big lake, it was wreathed in eddying, waist-high drift. I tried to tie my shawl around my head, as my ears were freezing under the flaps of my cap. But the greatest effort of will would not make my slow fingers come together. It was as though they belonged to somebody else—the north wind maybe. I wrapped the shawl around my head and tried to hold it there with the ends tight in my teeth. We came across the lake, a twenty-minute run, on a fast dog-trot, and all the way we were clapping our mitts alternately to our faces and ears. Twice we stopped, turned our backs to the wind and rubbed and punched the north side of our faces. Our eyelids were stuck together with frost when we gained the trees. It was like being in some quiet cathedral.

We were almost too stiff to light a fire. I had to put my hand in on my stomach for a few minutes, before I could hold the axe. We made the blaze a roarer with armfuls of branches, chunks of rotten stumps and whole small trees. Squatting on the brush we pulled icicles out of our matted beards and turned round and round like fowls on a spit. The sparks jumped out and burned our clothes, and the wafted flames scorched our eyebrows, filling the air with the strong smell of burning hair. But it was a warm smell.

While we were getting our pipes going John told me he had seen it so cold on Winnikapau that when they went ashore to boil up at the edge of the ice, a kettle of tea near the fire was bubbling on one side and skimming over with ice on the other. I was in a mood for believing anything.

White partridge tracks traced the snow near our fireplace. They made me think, not of pearly strutting birds, but juicy, stewed meat. While John went on with the sled I took the .22 for a little hunt, intending to catch up later.

I followed the tracks down a little brook, in what I thought was an easterly direction. Having seen nothing at the end of twenty minutes, when the brook petered out, I turned and headed for the sled-track. There was no sun, and the sky was that uniform gray that tells nothing, not even the time. At the end of twenty-five minutes plowing through the forest I still had not come to the track. I looked at my pocket compass and saw with horror and astonishment that I was going south-east. I was headed diagonally for the big lake again. My first impulse was to run, and the next was to follow my track back through all its windings eventually to the trail. But John says it's cowardly to follow your track back when you're lost. You never learn anything that way. I knelt on my snowshoe and, holding the compass, drew little diagrams in the snow with my finger. The main track ran roughly north-east and south-west. I was to the east of the track. I would go north and hit it as far on as I could, as I must be a long way behind John by now.

In twenty minutes I struck it. I was so mixed up I wasn't even sure which way the newest snowshoe prints would be pointing but they were going the way they should theoretically, so I whooped it up along the path. I saw where John had taken something out of a mink trap, and hoped it might have been a rabbit, but it wasn't.

We made good time on the track and at most of the traps we didn't even have to pause. Occasionally there would be a poor little yellowish-white weasel with a black-tipped tail, caught by the neck or nipped across the middle.

It was a treat to see John take the sled down the steep hill to the winding lake. At the top we took off our snowshoes and scaled them through the air with all our might, 'way out over the tree tops to the snowy lake below. I slipped and slid and dove down the hill in snow that was shoulder deep; John wrapped both arms around the nose of the sled, sat down beside it and coasted on the seat of his pants. Whenever she'd get going too fast, and there was danger of her getting out of control and smashing up amongst the trees, he gave a mighty heave, turned her up on her side, and bore down hard. In a way it resembled bulldozing a steer. This slowed her almost to a stop. Then he'd turn her on her bottom and the snow would fly again. We left a funny-looking track.

By noon our second camp was behind us, and late in the afternoon we struck the burnt woods wasteland. The beaver traps were empty and untouched. We were very disappointed, not on account of the fur, but because we wanted the meat. Frost was falling as we pushed over the bare hills and valleys, just a slow light featheryness drifting down as it often does, late on cold winter afternoons. Purple was filling up the hollows and distances. How I love that sad soft purple, the music of the eyes. Down some of the bare hills we both climbed on the sled and coasted. Snow flew from the nose like spray from the bow of a heeling schooner, and the axe blades glittered. Under us she flowed and wrinkled, and the feeling of speed was like nothing so much as riding a galloping horse.

Bread and tea in the flickering black and yellow of firelight and we pushed on till after nine when we made a rough camp and put up the tent, lopsided, on the ridge where we had paused to look back at the river on the way in.

This afternoon when we hailed the tilt Kay ran to the door for a wave. Then she dodged inside and clouds of blue smoke from the funnel told us what she was doing. It was like homecoming after years of separation across the sea. She even had raisin cake for us. It smote me again for the hundredth time that I had left her defenseless, and I felt like a villain, guilty of an irreparable crime.

"Child, were you lonesome?"

"Yes," she said. "But it was strange. Now I know what it's like to be all soul alone. I wouldn't have missed it. And now, isn't this minute good?"

THE pile of wood that I left for Kay is still here, a snow-covered mound against the tilt. She carried home and cut up her own wood all the time we were gone, saying she wanted to see if she could do it and make her aloneness and independence as complete as possible.

I guess she had one bad day when she went to the otter island and up the cut-off stream toward Sandgirt Lake looking at traps. After she got there it commenced to snow and the wind began to rise. She had one three-mile stretch to cross among the islands, and was afraid if it came on rough she might get lost. Some of the channels are bad ice, and the islands are hard enough to differentiate even on a clear day. In a blinding storm it would be impossible for anyone but John to find his way through the maze. She knew all this, and having reached the last trap, turned for home without stopping to boil up. It got pretty thick sometimes, but every now and again it would clear a little and she could see a quarter or a half mile ahead. When she reached here she was done, eighteen miles without a spell or a bite to eat, and she was too tired even to want to eat by that time.

She has had no luck with partridges or rabbit snares, and we are all very hungry for meat. We have to go a little easy on the flour now. We have a permanent sourdough kettle hanging on a nail above the stove. From this we mix up pancake batter and the crisp, yeasty cakes are a little more satisfying than bread. But one loses energy and endurance on a steady diet of flour. What we want is meat and plenty of it. I think at this point I could peel and eat a raw warm partridge gizzard the way John does.

166

K AY and I lashed up the sled and left for Victor's house this morning hoping to catch him before his next trip south to Harvey's, and so get passed on to Arch and the falls of the Unknown River. We didn't remember the way among the channels very well and, as usual, John's directions were a little more confusing than helpful. We found "the clifty island" and headed down the seven-mile whiteness of Flour Lake for a likely looking gap in the hills.

As usual there was new snow on the river, good snowshoe walking, but rimey and bad going for the sled. Every mile I had to "out knife and scrape 'er." And at the end of the next mile I'd be straining at the line, arms back wound in the rope, nose, it seemed, almost touching the snow. I could have sworn the sled was not just going hard but pulling backward, and I made up my mind it was thumbs down on the sled this trip. We are going to leave the tent, stove, and sleeping gear at Victor's, carry our food and take the consequences. Hauling a sled is toil and not adventure, and even a fool recognizes the fact after a few days. Now and again Kay took the strap across her chest and tugged while I walked ahead and recuperated. I was adamant with the stupid inner voice which tried to shame me.

While I was stalking a company of white partridges on a rocky point where the willows were drifted up deep, I spied way off a black speck. This was not unusual. It might be a rock or a snag drifted bare. But it moved. That might be the mirage, which, in the bright sunlight, was twisting islands topsy turvy, lifting them way off the ice, making

167

them disappear and reappear, or bend in spasms like fake, mechanical ocean scenery.

The partridges had some strange aversion to being shot, so we went on, sweating profusely and shedding caps and mitts, though it was about zero.

By and by we saw it was Victor, swinging along like a two-legged rocking horse with flapping feet, axe in one hand, gun in the other, bag on the back. And out from under the flap of the bag hung a mink's tail. Not much mirage about that grin in the midst of red cheeks. "Boy, you were leaning at it a little," he said.

Yes, he was going in to Harvey's day after tomorrow, and Arch was going to be there for Sunday. Providence had some intention of being good to us. God willing, and if we lives.

We were surprised to hear we had been heading for the right place. Victor guided us through narrow channels and among rocks till we emerged beside the main river. It was open and we trotted on hard ice beside the black, misty water where the sled became a bagatelle. We skipped over a cove where the ice bent under us, dodged some snow with water and ice underneath, and at dark were here in the new log cabin up among the trees with the fire going.

All the inside is startling new wood and the good smell of spruce. The new door, the bunk, the roof and the well-caulked seams are all objects of pride. While I went down for water, Victor split some wood. Lucky one, he doesn't have to scour the woods for sound dry turns. He is using the big logs of the old tilt for firewood. He has a buck-saw too, unspeakable luxury.

He had some old frozen porcupine ribs and a head, and much to tell us while they were cooking. Harvey's new house is at the end of the south path in from here, on the lower end of Unknown Lake, right at the beginning of Unknown River. Victor found Harvey's snowshoe track last trip in, and followed it right to the cabin. In the fall when Harvey and Arch paddled down the huge confusing lake, they were ten days finding the place, and almost gave it up. Arch has a new cabin on down the Unknown River in one of his old stamping grounds that he hunted and forgot about years ago. Victor went to Fred's a couple of weeks ago. His hair is as kinky as ever and he is getting so much fur and is so busy with it he can't get time to sew up the rips in his clothes. He wants to know when we are coming to see him, but I am afraid we cannot. Time is getting short. Victor has the sled here for John that Mathieu made. It is a beauty, very long and the bars "fancied up" with red paint made from roots and bark.

December 9.

LOAFED all day and went for a partridge hunt. Kay killed three, I bagged five, and Victor downed ten. We don't feel as sorry as we used to for the poor red-stained birds with drooping necks and matted feathers.

Last winter when a man walked through the village with a gun, home from a day's hunt, it used to horrify me to see the little children toddle to the doors and lisp, "Kill anything?" Now I think I understand it better. They never kill for sport. They kill because they must; and there is nothing evil about it.

169

We had a feast tonight, with two partridges apiece and haven't felt so good for ages. I hardly used my knife or fork at all.

December 10.

AT sunrise this morning we left with eight days' grub in two knapsacks. Kay carries the little one with about fifteen pounds and I have the big one with twenty-five or so. To cross the river on ice we would have had to go three miles up and then down again on the other side. Victor said we would do better to cross in the canoe, so we knocked some of the ice off her and dragged her down through the snow. The outer edge of the ice was covered with slush and water which froze on. It made the canoe so heavy we couldn't lift her and could scarcely drag her. To add to our difficulties the ice was very weak, so finally we all climbed in, broke the ice around us with axes till we were afloat, then chopped a channel ahead till we were in the clear water. Once across, we had the same difficulties hauling her up, and altogether we spent two hours at the business.

White partridges were everywhere, fluttering about the willows, but we didn't shoot any, as we didn't want to carry any more of a load and hoped to get a few later in the day on the burnt woods. In this hope we were not disappointed. The path took in over a hill which had two enormous boulders on its crest. All day we have come over rolling semi-barren land.

We will probably have to come back on this trip alone. If there is no snow it will be simple to follow the track and even feel it where it is blown out. But lately it has snowed every two or three days. Like John's this path is hardly marked at all. I asked Victor if he minded my hacking a blaze now and then. He said to go ahead, so I have been chipping trees all day. I look back so much, particularly when crossing lakes and marshes, to imprint on my memory gaps in the hills, or rocks and trees to head for on the way back, that it reminds me of the story of Hansel and Gretel. I am Hansel and Kay is Gretel and Victor is the bad old witch leading us deeper and deeper into the forest to lose us.

Just before sunset in the third lake of a chain we were following we came to a little tilt hidden away among the trees close to the bank. Its door is not ten feet from the ice and it is a wonder in the spring that the little log shelter is not flooded or swept away. Such occurrences are not unknown. Tilts are common, work-a-day affairs not at all sacred, and all kinds of things happen to them. Bears break the windows and carry the stoves out of them; trees fall on them and the gable-ends lean and gradually fall. A leaning tilt is one of the queerest objects; it looks like some personalized drawing in a child's story book of a house that is gathering up its skirts and galloping. Trappers have a superstition that leaning tilts always lean toward the water. This is not so, for they often sag the other way.

One funny thing the hunters do is to build tilts in the spring right up on top of the snow. In the fall the trapper returns to use his new tilt and it has settled itself snug on the ground. Wallace McLean has a tilt on Fig River that moves every year. The river, which is a good-sized stream with many lakes and tributaries pouring into it, has but one outlet through a very narrow cleft. It must be a sight booming through there in the spring. Anyway, it always jams with ice, and dams the river till it backs up and rises forty feet. Wallace's tilt is built on the highest land possible, and every year it gets moved. The second fall he ever furred the place, he arrived and found the shack turned completely around and one end up on a stump. He cut away the stump and she came down level in a hurry. The box that had been under the bunk was out in back and two of the stove legs were inside and two were outside. The stove must have floated away, for he never did find that. Since then the tilt has travelled nearly a hundred yards.

Victor's being an orphan has reminded me of something I meant to make a note of long ago. Among these trapper folk the youngest son inherits the family goods, not the eldest. The older sons are married, have built houses for themselves and made new fur paths for themselves far away (every generation it gets farther), while the youngest is quite naturally at home. Someone has to stay at home with the old folks and do the heavy work, haul the nets, drive the dogs and bring home firewood. Custom rigidly delegates the position to the youngest son, since he is the longest at home anyway. Even though he marries, he must live with the old folks and take care of them. Generally the old man's paths are within a hundred miles or so and the son can tend them and get home every two or three weeks. But he cannot go away for the whole winter like his brothers. In return for his fidelity the young son inherits the family house, traps, nets, motor boat, guns and furring grounds. It works out pretty well except in cases where the young son is married and the old mother is cantankerous.

I wish I might have known Victor's most remarkable uncle, Willie Goudie. Though he died more than five years ago people still speak of him as though he were alive. He died in pain and he died with a laugh. Parts of Willie's life-story make one wonder why God created man with such infinite capacity for suffering unless it is to wring so many tears out of him.

Willie built the second house in North West River, built it of board, hand sawn, built it high and big. There was one other house, and the Hudson's Bay Post. All down along shore between the post and Willie's house the Indians had a wide clearing for their summer camping ground. He furred a place up Grand River at the lower end of Winni-kapau, which his charming young son tends now. He was clever and cheerful and hardworking, and so was his young wife, Jessie Baikie. He deserved to do well, but no one did well in those days. The settlement grew slowly, on the ground that the Indians had cleared. The Mission built a hospital.

By and by the spectre of the north stalked into Willie's house. Tuberculosis. Willie's right hand commenced to rot away with it. No one could imagine how Willie would ever support his wife, two sons and a baby daughter in this land where a man lives by his two strong iron fists with ten nimble, muscular fingers. Willie laughed and whistled as always, and the doctor amputated his right hand. After the loss of his hand the circulation in that arm was never very good. It used to get so aching cold in winter, as a regular thing, that the pain made him sick and he couldn't eat. The Mission helped him, and his brothers, Allen, Albert, Arch, Jim, and Fred helped him, and Willie helped himself. He learned to chop wood with his lone left hand. At splitting firewood no two-handed man could beat him. He grasped the axe by the end of the handle, whirled it once above his head, and came down with the precision of a micrometer. He learned to paddle, and to fill his pipe, to set traps and tie a bowknot. His teeth and the stump became expert. He could pole a canoe up swift water, holding the upper end of the pole with his left hand and pressing the lower grip against his body with the handless arm. But he could only pole on the right side and this was a decided handicap when ascending a left bank. He went up the river two or three years, and once in a single canoe, though in company with others who helped him in the bad places where they always help each other.

For three weeks at a time he wouldn't see any one, and almost every bit of work he had to do was difficult for a man with one hand. Setting traps with two hands is bad enough on a cold day when it is torture to take off one's mitts, and the steel burns like a red-hot iron.

A trapper's existence is crammed full, for besides his work and travelling there is all the bother of keeping himself alive, hunting meat, baking, cooking, making camp and mending. Many days they work from five in the morning until midnight. Everything was more difficult and took longer for Willie. But the worst of all was skinning and stretching fur. He tried to hold the animal with his teeth and with his feet and with his stump while he plied the knife with his left hand. It was very awkward. Some of his fur he couldn't get time to dry and stretch, so he froze it and brought it home green, but this made a heavy load to haul. When he got a splinter in his hand it stayed there until it festered out. He tried probing for it with a needle in his teeth or stuck in his right coat sleeve, and it proved such a useless exasperation he gave it up in disgust. He made a path closer to home, up Big Brook, but it didn't pay very well.

One spring after several bad years, news came that foxes were thick off the other way toward Hopedale River. Fred and Albert and Willie decided they would go in there and stay all winter. During the summer they made a trip in with loads of grub and traps. There were more than thirty portages to carry over. Drenching rains hindered them and the hot sun which drains these northern men of their strength. They never complain of the winter cold, but every sunny summer day they complain of the heat.

In July the mosquitoes and stouts nearly murdered them, and in August came the little black midges which settle on one like a cloud, get in eyes, mouth, ears and nose, crawl inside one's shirt and trousers and socks and hair, drawing blood, closing eyes, and stinging like ten thousand never-ending needles. There is nothing quite like a portage under such circumstances, toiling up slippery paths, through tripping, grasping willows, across bogs and marshes, with heavy loads that gnaw and cut and ache, both hands full and the whizzing singing horde of insects drawing blood that mingles with the sweat. At the end of the portage they threw down their loads and bathed in the thick white smoke of a smudge fire whose choking fumes seemed to them like a blessing of Heaven. They put a kettle full of smouldering bark and moss in the bow of the canoe to drift back over them, and paddled down the narrow lakes like three strange little steamers.

It was a hard trip and they didn't get back to North West River until September, to be faced with the prospect of loading up and going in again to build cabins and begin their winter of work.

Willie's wife, whom every one calls "Aunt Jessie," told me many of these things. She went with him this time to stay until spring and skin the fur and lighten her man's burden. With her were two small children. Sometimes going along in the canoe they would be crying with the cold, and she in the bow, torn between the necessity to progress and the need to comfort her children, would reluctantly lay her paddle on the gunnel and put the little hands in on her breast. Before they reached the good fox grounds the lakes skimmed over and they went for a week beating the ice ahead of the canoe. Then a providential thaw cleared the water again.

The brothers settled far apart, as hunters must. Aunt Jessie helped build her family's cabin, for since girlhood she had been able to swing an axe nearly as well as a man. There were plenty of foxes, but they weren't prime at first.

When the north wind brought the deep snow and the ptarmigan, and the lakes began to freeze up and boom at night, Willie would be away two or three days at a time setting his traps. Aunt Jessie skinned and stretched fur, cooked, sewed, washed, tended rabbit snares and tried to make the cabin cozy. Those were happy nights when he came home.

Willie got a few foxes; then within a week they all disappeared. He got a scattered marten or mink, but there was never so much as the track of a fox the rest of the winter. In December he found a bear cave, woke the old bruin up, poked him out and shot him. Aunt Jessie rendered down the fat which makes a beautiful white grease that tastes better than butter, and of the skin made a sleeve for Willie, whose arm in the day's walk never ceased to trouble him.

First they ran out of baking powder, then grease and sugar and tea, until finally they were living on "dunch" bread and what meat they could get. Fred and Albert came for a council of war and they decided to go out with sleds for more grub and leave Willie to tend all the traps he could. They made the trip and returned, and so the winter passed. In the spring when they all got back to North West River and sold their fur it came to just about enough to pay the expenses. All winter the foxes had been thick around the village, one even came in and fought with a dog, and those who stayed close to home reaped a harvest.

Willie never complained, never asked for help, though his broad laugh and joke for every one made it a pleasure to be allowed to do something for him. About seven years ago he developed tuberculosis in his lungs. His oldest boy was already dead of it. In a few months the father followed. I wish I might have known him. God, if there is one, gave him grit, and slowly broke him to pieces.

December 11.

I AM taking notes tonight in my battered, eternal book under greater difficulties than usual, for this is the smallest tilt we have ever been in. It is much smaller than our tent.

Victor was behind, fixing traps this afternoon and Kay and I came on over two ridges and lakes to find the tilt. It was on a level shore dotted with big snowed-up boulders whose peaks, showing above the snow, were almost indistinguishable from the peak of the tilt. We walked up and down and up and down, until Victor came and shovelled out one boulder which turned out to be a tilt. The walls are only four logs high and the door is only two logs high. Arch built it long ago, and planned to have it seven by six. He cut the logs that length and of course the corner notches took up more than a foot, so it is less than six by five inside. Outside, by a piece of twine were hanging four weasel carcasses, one marten and a mink, which is Harvey's way of saying he has been in here and taken them out of the traps. The path really belongs to Harvey, but Victor, who is his brother, furs it on shares.

When we had wood cut up and water carried from the cascade brook, and snow shovelled off the roof so it wouldn't leak, we crawled inside. It was certainly a jam for the three of us and a hot tin stove. Victor says when he is here alone he sleeps diagonally from corner to corner, that being the only way he can stretch out. He cut up the bunk and burned it last year, as it was too short to be of any use. We each sat with our backs in a corner and our legs out straight in the middle, one pair on top of the other pair. We had to take turns getting each other's moccasins and leggings off. Somehow we all feel very good tonight and we don't care how bad the prospects for sleep look.

December 12.

VICTOR stretched out along the back of the tilt with his feet against the log wall on one side and his head against the other. Kay lay between him and the stove, which is in one corner by the front wall. I was at right angles to them along one sidewall, more or less across their feet. I kept my cap and mitts on and dozed off for a couple of hours with my head in the draughty doorway and my feet half-

178

way up the back wall. We tried to plug up the door with gamebags, but plenty of cold leaked in. When I woke up to stoke the stove for the seventh time, one stocking leg was, in some unaccountable way, scorched black. The way of it must have been, that along toward morning we hardly knew whose legs were whose. It sounds like pure discomfort, but in reality it was a great deal of fun.

It was a wickedly cold night and when we crawled out this morning the wind had a knife edge and the sun looked pale red, as though the chill had drawn the color out of it. I never tire of spitting on hard ice to see if it will bounce. It almost does.

The mercury rose with the sun till it was only about ten or twelve below, and a glorious day. From a hilltop we could look in three directions and drink in space and freedom and solitude to our hearts' content. Off on our left hand were the smokes from four different falls rising above the trees. The Grand Falls made a pillar of vapor that stretched up till it blended with the sky; the falls of the Unknown River were like small brush fires. Back of us we could see our track, a thin line across a lake, winding out of sight.

A snowshoe trail on a sunny day after a light fall of snow is a lovelier thing than I can describe. I often look back at it streaming from our heels, flowing back astern like the wake of a ship, a long winding track that scars the lonely limitless snow as a ship's track might scar the Pacific. Over glistening white hills and marshes and lakes it winds, a darker, serpentine ribbon, scallop-edged, filled with tumbled blue shadow markings. And every individual print is a beautiful thing. It is like sculpture and like a painting, endless impressions of an Indian craftsman's masterpiece.

Here is the broader webbed *babische* of the close-knit mid-dles, here the finer-knit *tibische* of the heads and tails, moulded into the snow, perfect in every finest line; there the round-curved frame of strong white birch and the lip of a tail, the head bar and the tail bar, the toe hole and a little cup, scooped out of the snow where the toes pushed through the hole at the end of the step; the blurred mark of the dragging tail, then another perfect, graceful-lined pattern printed in blue-white marble. The concave curve of a right tail nestles round the convex bulge of a left head and the purple ribbon is only a little wider than one snowshoe.

The prints speak a message, too, to whatever solitary wanderer may cross them ere the next big wind or snowfall (though none will). Are the patterns far apart? They were swinging with long steps, fresh and tireless, eating up the miles. Are they close together, left fitting into right so closely one racquet barely clears the other? They were hungry and tired and their feet were like lead, and they were probably cold, for the two go together. Are they deep sunk? Ah, he had a heavy pack, poor fellow. Does the tail of one swing far out sometimes as though the traveller had been taken with a sudden fit of pigeontoes? His thong is too tight or he is a greenhorn. And look here, he chews tobacco. The straps were cutting his shoulders. See where he sat on his pack and took a spell. Here he lit his pipe—a burnt match. In all the miles and miles of nature's own imperturbable manlessness, one burnt match dropped in the track looms as big as a house.

To add to these readings, men know each other's snow-shoes. Each has an individuality, a broad bit of sealskin mending, a different shape, a different size. They will say,

"Jim was here day before yesterday." I once followed a track with a man who kept up a running string of such comments as these. In addition, at the traps he would tell by the hairs and sign what kind of an animal they had taken out. Then he would say, "Tom took a turn ahead here, look at him drivin' 'er."

Travelling on a track like this is perpetual romance for me. This stump right here, this birch, this snowed-up brook; no, it is not these; it is on and on and forever on through the bright white wilderness and the shadowed trees. And best of all is to stand on a ridge and look ahead over infinities of nameless solitary country dreaming in the short winter sun. And who knows the glens and mysteries we may see way off over the hills, and the old Indian camps with buried heaps of rocks that were fireplaces in caribouskin wigwams long before the days of stoves and rifles. Something keeps calling, on and on to the farthest ridges that lean against the sky. And I am convinced that it is not just fancy. It is real and concrete. It is happiness, calling, "Come and take me if you are strong enough."

Of all men I think La Salle was one of the luckiest; to have drifted from the spruce-fringed lakes of Canada all down the Mississippi to the tropics; months and months of seeing round the next bend and never knowing in what strange paradise he might end.

And tonight we are in Harvey's big new cabin, with room to stand upright and pace about the floor. It seems by contrast as though it were a spacious hall; every log so gleaming white and straight and solid as though to say, "You couldn't knock me down with a twenty-pound sledge." "Button Bank," Harvey calls the place because he burst the braces buttons off his trousers hauling his sled up from the ice one rimey day.

When we arrived just at dark we stepped down onto the hard-packed "dock" and kicked off our snowshoes. Harvey was standing in the tilt doorway, straight and tall, his face framed in a cap with huge marten-fur ear flaps that hung almost to his shoulders. He smiled and we pulled off our mittens to shake his hand. It was like meeting one of God's elect, a picturesque, iron pioneer, intelligent in a world of blind instinct, kind in a world of tooth and claw, full of fun in a life of hardship. I felt like a boy with hero worship-itis again, though he is two years younger than I am.

Harvey first came up the river when he was ten; he hunted a living for his younger brothers when he was fifteen. He was an old hand in the river and had nearly been drowned twice at the age of eighteen. Here is a man who does not compromise, no mawkishness, no care about what people think. He has looked the grizzly daemon of fear and weakness square in the face, and, with his blue-flecked eyes that are more used to distance than print, licked him. You won't find the like of this one at the age of twenty-three in all the semi-Gothic universities in the forty-eight states.

I can never look at Harvey Goudie without wishing I had had four years in the woods instead of four years in college; without wondering if we are not pampered too long ever to get over it. A Labrador boy is a man at fifteen, and it has advantages over never being a man, even if you can't read and write.

Inside the cabin he had a good look at us to see how tired we were, and I felt that in our worn clothes, starting to grow ragged, and in our cold-roughened faces he found a newness and an old familiarity—that with his eyes at last he had accepted us.

The beaver stew for supper tasted almost too good to swallow, except that there was always more to roll around under one's tongue. After supper, the dishes are washed with a rabbit's foot and talk flows easy. Harvey is glad of the plug of tobacco I brought him and the pound of tea Kay carried. He was most out. But he has plenty of salt, nearly forty pounds of it, found it on an island in an aluminum kettle so big that the cover makes a good mixing dish; thinks Indians from the gulf left it five or six years ago.

Harvey and Arch had a time finding this place by the new all-water route. They have both been here in winter overland from Victor's, or up beside the rapids and gorges of Unknown River. But they had never been in the way they came this fall. I speak of Ossokmanuan Lake as Unknown Lake and the river that drains that lake and flows back into Grand River again as Unknown River. These are the designations the trappers use, and so I think they should be the accepted names. You see, the drainage plan of this region is much confused by the fact that Unknown Lake has two outlets, both tributaries of Grand River and flowing into Grand River at widely spaced points. One of these outlets is the Gabbro Lake–Attikonak Branch, as it is called, which flows north and enters the south side of Sandgirt Lake. The other is Unknown River. This latter river is almost one continuous rapid, except for falls, until it tumbles into Grand River again about ten miles above the Big Hill and some fourteen miles below the Grand Falls. Of course the shortest way to come here in canoe would be up Grand River to the mouth of the Unknown and up that to Button Bank. The Unknown is not navigable however, so they went over the Big Hill portage and all the way up to Sandgirt Lake. There they swung into the Attikonak Branch and paddled upstream still, through Gabbro Lake to Unknown Lake. All down Unknown Lake they came, camping wherever night caught them, utterly bewildered by the huge big islands which merged in the distance, and stood apart with miles of water between when they drew near. In the lake there was of course no current to guide them. Sometimes they wouldn't know which side of an island to take. Twice they chose the wrong side and found it was a point, and not an island at all. One of these points was thirty miles long, and led them into a dead-end bight whence they spent all the next day paddling out again. Several days there was a spanking fair breeze and they put up their tarpaulins and let 'er drive. Harvey had much the smaller canoe, and nearly capsized while filling his pipe on a squally day. He thinks the end of John's path is about two days' walk up the lake from here, but cannot recognize the cliff John and I saw, nor the high islands we crossed. He says they passed dozens of cliffs and scores of high islands. After five days down the lake they began to think they must be getting somewhere. The islands grew thicker and smaller, sometimes there was a little current between them, but nothing to point a general direction, and they paddled two days more in and out amongst them. Arch had said he could find the place. It was getting late in the season and Harvey was impatient.

"So one day we climbs up on a hill for a look-around. You see that big white-topped mountain when you was comin' across the wide maash? Well there was that mountain not so far away stickin' up fit to put yer eyes out, only from a different side. And I says to Uncle Archie, 'You ever see that hill over there?' And he says, 'No.'

"I was sure, me, I never see it before. But Uncle Archie, he should a knowed it all to pieces. He's spent half his natcherl life around here. One winter he was on his place further down, from December to March, all alone.

"So we shoves on. Uncle Archie, he said he were going to find this place if it took 'un all winter. I makes up my mind if we don't find it by next day I'm going to pick a likely spot and build a tilt and have my fall hunt anyways, even if I don't know where I'm to.

"We paddled around in circles all that day, and the next day about noon we got into another bight with nothin' in the end of it. When we got out again I says to Uncle Archie, 'So long,' and I paddles off one way and him the other. I didn't 'spect to see him again till after New Years down home. By and by, when he were just a speck on the water I hears two shotgun shots. I thinks he must a seed somethin' so I paddles back again. He'd spotted these little hills in back of here and that night we camped by the fallen in tilt."

Since arriving, Harvey has built the new cabin, made a catamaran sledge, a great long toboggan, and a whole set of new fur boards, scouted out country in all directions, set out his traps and made a better than average hunt. For weeks he lived in his tent, and, getting up at five every morning, spent two hours at work on his house before the day's march that would bring him home long after dark.

Two of his traps belong to his baby and three to his wife. Everything caught in those traps is theirs. The baby has four weasels and a mink, and the wife a marten. Like a good many children in North West River after the trappers

185

come home, his baby will probably be sick for a week of too much candy.

When we rolled in our blankets and there was no sound but the fire and the regular breathing, a great lightness and sense of well-being flooded me.

This has been one of the candle-lit, balsam-smell, happy evenings I shall remember for ever. If ever I am dragged back to the city again I shall gird myself in these evenings five feet thick and nothing can touch me.

The simple meal was better than a banquet, the cabin is finer than a palace, the molasses-stuck black plug in the pipe I have just laid down, is more fragrant than the finest cut tobacco, the shaggy, matted blanket sweeter than linen sheets. And if it seems so, is it not so? And what a simple, beautiful way to live in palaces and dine at banquets. No satiety, and how cheap! I shall say a prayer tonight and ask God to alleviate the hardships of the poor kings of earth. Stop their ears, O Lord, against the clanking radiator and the jangling phone, help them bear their stomach aches like men; may they find their wine as gratefully luscious as a tin cup of water and ice; help them tossing restless on their Simmons Springs to sleep as sweet as I do on the floor. God bless millionaires, multi-millionaires, kings, princes, and heiresses, for theirs is the kingdom of silk-lined hardships for ever and ever amen.

December 13.

ARCH came tonight to spend Sunday. He was surprised to see us. He is thin and weatherbeaten and gray-haired, but he looks healthy; not that wreck of a man we knew on the portage. We were way down the river hunting partridges and setting traps. We wanted to have lots of partridges for a big feast Sunday, two apiece, and the more left over the better, as we are all getting short of flour. But we had poor luck and will have just enough for one apiece.

There was a villainous wind ripping down the river and a snowstorm driving horizontal before it. We reached the tilt crusted white and literally freezing. Kay had refused to be a man any longer and stayed home to have a good time taking a bath in a washbasin and tidying up. She had a fresh, clean floor of new brush put in; a beautiful green carpet, lapped and arranged in a pattern the way the Indians do. Supper was cooked, the candle lit and the stove roaring. It was very different from coming home to a cold dark tilt. Having a woman there to come home to made it an event and something to remember on other evenings when it's dark until you make a light, and silent unless you sing to yourself.

December 14.

ARCH has been sitting on a box and telling me stories almost all day long. He and Jim lit out and took their families down further north to Davis Inlet a while back. They lived there two years and came back again. It's quite different further north, all barren, except a belt of trees a mile or so wide by the rivers.

He says when black bears are going to their caves in the fall they will hide their track in all kinds of ways to be safe in their hibernation from marauders. Sometimes they go to their caves in a snowstorm, leaving, as the only sign of their whereabout, stubs where they broke off branches to cover the doorway of their winter home. Sometimes they walk along a log and make a long jump one side to a rock or another log

187

and so throw off chance pursuers. Arch shot three white bears down north and one of them, badly crippled, tried to ambush him, but he saw it first. When white bears come ashore on the ice in the spring, they immediately head for the north again.

He has seen twenty-two-foot komatiks with a team of eighteen dogs. They must be like the teams a Hudson's Bay Company man has told me he has seen arriving in Baffinland from Greenland with loads of fur. In the spring out at the seal holes he has seen Indians in caribouskin moccasins, which absorb dampness like blotting paper, stand all day long in ice water ankle deep. Let us hope they had luck and, in consequence, boots for the next spring.

One fall the mountain cats went mad. They frothed at the mouth and ran in circles and died. It was something unheard of. They would attack a man, even though unmolested. One evening when Arch was returning from a hunt, he stepped out of the woods onto the ice and saw Jim's wife, Lizzie, across the bight chopping at the water hole. A noise at the edge of the woods startled him, and he turned to see a big cat bound over the ice and, ignoring him, make straight for Lizzie. She stood as though in a trance, and he yelled to her to run and get out of line. Then he dropped on one knee and fired. The cat rolled over, not ten feet from Lizzie. Its pelt was full of fleas, as they all are. Arch says he wonders they don't all go crazy. The meat had a peculiar smell and they dared not eat it. Out of curiosity he backtracked and found the lynx had been trailing him for more than two miles.

The two families didn't do very well with fur north, so they started back to North West River one spring by dog-team. They came to somebody's house every night, and from Davis Inlet to Rigolet every house had deer meat. The people they stayed with fed their dogs every night and wouldn't take any pay. Except talk. They had to pay in talk Arch says. Everybody wanted to hear all the news. Some of them hadn't seen a new person for two months. Hardly a night they could get to bed before twelve or one and they always wanted to be off before five in the early spring dawn.

Arch wanted me to tell him of life in the States, and asked me posers about all "outside." What is the Russian Revolution? It turned out to be a good bit of a puzzle when I was done with it, and Arch summed it all up with a thoughtful "m-m" and went on to something simple, such as, how do people get so rich. And then we tangled ourselves all up in business and companies and interest and banks—not sand banks or clay banks, banks that people put money in. All very strange indeed, and I commenced to believe, myself, that I was telling some Alice-in-Wonderland fantasy. He had never tasted honey and asked me how big a bee was and if it could make a pound of honey in a morning. How fast can an airplane go and what does it look like, and have you ever been in a railroad train honest? What do people in the States do for meat if they can't shoot partridges and the rabbits and deer are all killed up? He was much impressed that most people get two weeks' vacation with pay each year.

"Who pays 'em?"

"The people they work for."

"Oh my, I can't work for anybody else, but I can work like old fun for myself."

He could not get used to the fact that people in cities walk right by each other and never speak. That amazes everyone in this country. Like John, he looks at me with awe when I say that I have walked by ten thousand people in one morning and not spoken to one of them.

KAY and I left with Arch to go to his place this morning. She had nothing to carry today as we've eaten up the small bagful and more. We are going back alone to Harvey's Thursday. Harvey is coming to Arch's a week from today and they are going to start down over the hills beside Unknown River for home as their grub is getting short. Victor left this morning to go back to Grand River. He is starting for home with Fred next week.

It was a cold windy morning with a leaden sky and we all had our shawls on, which made us look like three old Italian women. Arch said it was shortest to go over the big mountain, as the river winds so much. The wind blew us down the river so fast our feet could hardly keep pace with our bodies. About two miles down we turned off on a brook to the north. Its valley brought us to the foot of the mountain, "Mount Fine Lookout," they call it.

We were the best part of the morning toiling up the slope through the deep snow, single file, drawing ourselves up by the thick little spruces, tramping the snow to marble steps as we went.

The top was a battleground of the wind, treeless, cut up by small cliffs. It was blown absolutely bare of snow, but the ground was covered with a layer of ice. It was like icing on a cake, and the frosted grass sticking through was the grated coconut. On the last slope it was so slippery we had to cut notches. And then we were on the summit in the bitter wind with half the world unrolled like a chart below us. In every direction stretched the labyrinth of channels and lakes, black of the spruce islands and white of the ice. The ice is a table and the islands are thousands upon thousands of jigsaw puzzle pieces scattered out on its surface.

It was close to fifty below. We leaned against the wind and peeked at the view from between our mittens while our eyes filled with tears and our faces stiffened. We felt lashed and buffeted and frozen, as though we were standing there stark naked. The cold was like pressure deep under water. Arch had to rub a whitening nose with snow.

He showed us the bend we were cutting off, and to the eastward a lake where the river widened, and on beyond, blue with distance, the point where his house lay hidden.

Kay wanted to take a picture, so I tried to open the camera. But I could not do it. She finished opening it and Arch stood shielding her while she snapped two pictures, one in each direction. Then we threw the camera in the bag and ran.

In a deep gully overhung with cliffs we came to a company of barrens partridges. They are white, like ptarmigan, only smaller. Kay and Arch shot three between them. I could not get a cartridge in my gun, my hands were so cold.

Once down to the trees, we had a mugup and a warm. Our butter is gone, and we have only a little lard left. I remember when it made us shudder to think of spreading lard on bread. But now it tastes like apple jam and honey. Lots of the trappers prefer lard because it always spreads smooth and never freezes. Butter freezes and gets brittle and crumbly so that you lose half of it unless you eat it with a spoon.

While we were winding down the long slope Arch told

me that he and Harvey had often wondered how Kay was going to get down the river, how she could ever walk so far and so fast, especially if it was snowy on the river and we needed snowshoes all the time. No trapper's wife has ever walked down Grand River in winter or been so far up as John's. Arch brought his wife up to Winnikapau one winter, and John Groves had his wife just above there another year. But they had help coming up in the fall in canoes, and brought extra quantities of supplies to last until spring, open water, when they ran down in canoes.

"Well," said Arch, "I aren't a-goin' to bother no more about it. She kin snowshoe walk as good as us almost. I see I been goin' along too slow fer her all the time. I don't think we could leave her if we tried, d'you?"

I think there is more to it than Arch realizes. Kay not only keeps up, but she has a handicap. Following on the snowshoe trail she cannot step in our steps; they are too long, and that in a long day of deep snow makes a huge difference. The men take turns going ahead, and when they are behind they step directly in the head man's track. It is almost like walking on a pavement and they can recuperate for the next turn ahead. But Kay has to take shorter steps, and breaking the soft snow between the racquet prints is almost like breaking trail ahead all day long. In some kinds of going it is actually easier for her to walk one side of the track, breaking her own trail.

It was good when we got out on the broad lake expansion where we could trot abreast without the webs on the wind-packed crust. At its far end we skirted a small rapid, bordered with bad ice and water under the snow. If you step in such a place your snowshoe comes out clogged with pounds of ice, and beat it how you may, a pound or so remains. There is nothing to be done but hang it in the warmth at evening and let the ice thaw off.

Tonight we are at Arch's, a fine long cabin set deep in some tall silver pines. The path to the water hole comes out in a beautiful little cove where a brook enters. I should like to see some of these places in summer.

There is no blaze at the shore to mark the tilt. Arch says an Indian used to hunt around here who would steal the bark off a tree, and if he should go by the tilt some day without knowing it was here, it would be just as well. We had to go a quarter of a mile for wood, and he and I each carried home a turn on our shoulders. Arch had six partridges hung up in the tilt, three of which we devoured, larded with pieces of pork and cooked with plenty of rice.

He has given Kay his sleeping bag, and he and I are sleeping on the floor on a beaver skin, covered up with a tent.

December 16.

ARCH is an odd old fellow. He is the only one we have travelled with who goes at a leisurely pace. It is a welcome novelty. As we go along the shores we come to a trap every five or ten minutes. This he unsets and hangs up on its chain stake, for he is "striking up" his path, preparatory to going home. The pause serves to emphasize the point of a yarn. In the morning, before his eyes are more than half open or the kettle is on, he starts a yarn, and the yarns keep going off and on all day. He puts on his stockings and his legging and his moccasin, talking steadily. Then he remembers he forgot to put on his duffel sock and has to take off his moccasin and legging. Kay says we are two of a kind. If we went furring together I think we would have a gorgeous time and make about two dollars for our winter's hunt.

Within six or seven miles of here there are four falls of the Unknown River. The river forks, and both branches have two falls before converging again. We took the south branch and saw two of them today, the upper one quite small, but the lower a magnificent plunge overhung with an enormous bulge of ice whence the torrent leaped to lick three seventy-foot stalactite icicles. In the pool at the bottom, hundreds of small white ice pans, round like cookies, bobbed on the waves and swung in the slow circle of the eddy. At the brink the fall is split by a small island of rock. It was this that led Mr. J. G. Thomas, a young American whom Arch guided here in May, 1921, to call it the Twin Falls. Just to the north, not fifty yards away on the other branch of the river is another big fall which Varick Frissell saw in the summer of 1925 and called Yale Falls. The river was open at the time both parties came here. They had left their canoes at Grand River and walked in. Thus they could not cross. Frissell was on the north side and saw the Yale Falls, but could not get over to the south branch to see the Twin Falls. Thomas was on the south bank, saw the Twin Falls and small falls, but could not cross for a view of Yale Falls.

In February, 1929, H. G. Watkins and J. M. Scott, Englishmen exploring for the Royal Geographic Society, guided by Robert Michelin, visited Yale Falls, Twin Falls and the small falls. There is another fall, however, two or three miles above Yale Falls, on the north branch, which we are going to see tomorrow. I do not think anyone from

194

outside has ever seen that one. Watkins and Scott noted its vapor and plotted its approximate position, but they were living on their dogs and what rabbits and partridges Bob could kill for them, growing weaker every day and they had to get out of it before doing as much exploring as they would have liked.

Arch led us to a tree at the brink of the Twin Falls and dug for about five minutes in the snow at its roots. Finally he emerged triumphant with a bottle in which Thomas had written his name. Philemon Blake, Dan Michelin and Arch Goudie, all trappers, also had their names recorded in the bottle. Mr. Thomas had written, "I claim the distinction of being the first white man to visit these falls." The claim is largely a matter of pedigree. Arch and Philemon (every one calls him Pleeman) had both been here before him. Arch is about half Scotch, a quarter Eskimo and a quarter Cree; Pleeman is about seven-eighths English and the rest Eskimo.

Kay was not to be outdone. She wrote, "I claim the distinction of being the first woman, black, white, red or yellow to visit these falls." The red part of it is doubtful, though faintly possible. Indians as a rule would not go ten steps out of their way to see a fall. They avoid them and don't go touring around looking for them like stupid whites. In any case it sounded better to include the red and it is not likely the claim will be refuted, for Indian women seldom leave their names in bottles.

There has been talk of harnessing these falls or the Grand Falls to a lumber mill. I don't see any earthly way of getting heavy machinery in here or shipping out the sawed lumber and I think, happily, it is a lot of nonsense.

We are camped tonight not far from the falls. It seems pleasant and homelike to sleep again in a tent.

KAY had a curious mishap at noon when we boiled up. We had just come back from Yale Falls to our camping place. Up on top of the bank Arch and I were taking down the tent while Kay went down to the ice for water. As is often the case, there was water and slush under the snow by the bank. The river rises after it is frozen and water under pressure seeps up between the ice and the shore. The bank was steep and Kay slipped down and jumped onto the ice. Her left foot went through the crusty snow and embedded itself in slush. There she remained as though in a vise, toes curled up and heel jammed in. The pressure of the step had hardened the half-frozen slush to the consistency of ice and caught her there. We ran down and tried to pull the foot out, but it hurt so much we were afraid of breaking something. Arch took an axe and I a sheath knife, and very carefully, for there is nothing like ice to make a blade glance, we cut her out. Her foot was nearly frozen. By the fire she put on dry sox and stockings and dried her moccasin. We could see the instep starting to swell. She walked with a slight limp all the afternoon. It would be terrible to be caught so if one had no axe or knife within reach. The ice would soon break one's finger nails.

Early in the morning we left our camp and went down the narrow, frozen north branch of the Yale Falls. Returning, we broke camp, lashed up the sled and saw the upper north falls on the way back to the tilt. I will not try to describe their frosty faces. A waterfall is as difficult to describe as the aurora borealis, and talk cheapens everything. Only I must put it down that every one of these falls is a double fall, split at the brink by a rock or a little island. The Twin Falls is one double fall, and Yale Falls is another double fall, close by. Twin Falls is not a name meant to include both, it is one and distinct.

We decided to call the upper fall of the north branch, which is crescent shaped and very high, Goudie Falls, in honor of Arch, who knows more about the lot of them than anybody else. Somebody else will come along and call them something else, so what does it matter.

When we had reached the pretty cove in the elbow of the tilt point, we found its surface crisscrossed with fresh tracks where some one had been trying to find the snowed-over water hole. Whoever it was, he had not succeeded, and had ended by chipping up a kettleful of ice. Arch's first thought was of the old Indian, and a fear for his grub and fur. Then he recognized the prints as those of Harvey's snowshoes. We gave a yell to the tilt, wondering why this unexpected visit. No answer.

Inside, we found a note on a fur board. Arch gave it to me, saying, "You can read faster than me."

It said: "Victor got sore legs and come back in the night Monday. I got to go out to the Grand river leving friday. I am going down home that way and will wait for you at Victors til Tuesday night. Send word what you think to do. Grub with us very short but Victors legs is better. I am going bak this evening."

The stove was still warm. What a walk, over the mountain and back in one day. Arch was stunned. He didn't know what to do. He didn't want to stay in here alone. He didn't want to go home by way of Victor's; it was eighty miles longer than going down beside Unknown River. He had to get his reserves of food at the Big Hill soon.

Mechanically he began to mix up some bread, and the wet, sticky paste was as formless as his thoughts. Round and round the knife went, pushing more flour into the pool of water in the hollowed center of the bowl. Now it left a gluey, closing path. He wiped the knife clean with dry flour, and the dough took spring and form under his fingers and fists.

"I could finish strikin' up tomorrow forenoon," he said, "if you would be gettin' the sled along. We'd be late but we could get to Harvey's sometime after dark."

"All right," I said, and was glad I could be useful. It isn't often I've been able to help a trapper. They are generally helping me.

I believe if a trapper had a broken leg he would manage somehow to strike up his path before leaving it. No man knowingly leaves a trap set on a place he does not intend to return to that season. Arch may come back here in February and March and he may not. It is a long trip up here again for the short spring hunt. Anyway he is striking up. There are no game wardens, nothing compels them to unset their traps and avoid needless slaughter, only the code they have made for themselves.

Daylight still lingered. Kay set about baking the bread, while I went up to the rapid to help Arch put his canoe on a scaffold high between trees where the snow will blow off and not lodge on till the weight breaks its back.

Now it is getting late. Arch is still busy putting his fur

in bags, patching a moccasin, getting ready for the long dash home.

It is going to be a question of food from now till we get to Victor's. We have nothing left but tea, raw tea, and the materials for bread—salt, baking powder and flour. Harvey is as short of flour as we are. I don't believe there are ten pounds of flour between the five of us.

December 21.

AT sunrise, it seems a year ago, we left Arch's point. Arch went off straight into the woods with a bag and an axe to finish striking up his last short path. We went over the big lake with the sled. It had a fair load, and I wasn't fresh when we came to the farther end. From there it was an eight-mile pull up grade to the mountain top. With a sled it would have been much easier to have followed the river than gone over the mountain, but I didn't know that at the time.

We were only half way up at two o'clock. I was wringing wet and immediately freezing cold when we sat down for a cup of tea and a small piece of bread. We went too high before boiling up. What little dry wood we could find was sheathed in ice and would not burn. My legs were trembling with weakness, and my hands were sore from yanking at the line. Kay helped me up the steep banks where we floundered and slipped back and sank to the shoulders in drifts. Every inch was a battle gained.

At sunset we were at the top, drinking in the stern, endless panorama one last time. The cold was intense. Darkness was softening the infinite miles of ice and islands. O you wilderness land of cold clean distance, you pitiless

Labrador of winter twilight, we shall love you forever, yes, forever with the love of children and savages, you land too strong to be spoiled by men, you land of fathomless beauty.

It was like a prayer, that last look from the mountain. We were no longer civilized, we had no heritage, no future, no thought of our thoughts. We were just us in the freezing dusk, escaped for one clear transcendent moment from all men and all time.

There the track was blown out and we lost our way among the cliffs. It cost us twenty minutes more of precious daylight scouting out a way that was practicable for the sled. Here and there were signs of Harvey's track, wandering and retracing itself. He told us, later, that he had been mixed up among the rocks in the dark.

The last light was fading as we went down the other side. Going down the first icy slope to the trees I had the sled on its side and a good grip on the curl. Over a hummock it got away from me. I grabbed the trailing line, fearful Arch's precious gear would be smashed to pieces down below. The sled and I both turned a somersault and landed in a drift between two trees.

Coming up the slope earlier in the day the head cross bar, to which the hauling line is attached, must have loosened with the yanking. It was now completely off. The lash line consequently came loose and the load was spilling out of the wrapper all over the snow. With some twine, which is the handiest, most indispensable thing a person can carry in pockets already stuffed with handy indispensable things, I bound it all together in an inextricable snarl of ingenious, or lubberly (depending on the viewpoint) knots and counter braces. Kay went on to find a way down while there was a little light. I could follow her track in the dark.

So we progressed, my cross and I, slithering up against trees, too slow with the sled on her side, too fast on her bottom. The gun hooked into a tree and came off, a kettle with it. The wrapper received a long gash on a sharp stub. It was now pitch dark. Once the sled knocked me down and ran over me, but I caught the tail going by and hung on like a tackler to a flying halfback's ankle.

Nearly down the last bank I heard a step behind me, and there was Arch, silent like an Indian whom you never hear or see approach. Suddenly he is there.

At the bottom we lit a fire and rested by its light. When we left, Arch put my axe on the sled. At the end of two miles the axe had disappeared. He fished out a flashlight from the sled and I went back to look for it while he took the sled and went on with Kay. The snow was deep and very light, and I couldn't find my axe though I felt in the snow wherever there was a mark.

By trotting and walking in spells I caught them just before they got to Harvey's. It was ten o'clock and snowing, and we were pretty glad to see the light at Button Bank.

Harvey said he and Victor were expecting the two of us, but had given us up for this night. Just after dark they went down the river to the brook and fired off shots to aid us if we were lost.

Victor told us he left Monday shortly after we did. In the afternoon when he was more than half way to the tiny tilt he twisted his knee. It grew worse, and he was afraid if he pushed on he might be laid up for a week or more without grub. So he turned back to Harvey's where there was help if he needed it. It was late in the night when he got there, using a forked stick for a crutch. His knee was stiff next day and badly swollen, but better now. The double strain on Harvey's last shrunken flour bag was fatal to its looks.

They had no partridges and we were all craving meat. I had to bake for next day, and then fell asleep like a log.

In the morning we pawed through Arch's load and all over the light snow on the dock. The camera with its priceless pictures from Mount Fine Lookout and the pictures of all four falls, was gone, slipped off on the mountainside probably in the dark. Harvey and Arch told me I must not go back and look for it. It would mean another day, we were all short of grub and the chances were I would not find it anyway. They were going on, no matter what I did.

I thought about it for half an hour while they loaded. I would gladly have gone hungry for an extra day to get back the pictures. What decided me was the new snow and the small chance of finding the camera if I did go back. It would have been worse than looking for a needle in a haystack. I decided to be sensible and bear the shame.

Arch had to mend his sled, so we went on to make a track for them. The old path was snowed completely over and it was deep, hard walking even where we could feel it underneath. We found the way all right, except at the far side of a lake, where some old blazes led us wrong. We were hungry all day, and our stomachs rumbled with emptiness. When we stopped to boil up we amused ourselves doing as the trappers do when they are on short rations. One carefully halves the little flat cake that is to do them both all day. The other takes his pick, thus assuring absolute fairness to both.

Being hungry rouses in one the most elemental motives. I never understood it before, and now some of the trappers' ways take on added significance. I realize now that among hungry men, no matter who they are, the slightest cause for resentment over food must be avoided. If anyone feels cheated and says nothing, that is worse than a fight. I remember now, though I thought nothing of it at the time, that whenever some of us have been together and there was plenty of meat the men would eat unheard-of quantities. No matter how much there was, some one would "dry the pot" and some one else would wipe up the rich brown gravy with a piece of bread. But if there was not enough, say a half a partridge each, there would always be a leg or a wing or a neck and some gravy left over. Every one would say, "I got plenty, me," and the precious mouthful would remain untouched through tomorrow's breakfast and finally be thrown away. There is nothing more illuminating than a good taste of hunger. I realize now how strong and square they are to be generous with their grub when they are short.

We saw no sign of partridge in the whole day's walk, and not a rabbit in a trap. Before dark we were at the tilt, with wood cut up and water from the brook. I had cut a turn of wood, tent poles and some brush for "the boys" when they pulled in with their sleds about two hours after dark. They were very tired, except Harvey who is never tired.

The lean, too-short sleep of utter fatigue was ours for a few hours. I woke several times chattering with cold, to stoke the fire and fall asleep before I was warm. And in my sleep, by a deeper restfulness I could feel for a little while the purple-robed warmth hugging my bones and then the thin sharp cold that sets one's subconscious on edge and makes sleep a tiresome labor from which one starts with relief as from a bad dream.

"My belt is in two notches and Kay's the same. We are not the same people we used to be. We couldn't have stood this if we had not worked up to it gradually," is all I wrote in the black book that night.

We had the kettles boiled and everything packed up while it was still dark. "Prima luce Cæsar castra movit." The snowshoe rhythm again, to which thought and muscle bow. We wanted to pass the first tilt and get out to the river, two days' walk in one if we could; Harvey said it smelt like snow.

It wasn't exactly pleasure, but it was good to feel we were living our lives and not giving in, and no burden to any one. We had said we could travel this way and we were doing it. I am so proud of Kay that sometimes I can hardly keep a straight face.

The sun was well on the down swing of its short arc when we struck the chain of lakes and threaded our way straight to the tilt by the shore. It was hidden in trees, but we had looked back many times to mark the spot when we were on our way in. Somehow we all got inside and munched our bread, dipping it in tea by way of butter. A bitter wind was sweeping the lake.

I put my empty bag on Arch's sled, and from there on took spells hauling for him. Harvey had by far the biggest load. He and Victor were hauling double, he ahead and Victor a step behind him. I've hauled that way and it is the worst kind of slavery for the hinder one. You have to watch the other fellow's heels eternally and keep step, up banks, down banks, over logs, under trees. If you get out of step you take all the strain or none, the sled runs up on the tails of your snowshoes, you fall and it butts you, still pulled on by the head man, head foremost into the snow, where you lie tangled up and weighted down, with your snowshoes hung about your ears.

At first there were woods and the long shadows, then darkness and an overcast sky. "It's going to be a black night," said Arch. "Aye, and snow," added Harvey.

Then came the burnt woods, barrens interspersed with skirts of wind-stunted scrub wood, desolate-looking places fit for no man. Snow began to fall and the sleds ran harder. We all walked with the least possible effort. Up the hills we advanced a step, then pulled the sled up with our arms. The sides of the bare hills ahead looked in the darkness like flat white lakes in a hollow. A bitter disappointment when we got there.

Several hours later we were in the midst of the boulder-strewn valleys and their pitfalls. Later in the winter the snow will be packed hard over all the irregularities of the rocks. Now it is "hung up" between the boulders, with hollows underneath. We could not see where we were putting our feet. We walked blind and tense, expecting to fall. Hours went by. Every five or six steps, every hundred yards, every other step the hollow snow gave way and dropped us into a pit between boulders. It grew harder and harder to rise from the hole of cold fluff. Arch unpacked his flashlight which aided us with its moving pool of yellow vision. But after a little it dulled to a dim red wire in a button bulb, mere mockery.

Kay was very tired and rose after each fall more slowly. She carried the flash while it lasted and we struggled behind with the sled. When the light gave out she tried coming behind on the track. We could not haul her on the sled in the rough going, and she would not have it anyway. She had said she would travel till she dropped, and now she was dropping and still going on. An iron will can support sagging legs a long time and stir others' hearts with unbelievable pain and admiration. In the soft bed of snow there was no pity. At last she fell and could not rise. I heard her lying in the snow, sobbing with rage. I lifted her up and murmured, "Poor, poor child." Arch was there too, a shepherd looking at an angel. He heard us but we did not care. He was one with us. We were two brothers and a sister. He brought the sled and we rested on the load while the snow sifted out of the darkness. It was a moment when time stands still, and human beings cling close together. I think a lifetime holds few such communions. But we had to go on.

By and by the going smoothed out and we caught up to Victor and Harvey, sitting on their sled at the foot of a bank, looking up at it, panting and streaming sweat. "D'you think we can do it, Uncle Archie? It is the last one."

It was amazing that they should know where they were, for the snow was falling thick and we hadn't passed so much as a fringe of scrub in miles.

Arch pointed to a gray rock in the gloom. "You see that," he said. "I ha'n't been here for fifteen years, but I remember shootin' a red fox by that rock. I know where I am."

As always at the end of a long march the object was not to think of getting there, not to think of anything, not to remember the thousand aches, just to walk in semi-consciousness. I was afraid Kay would give out. I don't know how she ever kept up. After she fell that last time I thought we should have to stop and barricade out at the next skirt of woods. But she grew steadily stronger from then on.

At the end of several eons we passed between the two big rocks on the hilltop and descended to the river. How we hoped it would be frozen straight across to the house. That would save us four miles. On the water there were peninsulas and plains of new ice, but the snow made the bad spots treacherous. It looked as though there might be a winding bridge across.

"Shall we try it?" asked Harvey, with his back to the wind. He looked the same as always, only his face was thin in the martenskin cap.

He took an axe to test the ice, and his flashlight, the last of whose battery he had saved for this. A little way off he turned and shouted through the snow, "Come along, Uncle Arch. You can haul me out if I goes through."

We could hear them making a chop ahead every step. We stood like tired horses who don't know how to sit, and waited a long time. Victor cut a hole for a drink. Just as I was getting a cup off the sled we saw the light wave and heard a muffled shout like a whisper, "Come on." By bending close to the ice we could follow their track. The bridge wound. Sometimes we felt that we were surrounded by the black, sliding water.

Twenty minutes later we beat the snow off each other and fell into the tilt. Seated on the floor playing cards were Henry Baikie, Alvin, Russel Groves and Cecil Blake. They were bound for home, and planning to spend Sunday here. We weren't very glad to see them and they weren't very glad to see us. Nine in a tilt is too much of a good thing.

"Hello b'y, hello b'y," they all said at once, "where come from today? Lord Harry you must a been drivin' 'er. Tired, eh?"

"No," said Harvey, lighting his pipe and putting on the kettle, "just a little thirsty."

They gave Kay the bunk, and the rest of us slept somehow. We were too sleepy to eat much. With a wan smile on her drawn face, Kay wriggled into her sleeping bag and arranged her cap for a pillow. What luxury it was to have a sleeping bag. "I think," she whispered to me, "a woman's place is in the home."

Victor had put away on a shelf a can of "hook outs," the black, soggy scrapings from the bottom of his pipe, saved to be dried and re-smoked in case he ran out of legitimate tobacco. Russell had been without a smoke for three weeks and he was trying some of this mess in his pipe. The last thing I was conscious of was Russell's face. It was turning slightly green.

December 22.

WE are back again at John's. Our last day here fills us with sadness. How ridiculous to leave all this. Where will we ever find a better place? The men have got the fever, they are going home. GOING HOME, they say it over and over again. John has the fever too. He is wild to get home to his wife, but even more to his little girl.

But it is not my home down there. Neither do I fit in the city where I was born. This is my home, more than any place I know, and I hate this enthusiasm for leaving.

Kay and I have talked it over very seriously. She feels this is a home worth keeping. She would be willing to stay while I go down and bring back a sled load of food. It would take at least six weeks, and maybe more, depending largely on the weather. John is not coming back here in the spring. We know where most of the traps are. We could hunt the place and Fred Goudie would help us to run the canoes down when he goes home in the spring.

But there is not enough food to last Kay six weeks. I should have to come back alone, and I am not sure I know enough. Besides, I couldn't haul enough grub to last till spring. We need more things to sustain life than Indians do. It is not so much that we are civilized and need comforts as that we lack their age-long, instinctive skill in hunting and primitive housekeeping. And that settles it.

John had all his traps struck up and was ready to go when we landed in here last night, hauling up his new sled for him. He was quite worked up about us as we were four days late. He said he was going to wait another day and then start hunting for us. Probably we were lost coming out from Unknown Lake on Victor's path alone. He was going to hunt for us as long as the food held out and then go home to spread the sad news. Oh dear.

Gordon Pottle was here. He stopped in on his way home and decided to stay and help in the hunt. I always liked Gordon from the days on the portage when I used to be going across with a load and meet him coming back light. While I tried to unscrew my face into some semblance of a human countenance he would say, "Boy that's some load you got there. The pond is just there, the other side a these trees." The worst part of the portage was meeting some one on the path who was going back for another load. It was such an effort to calm one's face and try to make it look like the face of a man in a Morris chair by a fireside, reading Charles Lamb. After a while it got so stupid saying every time, "Hot, eh?" "Steep, huh?" "Pfhew," that we passed in strained, embarrassed silence, the man without a load getting off the path twice as far into the bushes as need be.

Most of this last day has been spent packing, mending, washing, figuring out what we can leave to lighten our loads for the 350-mile haul. John is going to take half Kay's stuff and I the other. Heaven knows, she has pitifully little. Fortunately, fur is almost as light as feathers. We ourselves haven't much—twenty-five muskrat, fifteen weasel and three mink. John has two big bags full.

Before sunset I got away and went up the ripple rapid to a brook behind an island where we had a trap still set. It was covered with crusty snow. A mink had walked right over it unharmed, and I was glad. Even the paw marks seemed to smile.

It was one of those far-flung evenings that make you stretch out your arms to touch a finger to either horizon. The sky was a long crimson call over the wind-patterned snow and the tree tops, leagues away.

I think of the people in the cities going home from work, standing and sitting in trolleys and trains. Some of them have their eyes closed tight to shut out the day that has jerked their spirits a thousand conflicting different ways, to blot out the noises, the greedy faces and the horrible, colored signs. I feel as though the cares of all these people weighed heavy over the tree tops, as though some day some one must set all those lives free.

No one can say what an evening like this is, or what it

does. I can only say it is loneliness and solitude and beauty so sad it makes one's heart break with sorrow, and leap with gladness to have seen and been savage enough to feel. Whatever I say is only words. One has to be here in the cold, going home to partridge stew in a cabin, on hard legs, with the snow crunching, with months of the life behind one, to feel the red sky and the fading light creeping into one's muscles and brain and nerves to motivate one's life for ever after.

Kay met me in the doorway and we watched the night grow dark. At least we know what we are losing, know that if we never come back it is our own fault. And that is worth knowing. However senseless life may ever be, the spruces will still be here, drawn up straight or whispering to each other in the darkness, listening, waiting, not for us to come back, but for men to become better, for men to come and rub their cheeks against the shaggy bark, clasp the ageless trunks in loving arms and say, "This, oh this is good; better than the cumulative cleverness of the centuries. And at last we need not ask why."

Going home. There's something to roll on one's tongue and think about. John parodies the song of similar name, "There is many a sled grows rimier going home." Sometimes he sings whole sentences instead of talking, he is so happy. The fever whirls the men down the river every winter like clouds of drift in a gale.

Home in the north is ten times cozier than home in the south. It is an oasis in a cold, bleak world; there is no fruit on the trees here. It means a crackling fire, heat, glorious warmth even before food. It means love and sociability and news, precious germs of ideas, hints of novelty. It means a bath and clean clothes.

These people have a feeling for their homes that is as strong as life itself. And why shouldn't they. They have picked the spot where the water is deep to the shore and the hunting is good and the fishing. They cut out the clearing and built the house of logs with their own hands. And they have fought for it ever since.

Going home means getting to a miniature Heaven after four months in the woods. The long trip down is always fast, it resembles a gruelling race. Days and days of ache, weeks of weariness piling up, never enough sleep, never enough to eat, watching the weather ceaselessly, wondering when the deep snow will come and slow the sleds. There is hardly time for the alimentary functions. The passion, the cry, the driving will, waking and sleeping, is to get on. Nothing can stop them when they get the bit in their teeth, not even their own bodies, weeping with weariness. Swiftness, swiftness, lead-footed swiftness.

Arriving home is blessed rest from all this. One can sit in a house, safe, it seems, even from the wrath of God, and not give a damn whether it storms or not. One can watch quiet sunsets through the window and remember that man differs from a hauling dog after all. One can muse and forget to be keen and sharp as a knife. One can lump one's clothes in the corner, pick them up gingerly with a long stick and say, as though they belonged to some other fellow, "I am going to burn these."

I've seen the trappers arriving at North West River, three or four black pin points way off over the ice. The children run down to the shore and jump up and down in the snow and yell, "Ooo, Paa's comin'." The women get out the glass, steady it on a window sill and look long. By the time the specks are as big as tacks, she knows by the swing of the arms and the walk if her man is there. The travellers come up the bank, a smile on their lean, leather faces. And even their stained, frayed clothing looks weary. The children proudly take the sled and the man straightens and walks to his house. For two days and nights he does nothing but eat and sleep. Whatever time of the day or night he wakes, he eats a big meal and slumbers again. The dead, soporific slumber full of comfortable aches—I wonder if in Heaven there is anything as good as that sleep. The more rested he becomes, the hungrier he grows. About the third morning he appears in the doorway, dressed in clean clothes and new white canvas leggings embroidered with bright blue and red and green braid. He is a butterfly emerging from a cocoon.

The men who are married want principally to get home to their women. They want to hold them in their arms at night, there is a certain gnawing that craves peace. They are frank but not evil. It is all good, even this strongest urge of man.

Married couples in this country enjoy the blessing of being continually separated. The men are forever going away on hard, dangerous trips, deer hunting, down the bay in little boats, or furring up the rivers. The woman waits and works hard too, and is cold and afraid some nights alone and dreams something has happened. But you or I will never know this. Every fall they must part as inexorably as though fate had singled out this man and woman alone. The shotguns boom good-bye, and he paddles away, as gay as a boy, with never a thought but one or two of the rapids to come, and the fur he is going to bring home *this* year. And she turns back to the house and the children and the work. When he pulled away from the wharf he remembered to say, "So long," and she replied, "Good luck," very casually, as though he would be home for lunch and men are such a bother anyway. " 'Tis our fashion," one of them told me once.

In reality there is emptiness in the months to come. And oh the sweetness of coming home! A man is a bit of a hero and a woman a bit of a heroine, just by living life. Each is so and seems so to the other. Can you imagine what it is like two or three times a year to tumble into your own little nest, ragged, dirty, utterly weary, unquenchably hungry, frost-bitten, "done." It is too good to be true. Life does not grow wearisome.

The young fellows want to get home to see the girls, those black-eyed girls who are so shy to a certain point, and then so direct. They'd like to walk out with them tonight, down the frozen portage path, a thin white aisle between black spires, to the shore of the bight where they could look off down the bay in the starlight. And maybe coming back through the trees they'd slip an arm around her. Probably she wouldn't care.

And for them all, men and women, big and little, there is the Fair, the three-day midwinter festival the Mission arranges for the middle of every January at North West River. Teams come galloping in from Sabasquasho and Mulligan and Pearl River, the head of Grand Lake, Goose Bay and Mud Lake. A team once came from ninety miles away. On every komatik, kneeling or sitting on sealskin or caribou robes ride men and women and children in peaked fur-edged dickies. Perhaps there are so many of them that they have to take turns running and riding.

The town is full of fighting, snarling dogs, and at night they howl. A tremolo, piercing howl at one end of the village is answered by a long-drawn wail at the other and the massed chorus between these restless outposts overwhelms the shuddering stars with misery. People shiver in their beds. I think it is a throwback to the time when hair used to bristle on our spines.

In the daytime there are so many people to talk to it takes half an hour to travel fifty feet on the main path. The old folks shake their heads and say the place has got too crowded for any use, and what with the young fellows and girls skylarkin' around till ten and eleven a body can't git no rest.

Daytimes the men lie around on the counters at the H. B. C. store and smoke and yarn and occasionally buy some candy or a box of cookies, and tell about the otter they lost or the cross fox that got away. The women visit with their innumerable cousins and aunts, sisters and mothers whom Kay can keep straight, but I can't. After the old man has traded a little fur, they buy some stuff for a new dress maybe, or a few tins of tomatoes, that wonderful fruit from outside.

The Company puts up a barrel of flour for a shooting match, and the man who wins it has to do some extra fine shooting. All the girls make and fill supper baskets and the Mission holds a basket social. The young fellows bid for their supper partners and the old fellows nudge each other

215

and drive them up. No one is supposed to know whose basket is whose, but everybody does. The Mission puts on a play that is the wonder of the age, and afterwards there is cocoa and beans and cake for everyone.

But best of all are the dances in the schoolhouse; square dances with a fiddler in the corner tapping his foot and playing, "Turkey in the Straw," and "The Girl I Left Behind Me." The homemade desks are moved out and even the nonagenarians come. The men have on their new bright leggings and clean, beautifully smoked moccasins. The girls wear their very best dresses and the beaded moccasins on their tiny feet are tied with pert red bows. "Lancers," "Grand Chain All," "Swing Your Partners." Somebody calls out the figures as the four couples laugh and weave through the old-fashioned steps faster and faster. Johnnie Montague gets back around the circle to his partner, and "Home Again" he yells as he swings her right off her feet, whirling with short little steps. And the moccasins make a lovely whispering sound on the boards that gets into your blood, *tch . . . tch tch . . . tch tch.*

Occasionally they do the "Birdie," and the two opposite men come out to the center of the floor and clog, trying to outdo each other in speed and the intricacy of their steps. If one happens to be a Grand Lake-Nascaupee man and the other a Grand River hunter, all the spectators take sides. The sound of the twinkling feet thumping on the boards is drowned in bellows, "Now Grand River! Give it to her, b'y." "Hi Grand La-a-ke, Whee." I can see Dan Michelin dancing on his game leg like a madman, his forehead beaded with sweat, jolliness and excitement pouring from his round bronze face, and a long outdoor call of far places,

216

"Grand River!" exploding in the schoolhouse like the bursting of an ice dam.

Oh, it carries you away, no wonder they want to go home.

December 23.

"WELL, b'y," said John this morning, with his customary cheer when speaking of anything particularly disagreeable, "it's a dog's life from this home. It's git in the harness in the morning and work like a bloody haulin' dog till night and like it."

And so the furs start on their long journey to the grimey Jewish fur shops in the upper west twenties in New York City. I have seen them there, behind the dirty glass windows, the long glossy pelts from Patagonia and Alaska, from China and Baffinland, from Siberia and Hudson's Bay. And now it seems to me even stranger that these lithe, tawny beasts, so superior to men in grace and strength and keenness should be cut and dyed and plucked and haggled over by the little men who buy and sell. It is bad enough for a chicken to be a commercial commodity like so much pig iron, but an otter!

And what a far cry it is from here to that slim, elegant scented body that will wear a marten coat up Park Avenue some day next year; or the ermine wrap that falls from a powdered shoulder as the curtain rises. I wonder if she will ever think that those little white skins were brown in summer, and catching mice. Will she ever see in her mind's eye this orange-grained sled, worn thin on a long winding river road?

It is an odd thing that Labrador people never have fur coats, unless they be of harbor seal which is stiff and bristly,

217

sells for seventy-five cents and can be caught for nothing. The women are always hard put to it to find a stray fox brush for edging a dickie hood, or a bit of trimming that will keep the snow out of mitten cuffs. For the fur ears on caps they use skins that have been cut and shaved by mice, or fox skins that were half-eaten by another fox. They can't understand why people in the "warm countries" want fur coats. They like wool against the skin, and canvas to keep out the wind, much better than fur clothing.

The going on the river is good today, and the sleds come easily. I used to think that snow was just snow. But it isn't. It is a study for us now, like everything else, full of variety and vital interest. There are infinite kinds of snow to affect the slipping and walking. After a snowy night, the men can tell in the morning at a glance what kind of slipping it's going to be for the sleds, but I can't.

Sometimes the crust bears you up on snowshoes, sometimes the crust will not bear up under the racquets. Then each step is a delayed happening, for the hard surface goes down slowly and unwillingly. Another kind of crust is brittle. It trips you every step. The men call it "hookey." The crust that bears up without snowshoes, is, of course, one of the best. The crust that almost bears up but lets you through every now and then unexpectedly, is aggravating and makes you lame.

There is light new snow an inch or so deep that is excellent slipping for the sleds. They seem to want to go, to run of themselves. But the light frost which falls on cold evenings looks almost the same and is a chain to the sleds, "the pure rime," John calls it. Wind blows rime away and hardens the snow on the rivers and lakes. It is always better walking and easier hauling out on the open ice than in the woods where the drifts lie deep and soft and the wind cannot sweep.

On very cold days when the snow squeaks and crunches, it is "dry hauling." There is a certain sandy quality to the surface and the sleds run moderately hard. At noon on such days if the sun is very bright and the temperature gets up to ten below zero, the slipping becomes very much better. Generally in January or February each winter there comes a two or three day "mild" when the snow thaws. Then there are all kinds of wetness to contend with, easy-running wetness and wetness so sticky that the sleds pick up the snow right to the ice and leave a path like that of a rolling, growing snowball. In the winter there are a thousand different kinds of snow. In the spring there are a thousand more varieties. Different kinds of wood run differently. Birch is better in wet snow and worse when it's rimey than juniper. With runnered sledges, komatiks and catamarans, different kinds of shoeing have varying advantages and defects. Whalebone, ivory, iron, steel, tin, German silver, iced frozen mud, wide runners, narrow runners all slip quite differently and each is preferable to any other in certain temperatures on certain kinds of snow.

It is obviously stupid for men to haul sleds. Man is not built for it, the strain pulls his two-legged machinery awry. When a biped hauls, there is a great loss in mechanical efficiency. With a quadruped the strain is split up among the four legs, the pull on the backbone is longitudinal. The strain on the extremes of a man's backbone rather tend to break it in half.

There is absolute efficiency in a dog's horizontal position.

A ninety-pound dog can haul almost as much as a 150-pound man and keep it up longer. The dog requires nothing but a little food each evening. The man requires, tent, stove, axe, gun, sleeping gear, clothes, kettles and three or four different kinds of food. How superior dogs are to men in certain respects! It is the same way with the birds. Think how far the geese can travel without any baggage. We are really pitiful creatures to be so proud of ourselves. We spend most of our lives making ourselves comfortable.

Since dogs are so superior to men in the matter of necessary impedimenta and endurance it seems at first glance odd the trappers do not bring one or two to haul the sleds home. Most of the men have a team at home doing nothing, a bother for the woman to feed. But they have tried bringing dogs and found the average husky an unmitigated nuisance during the months of trapping.

For centuries husky dogs have been trained to haul, and they can do little else. They are tireless, fleet and efficient, a necessity to northern man, better for all around winter travel than airplanes, motor sledges, reindeer or ponies. In their sphere they cannot be beaten. But they cannot hunt. They have none of the instinctive intelligence of the little Indian "cracky" dogs that look so small and useless, and are so valuable to a hunter.

Huskies are born thieves. They will chew up snowshoes, boots, mittens, any kind of leather, pork, bacon, butter, lard, partridges or rabbits in the twinkling of an eye. Many of them learn early to rob traps. They gently push their noses in over the trap and pull out the bait, taking the greatest care not to get caught. They come along behind a hunter on his trap line, and as he baits the traps they eat out the bait.

They track up the snow for miles around and scare away the fur. They are here, there and everywhere, ahead, behind and on both sides, being able to travel at least four times as far and as fast as a man. Consistent beatings will not keep them from chasing companies of partridges and scaring them to flight long before the hunter has a chance to shoot his supper. The hunter may be gone from his main cabin for periods of a week or more. He cannot leave the dogs chained there. They would starve. He has to take them with him on his trap lines, and they in return do nothing but make him trouble. Moreover, most huskies will not eat mink, otter, fox or weasel carcasses. If the hunter brings dogs he has to come early to spend weeks netting quantities of fish for them, or else carry bags of corn meal and tubs of seal fat over the long portages.

On the so-called spring hunt, which lasts roughly from the middle of February until the middle of April, conditions are quite different. Most men bring a dog or two to help them up the river. And going home in April the dogs earn their keep hauling the catamaran sledge which bears the canoe. At this time of year there are long stretches of open water where the man puts the sledge in the canoe and paddles down the current. If it is smooth water and the dogs have sore feet or are tired, he takes them with him in the canoe. If he is heavily loaded and has rough water to negotiate he puts them out and they race along shore. Sometimes at the Devil's Hole, in Upper Mouni's or in the Horseshoes where the tide runs very strong, the dogs get left miles and miles behind the flying canoe. Then again come long stretches of ice where the sledge carries the canoe, and man and dogs all pull at the traces.

All in all, the trappers have found dogs worth while for the short spring hunt, during which there is seldom more than a month of actual hunting. But for the winter hunt, the dogs are no help on the way up the river in canoes, and they are a distinct disadvantage during the two months of work at the furring grounds. Trappers prefer to be without them and take the consequences on the long haul home. John Groves has the only ideal trapper's dog in this vicinity, a dog that can both hunt and haul. John takes the dog with him wherever he goes and makes of him a friend and pet. Most dogs of hauling size are considered work animals, necessary evils, not pets. But Yankee is an exception. He is a big, strong, half Newfoundland, half husky. From the Newfoundland side he has intelligence and a nose for hunting, from the husky inheritance, endurance and strength to haul. He knows enough to trail porcupines, but respect them; he has a different bark for partridges and for rabbits. He eats most anything, including bread, but will not touch food without permission and never, never steals anything or noses in traps. He retrieves ducks in water or out on bad ice. He will walk ahead or behind just as he is told, and is a demon for polishing off crippled running ptarmigan or tracking down animals that got away with a trap on one foot. Added to this he is a good sled dog and will come along behind on the track with a little sled of his own. I've seen him on a sticky day trying to start the sled. He'd run back to get slack and then take a flying leap ahead, straight into the air. The harness tightened with a jerk and the sled just began to move. Whining and growling, he crawled on his belly, his hind legs bent flat on the snow, trying to keep her going.

His faults are few. He baulks a little, as well he might, at steep down hills where the sled bumps into his hind legs and runs over him. And occasionally he can't resist the temptation to turn off one side and hunt, even though he is in harness. Generally he gets the sled snagged up in the willows and has to lie down and wait to be freed, but once while harnessed to a sled he chased and killed a muskrat, and often he has dragged the sled around in the woods and treed porcupines. He has been taught to guard a kill. Once when John forgot to call him on, Yankee stayed beside a dead porcupine for two days and a night until his master went back after him.

We came twenty-five miles today to Fred Goudie's house. Boiled up at Victor's and were slipping over the hard ice beside Louie's Rapid at dusk. The river and shores are so changed under the ice and snow it is hard to recognize them for the places we passed in canoe in the fall. Arch and Harvey, Gordon and Alvin and Victor are here, and John is glad, for if there is snow it will be easier over the portage to have plenty of men to take turns ahead.

We put up the tent beside the tilt, and the boys talked till late of all the happenings that have befallen them since October. They never mention hardship or loneliness.

Fred Goudie left a note for us. He is away in his south path for three days. Henry Baikie and Russell Groves and Ralph Blake went on for home yesterday.

December 24.

ALONG line of men with sleds, winding in and out on a snowy trail. Their arms swing very wide and their rolling snowshoe gait makes them look like sailors just off a ship. Sometimes they are all tight together, sometimes they are strung out over a mile or more, infinitesimal black dots on the lonely white river. An hour or so below Fred's we left the river and took the portage. If I were alone I could never find the way back through the brooks and marshes, over the ridges and ponds. Yet John found his way back over the portage alone the first winter he was up here, and in all the way he missed the invisible road but once—that invisible road that is sensed by distant hills, instinct and trained, unconscious memory. He went on the wrong side of one island, and, which is more important, he knew it immediately.

I remember Mark Twain said that Mississippi River steamboat pilots had remarkable and tiresome pictorial memories cultivated by constantly noting the river's changing sandbars. Just so it is with Labradormen. They figure out the day of the month by geography. On a certain day the big fish was caught above Porcupine; there was the day when Tom fell in Mininipi or the day of the early snow when Joshua, tracking the canoe through Upper Moonies, had to put on his snowshoes. From outstanding events such as these they figure each day's travel, counting on their fingers, and will tell you the exact day of any happening on trips up and down the river ten or twelve years ago. If they have been through a section of country once, they know it, for all practical working purposes, perfectly. Their feeling for location and direction is not to be acquired by an outsider in five, or even in ten years. Wherever they have been in all their lives they have been accustomed to finding their own way. In summer going up and down the bay in boats it is the same, noting harbors that are safe in a sou'west wind and bad in a nor'easter, charting in their memories shoals and tide rips and the distorted aspect of headlands seen through darkness and fog. Like other departments of their lives this feeling for place, this familiarity with the unknown, seems to me good to the roots. How much better it is to travel thus than to get on a train or a boat and be carried like a helpless babe to some other place whose name is printed on a ticket. In a thousand ways their lives are more their own than ours.

Early in the morning we came on three big companies of ptarmigan feeding in the willows by a brook. Everyone threw off his hauling line and untied his gun from the top of the load. Kay killed three, I got two and John downed seven. It is four days since we ate meat, and if we have any humanitarian feelings for the partridges, we are not conscious of them.

While he was staying at "our" house, Gordon Pottle bought an old shotgun from John. It was very rusty, and missed fire almost without fail. There were only two exceptions. Occasionally both barrels would go off when the breech was snapped closed, or rarely, if the safety was on, it would shoot every seventh time you pulled the trigger. Kay and I used to be in mortal terror of the thing when John carried it loaded in the canoe in the fall. John said it wasn't worth hauling home, but Gordon gave a mink and some weasel skins for it. He said that his father, who has something of a reputation as a gunsmith, could "take it abroad" and with the simple aid of a file and some old screws make it like new.

This morning Gordon got his new gun off the sled and went after the partridges with it. He snicked and snicked, and the gun refused to go off even when he pointed the muzzle in the general direction of the partridges and snapped the breech shut. We all stopped our hunting to encourage him, and the suggestions were not entirely helpful. John advised him to try to "hammer that old hen with the stock." At length Gordon threw the gun in the snow and turned on his heel. Then he came back, picked it up, put it on his sled and went on down the brook with bent, sorrowing head, while the guns banged all around him and the partridges fluttered. To our simple minds this is a huge joke.

We boiled the kettle by a brook where the ice was thin. There are so many of us we have to have two fireplaces.

Up over Louie's Ridge where we remember carrying four bags of flour just for fun, and by the cascade where we shot the whitefish long ago on a fall evening. It is good to recognize something. It makes it easier to imagine you are an old-timer. It has been a sunny day and I enjoyed the hauling. I love the motion of the sled ahead as it ripples and curls and twists, dips its tail and lifts its head, creaking like a ship. Kay, without a sled, found the day not too long herself.

Late this afternoon on the Big Lake we spied smoke hanging over the trees. It proved to be the camp of old Mathieu, the Indian, a big, dome-shaped *meetchwop* of canvas sled wrappers and tents and skins over a frame of bent willows.

For a doorsill it had two big logs and the inside was an oval, cozy room with a balsam carpet. Two tin stoves occupied the center and around the edges were the bags and blankets. They asked us in and spread a blanket for each of us. It made me think of being offered a chair. Mrs. Mathieu has a new baby, and she showed Kay in the little French calendar book his saint's day. She took Kay under her wing, so to speak. They carried on a low, animated conversation, though neither understood the other's mere words. They leaned toward each other like two sisters, and held hands and laughed softly and the tent was filled with a strange new feeling. Kay must have missed a woman sometimes. I never thought of it before and I don't believe she did either.

The French girl's baby is soon to come and her face has the drawn, peaked look. Mrs. Mathieu says the girl cannot live on meat like an Indian. They have had a bit of a hard time, no caribou. Their moccasins are bad and their snowshoes are knit with salmon twine brought from the Gulf against just such an emergency. They are beautifully knit with a pattern of binding at the toe-hole, as though it grew there under their fingers, irresistibly. But twine will not wear like *babische* and on days of crust they dare not travel.

We are camped near them and every one has contributed a little something to their welfare—candles, flour, matches, tea, beans and old moccasins, though we haven't any too much ourselves.

John is going to keep a promise and take us to the Grand Falls tomorrow, much as he hates to let the others go on. Keeping the promise is for him an internal struggle, for he is so constituted that it is a physical necessity for him to be ahead, always ahead in the line of march, never left behind for any cause whatsoever. Grand River and the falls are only six miles in over the hills from this point on the portage. Perhaps we shall catch the boys again before we get down home, perhaps not.

I had forgotten; it is Christmas Eve. How nice to be able

to forget it, to remember it ourselves, to make something of our own out of it, not to have Christmas rammed down our throat by a horde of merchants.

December 25.

WE left the camp up when we started in for the falls this morning. The rest of the boys were just filing off down the lake. "Tell them Traverspine I'm comin'," John bawled. "Have them cook codfish and potatoes for me."

Then he turned to us. "I'll beat them yet."

At the end of two hours' climbing little hills and slipping down the other side we commenced to hear the roar of the falls as though it were at our feet. Slipping down one hill I broke the stock off my .22 rifle. At the edge of a cliff we looked over. It was the gorge, called Bowdoin Canyon. We were too far down the river, so we circled back through the woods and came out at the brink of the falls. The river bends at right angles just below the falls in such a way that from the other side one can stand and look directly at the torrent, head on. But from this, the north side, one can only see the brink and the bottom, and no view of it as a whole is possible. We lay on our stomachs on a huge round mound of white ice and took turns holding each other's feet to peer into the witches' cauldron a long way down. Now and then for a second the vapor would part and we could see the foot of the roaring white column tumbling into a pool of black water 300 feet below. Then the mist lazily closed together again. Above the take-off, the river is a long steep slant of raging rapid. One would have to go five or six miles up to cross on ice. We would have come and seen the falls from the south side with Fred Goudie if I had not crippled myself so much. But I did and now there isn't time.

The roaring water drowned our voices and we couldn't hear each other, even when we shouted. The white mist was cold as the hand of death. It frosted our faces like three cakes.

The *Encyclopædica Britannica,* I believe, calls this the greatest fall in North America. It is a breath-taking sight, the boundless power of the frantic rapid, crowded between narrow walls, thundering down a steep slope to leap far out from the brink and plunge into the dim maelstrom below. But a dish of apricots we had for supper in honor of Christmas was also very good. It is unfortunate, when things have been talked about so much that one feels compelled to like them. For me the Grand Falls is an interesting incident of the trip, no more appealing than the fact that a tilt can be built without a nail or the knowledge that you get cracked heels if you don't wash your feet. As always, it is the travelling and the people met on the way, not the getting there. The people around North West River insisted that we were going up the river to see the Grand Falls. So be it. We have seen them.

In a clearing nearby stood a stump, capped with an aluminum kettle. Under the kettle lay a bottle filled with slips of paper and people's names. As we were shivering and chattering in the unaccustomed dampness, we built a fire to warm us while we looked at the bottle's contents.

It is odd how much better pencil writing withstands time's ravages than ink. The first names in the bottle are those of Messrs. Austin Carey and D. M. Cole, two Americans of the Bowdoin College expedition who came here alone in

1891. It is lucky that these blurred lines were not the last word ever heard of them, for while they were away at the falls, their campfire, which they thought was out, burrowed into the moss, travelled underground and sprang up, starting a blaze in their camp. When they returned they found their canoe and most of their gear and food reduced to ashes. It must have been an appalling discovery. To find oneself in the interior of Labrador, land of water and islands, in summer without a canoe would be almost synonymous with finding oneself dead. With them they had a pistol and some kind of shot cartridges. They caught a few fish and killed some birds and squirrels with the pistol—just enough to keep alive. They made a raft which they lashed together with their clothes and navigated with poles and rude paddles. They could not remember the river entirely, with its bad rapids that begin suddenly around sharp bends. It is remarkable that they got ashore above each one. At every big rapid they lost their raft and had to make a new one. At Winnikapau Lake they had to leave the raft again and take to the hills, a tortuous way, cut up with cliffs and brooks, rocky draws, thick woods and willows—and flies, a truly terrible road. While they were picking their way through the hills, two more Americans bent on exploring the Grand Falls, Henry G. Bryant and Professor C. A. Kenaston, sailed up the lake unseen. With them, as guides, in their 500-pound boat were John Montague who was years afterwards drowned in Gull Island Rapid and an Eskimo named Geoffrey Ban, from Okkak. Somehow the unfortunate and plucky Carey and Cole got down the river, rafting and walking and swimming, chilled by the icy water, scorched by the sun, swollen with fly bites, cut and bloody and emaciated, their clothing and boots in shreds. At Gull Island Rapid they had left a cache of food on the way up, which no doubt saved their lives. The tale of that trip is a little-known epic. Uncle Jo Michelin was cutting wood above Traverspine on the day they drifted down. He has told me they didn't look human, and the crew of their boat, which was waiting at Rigolet, couldn't recognize them.

There are more than fifty names in the bottle. About many of them we have heard, and it is like meeting old friends. Some twenty of the names are those of a party of Labrador-Ungava prospectors who were here the summer before last. A dozen or so more are those of trappers who copied the "sports from outside" just for fun.

The first white man to see these falls was John McLean, a Hudson's Bay Company Scotchman who still holds the record for remarkable canoe and snowshoe trips in Labrador. He gives an account of some of his experiences in a book called, "Twenty-five years in the Hudson's Bay Territory." In January and February of 1838 as factor at Fort Chimo he crossed overland from there to Hamilton Inlet where the Company had established posts in 1837, passing on the way through Lake Michikamau. The same winter he went back and reached Fort Chimo before the ice broke up. In the summer of 1839 he started out for Hamilton Inlet by canoe, reached Grand River waters and descended as far as the Grand Falls. He estimated that there were twenty-five miles of unnavigable water below the falls, and as he could not get his gear by this obstacle he was forced to turn back to Chimo. Somewhere he discovered an Indian who said he knew a portage route by ponds and lakes and brooks around the Grand Falls. The next summer McLean started out by canoe, portaged around the Grand Falls and reached Hamilton Inlet. He went back the same summer, and in the summers of 1841 and 1842 he repeated these tremendous journeys. Literally hundreds of times he nearly lost his life.

Twenty years after McLean first saw the falls, an Iroquois Indian, named Louis-over-the-fire, guided a Hudson's Bay Company employee named Joseph McPherson to the cataract, en route to Fort Nascaupee on Lake Petitsikapau. I do not know whether this Louis-over-the-fire and the trapper's legendary Louie are one and the same, but they probably are. Trappers have told me that it was Louie who first discovered the Big Hill portage. And it is also interesting to note that Mr. Bryant on his way to the Grand Falls in 1891 met Louie at North West River, an aged H. B. C. Indian who outlined for him the portage route. Louie died at North West River in November, 1892. For some years prior to his death he was in charge of the Company's "kitchen," a small wooden building, still standing, where any one who comes to the post to trade can put up free.

John told us that if one were across Grand River, the Unknown Falls lie only about seven miles walk to the south. The river on Lowe's map marked *Valley River*, which cuts the country between here and Unknown River, is only a brook which can be forded on stepping-stones. We made a note of this and put it in the bottle with our names. With the exception of trappers, we are the only party to visit the falls in winter.

From a hilltop on the way back John showed us where Grand River and Unknown River meet. We could not see the rivers themselves, but the indication of their junction marked by the hills. And not far away he pointed out the smoke from one of the Unknown Falls.

Back at the tent we had a mugup, lashed up and said good-bye to the Indians. They are starting down for North West River in a few weeks.

Part way down the Big Lake I happened to look back, and there between me and the sunset stood the vapor from the Grand Falls, a tall, red and gold column at least a mile and a half high. It was like an omen or a tale of Jehovah's might told in the Old Testament. It made one think of Atlas or Mount Olympus or something too grand and vague to be of modern times. Kay and I loitered and watched it long, until John was a mere speck on the ice. When we set out to catch him twilight was settling down. The dimming visibility made it seem as though he were leaving us two steps to one.

We only came six or seven miles and then camped in a thin skirt of woods. It is a bad place for dry wood, and the ice is too thick for us to get water. When we stopped walking the cold dark clamped down on us and nothing could keep us warm. It is always so making camp at evening. One is hungry and tired and thus more susceptible to the cold. On one's skin there always comes a faint dampness from exertion. This starts to turn to frost. The shivers creep up and down one's spine, hands and feet begin to burn and then to throb, until one's heart is like a gigantic pump, pumping pain. The difficulties of chopping wood in the dark, in deep snow, with freezing hands, are considerable. The rounded heads of my snowshoes are nicked by the nibbles of the axe. I shall never stop being wary of that silver-bladed guillotine in the hands of fate. Several times I have nearly gashed

233

myself again, and I've seen John come within an ace of cutting himself too.

The tent is up crooked, the strings tied to half-trimmed pickets and handy-growing branches of scrub spruces. The stove is also up crooked on its wobbly legs. The first little flames echo fitfully within its depths, like a living whisper in a long closed vault of the dead. We crawl into the tent and wait for the heat to come, beating our hands and feet, breathing deep breaths that resemble sobs. "Crying with the cold!" How often I've heard the school children in the village use that expression, heard the big fellows taunt the little ones with it, seen the little ones hide their tears like the Spartans they are and will be. What a simple phrase it is to be so filled with meaning. We sit in the dark, waiting. Our hands are too numb to fish in the bag for a candle or to light it if we could find it.

December 26.

WE are at the end of the portage and snugged away tonight in Edward Michelin's tilt on a bank above the river. In back of the cabin, hanging over us like a shadow, looms the black bulk of the Big Hill, stretching straight up to the glittering stars which must surely perch on the top. The log house is lost, like a pebble at the foot of a high wall.

We came to the top of the hill and found that Harvey and his gang had polished the precipitous path and pressed it hard as iron with their sleds and the seats of their trousers in their descent yesterday.

It took me over an hour to come down the hill, falling from tree to tree, holding back the headstrong sled whose will to speed would have been more seemly on some of the

234

long lakes earlier in the day. It was fun, and all down below me the silent trees seemed to be watching and wondering if they might not have the honor of smashing my sled to splinters for me. The sled had to be kept on its side all the way down. Sometimes the going seemed too slow hanging on from tree to tree and I sat down beside the head of the sled and wrestled with it while we dropped straight down. I don't know how I got so much snow inside my shirt. Once the sled gave a wriggle and spring like a thing alive, rolled bottom up, over to the other side and up on one edge, trembling whether to go one more turn onto its smooth-worn bottom and end its life in a graceful swoop to the base of an immovable tree. I was flying down the path flat on my back and couldn't slow her much. But she decided to behave herself, and settled back on her side where the lash lines, the coarse canvas wrapper, the edge of the stove and the side of the curl served as brakes.

When I sat on top of the load and coasted down the last gradual slope to Edward's scaffold, the first glimpse of the river was like a look into an enchanted valley. Everything is different down here off the Height of Land. The river is folded deep in a crease between hills such as we have not seen in months; there are many more silver pines and birches, the snow is not as deep, the air has a different feel.

When we arrived we had not a single grain of flour and no meat. But our reserves are here, hanging from the rafters in dirty canvas bags; a third of a bag of flour, some beans and pork, sugar, candles, a pound of sweet chocolate and a can half full of jam. God is good to give us tasters and stomachs and I am unashamed of the pleasures they bring. The only ones who must deny this are those who get more pleasure out of gastronomy than I do, who know few other pleasures, who know no other pleasure, who know no pleasure at all. Oh, let us stop this. Whose opinion is worth nothing anyway.

Edward left us a note saying he was leaving for home December 22 and hoped we would find our stuff in good shape as he had tried to keep it dry, but the mice had cut the flour bag a little. As usual, "not much fur with us and no strange news." Graham Blake, who was furring on the portage and over toward Michikamau with his brother, Reggie, cut his foot with an axe. Reggie had to leave him three days in a tent, to go and get more food. When he got back the foot was going septic. He hauled Graham down here and Edward cured him with juniper poultices. Edward got ten mink in one haul, but as usual, "not much fur with us and no strange news."

We dined late, on plenty of boiled pork and beans and fresh bread. After living in the tent a few nights, Edward's house seems the size of an auditorium. It is bright out tonight. Ghostly mist from the black channel in the center of the river is rising to a silver moon. It is my turn to stoke the fire. John wants to make a long day to Goose Cove tomorrow, so that we can spend Sunday with Bill Baikie if he is there.

December 27.

THE tilt roof is deep under blobs of snow that hang from the ridge like overstuffed saddlebags. The stovepipe funnel cannot reach above them. All night its round mouth alternately gapes and glows in the basin of snow its hot breath has melted. Toward morning its mouth grows completely black and silent. The cold tin stops contracting and crackling. There is no sound in the valley.

Then a blue wisp curls up from the funnel. Sparks follow, drifting up among the branches like playful stars that mock the stately old ones, then a steady roaring flame that crimsons the deep snow on the roof.

Inside the tilt, sleepy eyes are rubbed, a candle throws its soft, dull light, the teakettle and the bean pot go on, *scrape, bang*. Socks and mitts come down from their pegs over the stove. Some one crouches and goes out the door, stands in flannel shirt and woollen breeches eyeing the stars and shivering. His breath rises in white clouds in the deep blue darkness. The night is on tiptoe, vibrant; yet silent. From the river, hidden deep under a valley full of vapor, comes an occasional gurgle or the sound of icepans grinding. The person by the door rubs a double handful of snow in his eyes.

It is warm inside, and the smell of the singing teakettle is strong and pleasant. Moccasins and leggings are on and tied up, sleeping bags are rolled up and piled in a corner with the food bags. Breakfast of tea and sugar, bread and butter and beans is soon done. Two eat a few spoonfuls of beans, the woman eats none. "Eat light to travel far," the Indians say. One of the tilt's frying pans is hung up on a nail with the sound of a distant bell, a box is shoved under the bunk, the drywood we have cut to replace what we burned is stacked neatly in the corner. Coats and caps and mitts are fitted snugly on, a shawl over the cap and around the neck, a scarf knotted tight around the waist. Muscles are fuzzy and half asleep, and do not want to go.

Outside, the thin, naked sleds stand upright, shivering

against a tree. *Bang,* they slam on the hard-frozen dock and the wrappers, stiff with cold, cover them. Every bag and kettle has its familiar place, and the wrapper covers the lot as though to keep them warm. A candle on a stump hardly quivers, the morning is so still. The lash lines, stiff with ice, creak and squeak as they are hauled taut by tender, bare hands. Two load one sled, and one the other, and they do it swiftly.

Now all three are crouched inside, hands on the dying stove for a minute. "Let's go." Snowshoes clatter in the stillness and the sleds begin to whisper on the snow. Down the bank at the edge of the ice there is water under the snow. One of the sleds gets wet, and a sheath-knife in a mittened hand scrapes ice and tiny orange shavings from its bottom. Three go on, out over the snowy river in the mist-filled grayness toward the black middle channel, two with sleds and one without.

Out beside the water they find hard ice for a roadway. A moment's pause and the snowshoes ride on the sleds. The ice is covered inches deep with big, substanceless, starry frost crystals through which they leave a dark track like the track of barefoot boys on dewy grass. Hour after hour the three little specks trot at a shuffling jog, or walk with long steps through the icy fog. And the sleds rumble over ice and whisper over snow. For thirty-five miles they are to hold this pace. How many will there be at the finish?

Tumbling North Brook [Portage River], where it foams into the river, has refused to freeze and they must follow the brook up and jump a four-foot ice crevass to gain the other side. The awkward one spills his sled into the crevass. It lands in the brook and its tail and part of its load is sheathed in ice. There is plenty to haul without hauling ice.

At ten-thirty the dim sun rises high overhead against a tree-crested mountain. At two it sets again and the deep valley with its own secrets sinks in shadow. The three fly on silently, and all day long vapor slowly curls from the black, coagulating channel. White icepans floating, race them, now fast, now slow, spinning leisurely; in eddies and bends of the channel the pans carelessly grind the edge of the main ice and shave from themselves clusters of crystal spindles which they leave behind, dully gleaming at the water's edge.

Twice the three pause by a fire to gulp some tea, not for pleasure, but for strength. The path of bare ice vanishes, the river is snow-covered and frozen all across; then it opens up again. They follow now one side, now the other. The deep snow is crusted but weak. They run and walk, run and walk. Sometimes the crust bears them, often they sink to the knees. Still they try to run, hoping each next step will bear them. Their pace falters, accelerates, they stumble, they speed. Darkness falls and the black water and the black ice blend as they cross and re-cross and tap with a stick where the ice sounds hollow. The one ahead tightens his belt and mutters in his beard, then runs for half-mile stretches. The two behind consult in hurried whispers, and the woman says, between clenched teeth, "No! I'm good for it."

Tight to the flying heels they stick and never a gap opens up. And they mutter too, and a savage beast raises its head in them and they hate to the point of murder the sturdy blackbeard, driving ahead through the gloom. They forget that he has taught them as a father, they forget that he the

239

primitive and they the civilized have met and laughed together like brothers, they forget that lightly, out of whimsi-
cal kindness, he has made them a gift—the wilderness. They
would like to sink their fingers in his throat.

All three are panting, noses freezing, faces hung deep
with frost, and under the layers of clothing backs are running with sweat. *He shall not leave us, he shall not leave us*
the hurrying mocassins of the two in the rear say on the
snow.

Oh John, my friend, my brother, why would you leave
us when darkness closes in and the ice is bad. Why would
you like to come back hours later and find us and help us to
limp in, taking the sled and humiliating us. I know. You
are too wild for the like of us. You are used to being alone
and free. Our presence is a chain sometimes, and you hate
us. Well, we cannot help that now. You will show us that
you are superior, here on the river in your own land and we
are weak fools who think long words can take the place of
iron legs. For you, this evening, we are all the people "from
away" who know so much, who have curled their lips and
called you "natives" and "breeds." Will you leave us,
though, you devil! That depends on how far Goose Cove is.

The crust breaks and bogs us as we run, and we think we
have no strength to spring up on top. It breaks, we spring
again, and again, and again. Come, we will run forty steps
and walk ten. We cannot do it. We have done it. Now,
again! Always the bumping, bending sled of Blackbeard
flies ahead. The Blackbeard never turns, never speaks.

A full moon rises, and the river road gleams and the cold
cuts deeper. Now it is in our feet and hands, gnawing. Huge,
blackrock Whale's Head glowers down on us from the moon-

240

lit sky. And still we walk and run. If my sled should turn over in a rough hummock, the gap would grow wider and I could never close it up.

"How far is it now, John?" one asks humbly.

"Two miles," he answers curtly, in a low voice. Slower and slower the single file trio moves. The sleds that were light in the morning are lumps of lead.

Suddenly, the one without a sled sails out in front like some gallant race horse on the home stretch. This is an affair of the will. I hold my breath in wonder.

"I'll see you there," she says quite evenly. Our steps quicken after her, then slow again and she vanishes around a bend.

Twice in the last mile, Blackbeard and I must sit down on our sleds, heads in hands, letting the cold gnaw if it wants. Each time I am half afraid I may not be able to stand up again. At last we see the light high up on the bank and we crawl up the steep path to the open door and say, "Hello, Bill." She has been there twenty minutes.

Bill Baikie's house is the biggest, most comfortable cabin on the river. It has two good-sized windows with real glass in them, two bunks, about twice the usual floor space, and a board floor. Harvey and his gang are here, arrived this afternoon after a short day from Round Island. Bill is playing host. He finds a place for everybody on a bunk or on the floor, he gives us tea while we pull the icicles out of our beards and dry our streaming faces. He is laughing and there is much talk, but we hear it as if it were in another room; and we are not hungry either. We must go out once more and down the bank to unlash the sleds. The tent is hard as iron from its fall in the brook, and we can't put it up. Ten in a tilt again. John volunteers to sleep under a very low bunk where he can hardly wriggle. I cover his feet for him with his blanket and we laugh together. Oh John, my brother, something between us is stronger than hate and as deep as the sleep that buries us.

December 28.

IT is Sunday again and we are staying. The other boys left early and John got up to re-enact the codfish and potatoes ceremony. I merely rolled over.

Today there was time to think a little, and enjoy a lot. Every moment was precious and every yawn and stretch. Bill gave us some caribou meat and we spent the day eating and reading and lolling. He's a jolly fellow about thirty, full of yarns and jokes, and one of the best hunters in the river. He makes two thousand dollars out of fur in a good year, though of course there are some years when he doesn't make five hundred. This may sound like fairly good money, but one must realize that these people pay a duty that ranges from ten to one hundred per cent on almost everything they buy. He always expects to be kidded a little about the girls, for it is a stock joke that four girls have refused to marry him; but I don't believe it is entirely true.

Tomorrow he plans to leave, and meet his brother, Donald, and his partner, Dan Campbell, a day's walk below here at Fox Island. They have been furring in to the north of Winnikapau all the fall. We will stick together the rest of the way down and Bill will automatically be boss, as he has made the most trips up and down the river. His platform is early starts and camp before dark, which is very wise. There is nothing worse than groping through the woods in the deep snow, looking for a dry turn of wood in the dark.

Part of the afternoon I was reading one of Bill's books, a book about the wild west with plenty of gun-play. Like most of the books in trappers' tilts, the flyleaves are covered with figures, calculations how much their fur is going to be worth. John told me that the second year he was up the river he taught himself to divide. He knew how to add all right, and so figured out the total value of his catch by the last prices he had heard. It came to $1500. But how calculate his two-third and the owner's one-third? He added 1500 three times. No, that couldn't be right. Finally he took fifteen matches and counted them out in three piles. Ten for himself and five for the owner. Ten hundred for himself and five hundred for the owner. And when he got home the fur prices were about half what he'd calculated on, so his figures were all wrong anyway.

Strange how long we remember our happy days here, and how quickly we forget the bitter ones. The main thing I remember about yesterday is the moonlight and the frosty faces and the joy of getting here. John doesn't get philosophical very often, but he often remarks how quickly one forgets hellish days and hungry trips. Because of this we can start out on other trips with the tight, joyful feeling of exhilaration in our hearts.

December 29.

WE are at Fox Island, Bill's lowermost tilt on the river, all ready for a whack at Winnikapau Lake tomorrow. We all felt refreshed and strong as horses today, swinging down the river and into the channels among the islands where we sailed in September.

In the afternoon, coming around a long low point to the tilt, we saw the blue above the roof that signifies man. Donald and Dan were here, windburned and tough and full of fun. They came out of the hills today to keep this rendezvous with Bill, agreed on months ago, and they were so glad to see us they let go a shotgun as we came into sight.

A scarlet sunset fired the cold sky beyond the sharp black treetops. Thousands of men have died, one can't help remembering, beyond the black ridges in wilderness such as this, not to gain riches for trading companies or themselves, not to make maps or win distinction or find new homes; just following the sunset or the sunrise. They both lead to the same place.

It is my turn to bake tonight and the cakes are slow. When one side is browned in the frying pan and the cake is stiff enough to handle I stand it up on chunks of wood and let the raw side bake against the side of the stove while another starts to stiffen in the frying pan.

It is the river custom to take turns baking, and when there are five or six to bake for, the cook gets little sleep. It matters not at all to him if the bread is a trifle burned or a mite heavy. The hours of sleep are more precious. Sometimes the baker gets six or seven cakes going all at once; two in frying pans on the stove, two propped against each side with slivers stuck in them to keep them from leaning directly on the red-hot metal, two more on chunks of split wood under the stove and just for luck a "serpent" of dough wound up around the stove pipe. Woe betide the baker if he falls asleep while the stove is roaring.

I've just been outside and the air is so cold it burns one's lungs. The moon is climbing, and way out on the ice there is a light. It winks like a campfire. But of course there is no wood out on the ice and no one to kindle a fire. I know it is an ice crystal shining above the snow in the reflected moonlight, one of those cut diamonds as big as your head that shines in sunlight with blue fire. Often before on nights of moon we have seen these winking ice lights, miles away. Sometimes one has to walk a hundred yards before they wink out. Then it is fun to walk back again to the point where the light comes and goes with a mere movement of the head. It is like some invisible threshold, on the other side of which lies magic.

December 30.

THERE is a section of upper Winnikapau that remains for us a bit of nothingness shrouded in dark. We passed it in the night going up, and again in the night going down. This morning we were up at four and off at five. By our time, which is neither God's nor other men's, it is light at eight and dark at three in the afternoon. In pitch darkness we skirted the upper cliffs that rim the lake, and had polished off nine miles when dawn broke over the mountains.

Most of the river men agree that they hate to walk Winnikapau worse than any other stretch. On the river we pass a point at the end of several hours at most, we round a bend and see a new vista and feel we are getting somewhere. But on this thirty-five-mile plain one walks and walks and gets nowhere. The landmarks are huge rock headlands, bulging out against the sky like insulting chins. At the end of hours and hours of trudging they are neither sharper nor bluer than before. They are not interested in little black bugs with flapping feet and tails. They are cool and tantalizing and inaccessible. The mountains of the moon are not more aloof than these. Shadows of clouds float over them, partridge hawks from rocky eeries circle miles up in the sky. But nothing changes. They have stood alone so many tens of thousands of years, immovable under the lash of ninety-mile hail storms—how can mere man approach them.

The way to enjoy Winnikapau, like a thousand other things, is not to look ahead too anxiously, to look about to right and left and behind and at one's feet, to keep a steady pace and think of other things. What are they doing at home now? running for the train maybe. How graceful the shape of a snowshoe is, like the curve of a silver gray gull's wing, not really, but to me. How the snow sparkles, why should this sparkle be any less valuable than the sparkle in a $10,000 diamond. Will we ever have a cabin of our own on the shore of a lake such as this, with flowers beside it in summer. What a funny little gait Bill has, he swings his hips and shoulders to save his legs, look, he's hauling now with the line across his head; I must try that, too, the change rests one, the strain is more along one's body, it is more like being a hauling dog, if possible without fur, a hauling dog, a hauling dog, keep 'er going b'y, how the damn sled drags, oh hell, forget it. Surely we'll boil up before another hour. Guess I'll sing for awhile.

At the end of several hours a casual look ahead is allowed. Sure enough we are a step nearer the big chins. The trees, where the sky shows through, look like stubble that has lacked the razor for three bristly days.

Bill is known as a good traveller. He keeps a steady pace that eats up the miles, figures his distances sensibly and knows the river well. Only we are not used to going so far in the morning before the first boil up. Kay and I were going ashore to boil up by ourselves when the boys turned in toward the rocks this morning. Travelling on a diet of bread and tea, with an occasional meal of beans or rice, keeps us hungry most of the time. What we crave is meat and we can't get it. A meal of bread and tea doesn't stick to one's ribs long. All of us are hungry for an hour or two before we finally stop each time to make a fire and eat, but we have gotten used to it and never stop until we begin to get weak.

Kay and I used to get very worried along about ten in the morning. We would feel absolutely finished and wonder to ourselves how we could ever go on until dark or after. But now we have learned to count on the boil-ups. After our tea and toasted bread and a little rest by the fire we are not only as good for it as before, but better. That is the best time for all of us. For three or four hours after the first halt we feel as though we could go on forever.

John has a favorite expression of greeting or farewell which he picked up one winter when he met Peter Lafont on Winnikapau. The old Frenchman hadn't seen anybody for so long to check up on his dates that he didn't know whether it was Christmas time or New Years. He simply grinned and repeated over and over again, "Happy to you."

There are three men furring around Winnikapau these years, but like all the "valley trappers" [those who fur below the Grand Falls] they came up two or three weeks after we did in the fall and went home a week or two ago. Jo Blake, whose house is a couple of days below here, is one of the jolliest of the valley bunch. One winter when the Height of Landers spent a night at his place on the way down, he claims they left his big tin mixing dish all stuck up with dough. The next December when they pulled in to his cabin they found a note in the dish saying, "I washed my feet in this just before I left."

We are camped by the willows, right on the ice in a not very sheltered cove, a bad place, it seems to me, if a blow came on. The snow was not deep enough to hold the pickets securely, so we put down a heavy log on either side of the tents, drove the pickets in the snow outside the logs and there they held firm. In Bill's tent after supper we had a powwow, discussing an idea that would change life in Hamilton Inlet fundamentally.

In February, in the month of deep snow and hard hauling, to the knees with snowshoes on, most of the trappers will make the long trip up the river again. They have heavy loads, for they must take enough food to last out the hunt. Sometimes the trip takes a month. For weeks on end the northwest winds sweep the river, or it snows one batch after the other. It is the hardest journey of the year—and for what? A short hunt during the month of March when the fur is starting to fade, and the long trip home again. In the bright sun of March foxes are starting to fade, and by the beginning of April the mink and marten skins are almost stage. They will bring less than half what they would have if caught in January. And spring is the breeding time. Many a trapper, skinning a she-marten that carried three young ones, has wondered whether he wasn't penny wise and pound foolish. Instead of one faded skin this spring there would have been the chance of four dark, glossy ones next winter. Often times this "spring hunt" doesn't pay. In brief, we decided it would be better all around for the trappers to bring more grub and bigger trout nets in the fall, stay up the river until late February and then go home and stay home.

We waxed more and more enthusiastic. John decided they would have to do something to keep from getting fed up with the work and the loneliness. Each one would bring a Christmas box with rum, raisins, cigarettes, a can of tomatoes and some candy and a story book for a big celebration. They would agree to get together from a hundred miles around and have a big time for a week.

Bill, leaning on his elbow by the stove, commenced to chuckle. "Yes," he laughed, "some poor devil, three days walkin' in deep snow, get to the tilt done out, nothin' but a note, 'Got lonesome, come on, b'y.' "

John started to rock with glee, "Oh my, oh m-y-y, hello up the bank, no smoke, stove cold, lonesome fer the girls, bound fer home, oh ho ho." They laughed till the tears ran out of their eyes and that was the end of the plan to make life more efficient and less fun.

We came twenty-eight miles today.

December 31.

WHEN the boys and Kay pulled out this morning I got left. On my sled I carry the tent and stove so that if we should get left very far behind at dark or lost in snow we would be self-sufficient. But unfortunately these are the last things that can be packed when we break camp, and I cannot get lashed up ahead of time. In the morning it is a rush and I am slow. We woke up at five and were gone at six. My hands were numb for tying the lash line and I was five minutes behind taking the trail out onto the lake. It was an unusually black morning, though a star showed here and there. By lighting matches and feeling the snow with my bare hand I carefully followed the track of one of Harvey's gang, who must have gone across the lake to hunt partridges when they passed yesterday. Anyway, I came to the shore and the woods and some feathers. It didn't matter much, so I turned and headed down the lake. After awhile I heard some one say hello and there was Kay standing quiet, waiting for me in the middle of the breathless, endless lake. *Winnikapau* is Indian for "lake of the foul smelling willows," but to us it means the lake of strange partings and meetings in darkness, night storm, rainy dawn, endless snow, morning stars rimmed with mountains half unseen, stirred up with frosty silence in two minds that think of "Night Among the Pines" and Robert Louis Stevenson. ". . . there is a fellowship more quiet even than solitude, and which, rightly understood, is solitude made perfect. And to live out of doors with the woman a man loves is of all lives the most complete and free."

Tonight the two candle-lit tents stand side by side on the edge of a pond, the Beaver Pond, deep among hills far back from the river. At dusk, coming to the ice the pond was a pool of cream in a bowl of blue and white hills. Far up, the fine-etched birches drew hair lines on the snow, all vertical and pointing to the sky.

We are nearly over the winter route across "Paagy's Banks" and it is the end of another long day. "One stitch and another and the longest tear is mended, one step and another and the longest journey ended."

Lucky for us we split up our remaining raisins and chocolate into thirds and Kay and I kept ours to give us strength.

We carry a supply in our pockets and they do not freeze. Below the lake the river was wide-open rapids, right to the banks. We hauled six miles over bare-blown rocks and along sidling banks where the sled was upside down as much as right side up. Kay took a line on the stern to keep it from rolling over and over into the fast, black water.

At the end of that we sat on the sled for a cup of water and a bite of chocolate while we looked at a hill straight up from the river. The boys were gone up it and out of sight. Below this point the open water continues and the "clifty" river bank is impossible going for sleds. The winter trail cuts up over the hills for ten miles before coming back to the river again. The first part of the climb was up a solid ice cascade where we cut notches and hung onto trees and crawled. Every willow branch beside the brook hung limp and broken.

"When a man gives out you feed him," a Pyrenean guide once told me. Our chocolate stood us in good stead, and together we dragged up the brook. The last half of the ascent was rock and sand blown absolutely bare. John came back and helped me. The hauling line where it is tied to the sled, bit half an inch into the wood.

Tonight our arms are bruised from the lines and our sleds are scarred. John cracked the curl of his toboggan in a sharp little gully and Bill is busy with awl and *babische* sewing a thin birch patch over it for him. He says trappers should patch their knees that way, perhaps wooden patches wouldn't wear out.

An old trapper once said of outsiders who were tripping up Grand River, "Goin' to the Grand Falls fer pleasure, hey? They'd go to Hell fer a pastime."

251

FROM the tops of the high hills we saw the river, miles away and below us, half hidden in winter mist, mightier than a god; where Shoal River flows in, a sweeping cut through the hills that speaks of power. All the view is gigantic, epic, like the setting for events too great to be comprehended by men. We are lost in a region of grim distance and snow and cold, where the trees have been twisted and crippled.

Like children we quickly forget it, slipping down the hills to the river. Where the slope was fairly clear of trees Donald showed me something new in handling a sled. We let them go down backwards. The stern dug in and they brought up at the bottom in a drift. We followed, tobogganing on our trousers, each making a soft new track to slow the speed. "Come on, b'y," said Donald, running down another hill with fourteen-foot strides. But I think a person has to be raised to it from childhood to run on the racquets full speed down hills. On a steep upgrade the snow was shoulder deep and fluffy. Donald was bent way forward, arms in back, wound in the line. When he gave a heave the snow slipped out from under him and he plunged on his face. We laughed at him and did the same.

Back at the river there was no ice and we cut into the woods again, through snarls of willows and trees so thick we had to crawl on our bellies under their lowermost branches. The willows grabbed at the sled with crooked fingers, they ripped the wrapper and tore the lash line loose, they pulled off the axe and twisted the gun crosswise. They made me raving mad and I cut and slashed at them with the axe. They whipped our faces and tripped our feet and pushed us backwards and sideways and jostled us like people in a hostile crowd. The story of Job McKenzie in the rough ice, shaking his fist at the sky and telling God to come down and fight, did not seem at all ridiculous. The sled got snagged and I yanked till something broke. My old green sweater-shirt got plucked out of the load and I would not go back for it. Kay came along and picked it up and I was ashamed and pretended I did not know it had come off.

By and by we tumbled out onto a frozen brook and there was Bill, talking to a stranger, a black-haired boy in ragged leggings who leaned on a long paddle. It was John Pottle, seventeen-year-old hunter, who at Bill's hail had dodged the ice pans and paddled across from his house on the other side to give us a lift in his canoe. After the greeting he turned to Bill. "The River, she's bad just yere," he said. "The ice is wore right to the gums. Pack your sleds in and I'll take 'em down to the ice. Yes, there's ice around the Marble Cliff."

He is staying on another week. This is his first year alone. He is quieter, more reserved and deeper than the mischievous boy who used to tease the kids in the village. The woods are busy making him a man, and something in him is responding.

We unloaded the sleds and packed them into the canoe. She was very deep when John Pottle and Bill swung off into the tide. The rest of us crawled over the rocks and around a bend, glad to be relieved of our sleds even for a little. At one point we had to climb a steep ice cliff formed by the seepage of water from above, "quarr water" they call it. There were axe-cut notches in the ice, up which we crawled, cautiously, as the bottom of the slide went sheer into the water. The only way to get a sled up the chute is to climb up with a long line. Two men at the top with their feet braced against trees can haul her up hand over hand.

By the breaking of a line John Groves lost his sled here ten winters ago. On it was lashed two thousand dollars' worth of fur. It must have given him a sickening feeling to see it splash and watch the current roll it faster and faster down the river. Many men would have thought all in a second of the long hard four months wasted, and the thousand miles or more of snowshoeing, and how rotten hard a man's luck can be sometimes, and then in a flash of what a good story it would make for the boys lying round at the Company's, especially if made light of by the teller, as though the blows of fate could not discourage him. But John Groves isn't like that. He grabbed an axe from another sled and sped down along shore, hurdling rocks and jumping from slippery ice to slippery ice like a ten-year-old, not a man of forty. At the next point an eddy caught the sled and brought it close. John Groves was there, to the waist in the tide, and he hooked it with the axe head. It doesn't seem right to say that fate brought it into the inshore eddy. For he has always made his own fate. Storms, weariness, nothing can swerve him from his purpose, and of all the men in the Inlet he still makes the best living. Some say that with trapping and trading he has made his fortune.

Some day I must try to put down his story: how he and his brother at thirteen and fifteen were left to support their widowed mother alone at the house in Goose Bay. How they trapped and fished through the ice and hunted meat. How the neighbors (ten and twenty miles away and struggling for existence themselves) tried to help with dog harness and

254

tools and nets. How he and Charlie used to camp alone every spring at Sandy Run, sealing for nearly a month, and their only boat a rickety punt; camped alone on Sealing Point with the wide cold bay and the snowy mountains watching them and caring nothing whether they lived or died. And the sunny days with the white ice dancing down the bay on the blue water, and the lowering days of wind and fog and sleet, and the icy nets. How could they handle 300-pound harps, even get them into the boat? But they did. And every now and then they'd take a load of fat and skins to North West River, a trip that might have drowned them twenty times. How he learned to knit nets and build houses and boats and canoes, how he learned to cut and pile his 150 turns of wood a day, and drive the dogs and make stoves and funnels and work with iron. He can make as fine a knife as you would want out of an old saw. How he studied the ways of the geese and the fish and the animals, how he learned to snowshoe forty miles a day and do without sugar for months and flour for weeks. It was he that searched out the best fur paths on Grand River. He could skin a marten in two minutes by the clock. There is his marriage and his resolve never to be in debt like the others; the winter up the river with his wife and year-old boy at Goose Cove; the trip down, running rapids, only a few weeks before a baby girl came. How he tried fox farming and kept tame bears that ran all around the house. The first trading venture and the Hudson Bay Company's attempts to squash him out. Then he bought a schooner and there were many summers sailing in and out the bays trading goods for salted salmon and furs. Trips to St. Johns followed, and always the effort to become better educated, to read and figure with ease, to learn to deal with the merchants of the city. How he sent his children outside to be educated, and how, convinced of the superiority of the people from away, he went to Canada and tried to live in a small city. He lived in a flat instead of a wide house beside the lapping water, across the bay from the blue mountains. He was lost, he was sunk, there was no work he could do and like, no air he could breathe. He, a Titan in his own land, trying to be a hodcarrier, riding out in an automobile on Saturday afternoons to a mud pond to shoot a miserable duck or two. He could not stomach that, and came back to his own land of the sparkling ice in springtime and the hard free life that he has made and been made by. He goes up the river every fall and there is no one like him in the rapids. He goes down the bay twice a summer in his boat for freight and he needs no help. One cannot convince him of the inferiority of the people from away. He is a man if I ever saw one.

There was ice around the Marble Cliff as John Pottle said, but very little, a narrow shelf not as wide as a sled, beside swift tide. Two of us had to take each toboggan by lest head or tail slip in.

Below, there was more ice to go on, though in places it was weak or narrow and sloping toward the water. Often, hauling our sleds diagonally along sidling ice, they dipped their bending tails. John's slipped off and sank to the nose, which iced it up badly. Kay and Donald were going along, one behind the other when a big section of the shelf they were on cracked off and started floating down the river. They ran and jumped ashore across the widening crack and Donald yanked his sled across just before it was too late. We kept our eyes on the pan and watched it break up down below.

Squirrel River is an innocent looking stream about fifty yards wide where it enters the north side of Grand River. I was ahead when we crossed its mouth this afternoon.

"Run, run," yelled Dan Campbell, who was directly behind me. I looked around to see what was the matter. "You got to, we always runs across here." I ran, with the sled clattering behind me on the rough ice, which stuck up through the snow, and I noted on either bank of the stream and clear across Grand River way up among the trees, huge blocks of blue ice eight feet thick, tossed there by some terrifying force.

Three times a winter, without warning, this little river bursts with the speed of a whirlwind and the strength of a giant. In some ways it resembles a glacier. It is a curious phenomenon and I cannot explain it entirely. The river is not more than three feet deep at its mouth when it is open. It freezes all its short length, nearly to the bottom. Then the irresistible water from up above starts to flow down over the ice, freezing as it comes, until the ice is as much as nine feet thick. The ice piles up and piles up at the head until the water is compressed. Perhaps it is compressed under the earth, I do not know. But three times a winter there is an explosion. A solid wall of ice rushes down the stream, sweeping it clear right to its bed, and piles up on the far side of Grand River. There is a sharp bend a short way up the stream and it is impossible to see the broken ice blocks coming until a few seconds before their arrival.

Bill once saw the river go out before his eyes. He had to

257

camp and wait a day for it to freeze hard enough to cross. Fred and Arch waded it without boots one winter several hours after it had broken up. They plunged in, to the thighs, carrying Fred's sled between them. Then they went back and carried Arch's sled across. There stood Fred's little hunting dog on the other side shivering. They called him, but he wouldn't swim, so Fred made a third trip while Arch built a fire. He agrees with John's contention that very cold water, being almost ready to freeze, is kind of thick like soup and hardly penetrates a pair of woollen trousers at all.

There are lots of stories about Squirrel River. The best one has to do with a dream, a typical trapper's dream in which the characters are animals, and the setting Nature. They are always dreaming dreams of storms and hunts and birds and beasts, all of which they interpret. When we were up above, John was forever dreaming such things and had a whole code of interpretive symbols. To dream of his friend Judson Blake meant bad luck for three days. A dream about a fox meant, "mice are shaving your fur in some trap tonight." He would be off long before daylight that morning. Indians meant plenty mink, and if they were especially pigeon-toed it signified that there were caribou somewhere in the vicinity. He took his big rifle with him that day. Caribou stood for marten, and if he dreamed of rain, watch out.

Dan Michelin, whose ground includes Squirrel River, used to have five traps above the stream, which made it necessary to cross and return every round. One December night he dreamed about a white bear. He had dreamed of polar bears before. Once he fell through the ice next day, and another time following the dream he caught his left thumb in a No. 2 trap. This bear was unusually large. He was a dirty, yellowish white, with an open red mouth, shining yellow fangs and wet hair over his eyes. In the dream Dan met him in the woods. The bear approached on all fours, rolling his head from side to side. Dan's gun was unaccountably lost in the snow and there was no time to find it, so rapidly the bear shambled on. He ran in and out through the trees in a big circle and back to the starting point to sweep through the snow in passing in a vain hope of connecting with his weapon. He cannot remember whether he had on snowshoes or not. It was a long chase over hills and through willow thickets. He was absolutely terrified when he awoke with the bear's breath warm on his neck and his back tingling with the expected rip of claws.

A chilling certainty of impending catastrophe filled him, strengthened, no doubt, by the fact that he had seen no other man for a month. Though it was yet dark he got up and loaded his .44 and determined to keep it loaded until the thing happened.

All that day he travelled warily, expecting a tree to fall on him or the ice to break, or the axe to slip. Nothing happened to break the monotony of a gray day. It was worse than an accident, for there was no way to avoid the approaching stroke of fate, no way to fight whatever was going to happen.

In the night he barred the tilt door and brought his gun inside. The dream of the white bear came again. This time the animal was crouched behind a stump, waiting. Dan awoke in a sweat and went up along Grand River in the morning feeling hunted. About noon he came to Squirrel River, crossed it on the dead run and went to his five traps above. Coming back, he had all but crossed the stream when he put his game-bag down on the ice and went up to look at two traps on the bend. Walking back to the bag he commenced to think it was all nonsense, this presentiment of danger. Nothing was happening, why, he was like a kid alone for the first time in the woods. Hell, he wasn't scared of a bear, *white bear!* The familiar fear clutched him. He turned, and around the bend majestically swept the wall of churning ice. He grabbed up his bag, took eight tremendous leaps to the shore and scrambled up the bank. Swirling water was touching the tails of his snowshoes when he turned to look. The middle of the river was a jumble of rushing water and grinding ice blocks tossed like leaves.

It was last spring that he told me this, one long wet afternoon sailing in from the seal nets. "You b'y, with your learnin'," he said, "you don't put much store by a dream I s'pose. You thinks dreams is dreams and alone in the woods they gits wirkin' in a feller's head."

He tapped my arm with his pipe stem and the crinkles around his eyes deepened. "I tell you, lad, but fer the white bear I'd be dead."

Through the age-long afternoons which grow colder and darker each minute, we walk and haul toward a camp, forever weary and with a gnawing in the stomach. We wonder if we will have the strength to get there. We always do, and it is most important not to voice this wonder. When we reach the camping spot at last, we must put the sled lines across our heads and haul up the bank, slowly, gasping. If we are too weary, we unload the sleds on the ice and carry bundles of gear up to the trees bit by bit. We thought we were weary to the point of exhaustion and hungry to the point of weakness, but from somewhere we unpeel another layer of energy and work for an hour making camp. The strength comes and keeps on coming. We must tramp a place for the tent site, break many armfuls of brush for a floor, cut poles and pickets, put up the tent, set up the stove, unload the sleds, chop a hole through the ice for water, if possible. Each one has his job and goes about it doggedly. When the tent is up and the blue smoke starts pouring from the funnel, it is a good sight. The worst job is carrying in the firewood log. To fall in the deep snow with a 110-pound log across one's shoulders and one's snowshoes inextricably snarled in a snowed-over scrub spruce is an experience in exasperation. John brings home the wood for our tent if darkness has come and drywood is hard to find. Through the blackness he gropes, feeling the rough trunks with his bare hands, chipping pieces out of the wood and tasting them to see whether their brittleness is of frost or of dryness. He can find wood where I would freeze. It is most important to get a sound, slender, straight dead spruce, or better still a juniper, for the comfort of the night depends on the quality of the firewood. Balsam is no good, for it burns up too quickly and so does spruce that has started to rot. Birch is almost invariably green or rotten. Often I have brought in a gnarled, crooked-grained spruce which we could not split without great danger to the axe helves. We cast it aside and got another stick. If we are camped in a spot where the drywood is not hard to find, I take my turn, and often and often John will tell me where to go, "over that little lump there," or "down around that there bend," or "up amongst them rocks by the quarr water." He has camped in the vicinity before, perhaps seven or eight years ago. He does not think of this as an infinite, brooding wilderness, but as a long chain of familiar, well-remembered marks. He recognizes a draw between the endless hills, or a curious shaped rock by the river much as a city man recognizes a trolley crossing or a street corner.

After our hour making camp we crawl inside the warm tent. All day we have thought of this. And now it is anticlimax. We are no longer hungry, we do not want rest from our weariness. We are only clods who endure, who are in the habit of enduring forever without end. We have to rest before we can feel our weariness, we have to eat before we can feel our hunger.

Right away we eat bread and tea. Bread and tea are what we live on. We neither like them nor dislike them. While we are eating we put on pork and split peas for a real meal when we shall be a little rested. Every night John offers to bake the morrow's bread, but I generally manage to take my turn. Many and many a night Kay falls asleep after a little morsel of bread and a cup of tea. She does not wish to be awakened when the peas or beans are cooked. Next day all day she travels her twenty-five or thirty miles again on nothing but bread and tea. Often John and I fall asleep, too. Hunger and cold wake us up about midnight. We eat enormous plates of food, have a smoke, stoke up the fire and fall asleep for a few hours more. Some of the peas we save for Kay to have first thing next evening, or at one of the boil-ups during the day. They will freeze in the pot and not spill even if the sled capsizes.

No one can eat much for breakfast, only a little bread and tea. Two mornings now, after his light breakfast, John has slipped out of the tent and vomited it up. Then he loads his sled and goes off running. If ever he is sick or tired, he travels faster that day. If ever he is lost for a few minutes in the woods he strides through the trees as though he would knock them down.

He and I take turns keeping on a fire at night. As is the custom in this region, we depend for warmth, not on sleeping bags but on a fire in the camp stove. He has only a Hudson's Bay blanket. Kay and I each have a similar blanket sewed up like a bag and slipped inside bags of seven-ounce duck. They weigh about ten pounds apiece and roll up small.

A quilted goose-down bag, or a bag of summer, hairy caribou skin is, of course, much warmer. They say one can sleep in the snow when it's fifty below, in a caribou bag, and they are very light. But, unfortunately, they are too bulky for a hand toboggan. The sled must be narrow to fit in a snowshoe track, the big roll of such a bag sticks out on either side, or at best takes up half the sled. We have many other things besides sleeping gear to pack on the sleds, and a too-much-loaded, top-heavy sled is worse than a few chills down the spine.

Night about, John and I take turns with the fire. The man off duty gets in his bag or rolls in his blanket with all his clothes and a sweater on. The other sleeps on top of his bag. Every two or three hours, depending on the temperature of the night, the cold wakes him up. There are still plenty of embers in the stove. He rises on one elbow, opens the tin door, shoves in two or three chunks and drops asleep again. After a week or two a person gets so used to this procedure that he cannot say in the morning how many times he has fixed the fire.

Hunters when they are alone never sleep in their bags

unless they are in a well-chinked tilt and it is a mild night. On a cold night, no matter how tightly they roll themselves in their bags the cold will wake them eventually. The only difference is that the fire is black out. In a tent it is even more important to catch the fire before it goes out. If there are no embers one must light the candle, fumble with matches, shavings and splits, start a new fire and get thoroughly awakened and thoroughly chilled in a below-zero temperature. The coverless course, idiotic as it sounds, is the most comfortable and the most practical. I have often read that it is very dangerous for a person who is extremely tired to fall asleep, as he will sleep on and be frozen to death. If this were wholly so we would have been dead twenty times. I think a person must be numb and nearly frozen to begin with, or sick and very weak for the cold not to wake him.

It is snowing hard tonight and the trees are filled with the hissing whisper of driven snow. Whenever we wake up we must beat the canvas from the inside to knock the snow off. If the tent gets wet and freezes, we will not be able to fold it up and get it on the sled in the morning.

January 2.

Toward midnight the cold choked off the snow, but it began to blow. Forty below and a wind this morning whirling drift down the river as high as the trees.

Our camp in the mouth of a brook under the lee of a high bank looked too good to leave. In Bill's tent the funnel squeaks as it is taken down out of the tin collarpiece. We hate that sound, for it is the signal every morning that camp is being broken and our stove must come down too. Some one holds the stove by two chunks of wood, carries it out and dumps the embers. We quickly rake them together and start a blaze on the snow. It seems like our last hold on life.

The bow-knotted strings are loosed from the pickets and our poor, defenseless house collapses in a formless bundle. There is little rest on days like this. We take down the tent and stove, knowing we will not be warm until evening when they are up again. The tracked-up snow and the sheltered brook look like home. Out there in the half light are the river and the wind.

We had to warm our hands twice at the fire before we could get our sleds lashed up. Out on the river the gale nearly knocked us down, but we were grateful that it was a tail wind. I turned for a last look at the camp that was. The fire under the bank was winking in the dirty dawn, small and yellow and lonesome. Then the stinging drift erased it.

We had our dickies belted tight and the fur hoods up. Our windproof overalls encased our legs. Bill soon tied a sweater round his waist and let it hang down behind, remarking laconically that his "starn was froze." We ran for a long time before the pain came and the bursting sensation of internal pressure, and then the flooding, soothing warmth.

There is more rest in running than anything else. When we boil the kettle there is no let-down. We come away colder than before, with our eyebrows singed and our clothes scorched and our backs numb. John's teeth are chattering so, his pipe wobbles in his mouth. He takes it out and, flinging his head back and his face up to the flying storm, sings in a laughing, nasal, top-of-the-lungs shout:

> "Oh! A trapper's life would just suit me,
> It is so healthy and so free,
> And oh we gets a lot of fur
> And quickly makes our fortune thur."

Signs of Harvey and his crew have been growing more frequent, but the wind and drift blurred their trail. Suddenly, a little after noon we came around a wooded point and caught them in a little cove, crouched around a streaming, comfortless fire, gulping tea. Their sleds lay at odd angles on the ice, dishevelled and snowy, seeming to droop like tired horses that wait.

"Hello, b'y."

"Hello, b'y, yourself. **Bound fer home?**"

"Thinkin' about it."

We did not stop, and they were soon after us. Young Alvin is one of the speed merchants of their party, for his sled is very small and very light. Harvey has a sled nearly twice as big, and heavily loaded, but no one can keep up with him. From then on our pace was even faster, on account of the well-concealed, good-natured but iron-hard rivalry between John and Harvey to lead the line of sleds. From then on we came at more of a run than a walk. The snow was rimey and the sleds ran very hard. No one stopped to scrape off the rime. We covered our faces with our mitts and beat our hands and loosened our snowshoe thongs to ease our cold toes, but we kept on hauling and never lost a step for hours and hours. I don't know how Kay stands the pace, I don't know how any of us stand it.

Night comes, and at last the tent is up, the fire going, enough wood cut for the night, bare sleds stuck up, snowshoes hung on a limb, guns and axes upright in the snow, a waterhole cut and a brimming kettle on the stove. A moment more of cold is immaterial. Numb hands and dead feet count for nothing now there is warmth for them. One last look at the bleak river, growing terrible in the darkness of the deep hills, a valley taut with cold, under icy stars. Now, Old Devil, be as cold and blowy as you like.

The cold sinks into us and becomes part of our minds and bodies, waking and sleeping. For we are more often cold than warm. It keeps us tight and alert. We wake at the touch of a finger and immediately know where we are. In the nights, dead with fatigue, we wake up chattering with cold, to scratch a match, light the candle and kindle the fire, biting our lips and trembling in haste. I think we are as devoted fire worshippers as any since the world began. We glory before the yellow, red tongues that lick up through the curled shavings (which we draw every night before going to bed), and the crackle of the kindling, and the tin stove roaring, chortling and trembling on its legs with joy to be alive again. At the end of the day we are not thinking about food or rest. We want heat more than anything. We keep shoving in the wood until the stove is glowing red and the tent is stifling. We lie on our stomachs with our noses pressed in the brush for air, and the hotter it is the better we like it. When stoking the stove, if embers roll out the door onto the brush we pick them up in our hands and toss them back in again. They do not burn us. Fire is our friend, fire is life.

267

I asked John tonight, "Why do you travel so fast, why do you kill yourselves this way?"

He looked at me with scorn that I should admit not liking it, and answered, " 'Tis our fashion I suppose," and turned away.

I'll not pretend to like this pace. I'd like to climb the hills and look around, follow up brooks, dig under the snow for berries and take a day off now and again to think and dream. Even now we enjoy it some, Kay, too, though it is wicked that she should have to travel so. There is such a paradise of beauty all around to be enjoyed, it seems a shame we cannot have plenty of time and be rid of the tight, desperate atmosphere this grinding speed creates. So much for what we'd like. We said we'd travel their way, and beggars can't be choosers.

Nor anybody else, travelling here in winter. There really are good reasons for haste if one wishes to see them. In the first place, we have fairly good going, nearly half the time we can go without snowshoes. Sometimes we can run and walk on hard ice. Deep new snow is certain to come soon, bad walking, rime, killing turns ahead. The farther we get before the next snowstorm the better.

Then there is always the question of grub. If you take a heavy load you must go slow, as it is twice the work. You have a lot of food, but you need it. In order to haul it you eat it up and the net gain is nothing. Besides, travelling slow there is all the extra work of all the extra camps that are made and broken, all the hours wasted, and all the snow-storms encountered. To a certain degree, the more comforts, the harder the trip, for comforts ride heavy on the toboggan. On the other hand, with a light load you've got to go fast, and with luck you can. The total of the trip is less work and more days home. The winter trail is not very comfortable, however you go about it. Perhaps they think it is best to grin and bear it and get it over with.

Habits of solitude have a connection with thirty-five and forty-mile days, I think. The presence of another person is in itself an incentive to work to avoid being criticized, and at the same time an incentive to loaf and enjoy sociability. Remove this influence and a man cannot work moderately. He either works like a Trojan, or he works not at all. The days slip by so stealthily, and if he has some kind of work or accomplishment on hand, it gradually absorbs his waking mind and even his dreams. There are no calls to meals except from amidships, no arbitrarily timed amusements, no distractions, no one to talk to or consider in the slightest, no one to get tired or sick or cold or slow him up. Finally he finds himself working to the limits of physical endurance, never stopping until the demands of the body are positive shouts. Then again, if he does not feel like working, the only amusement, the only change or rest from himself is to indulge every whim and do nothing, absolutely nothing.

A trapper has to do a certain amount of work to keep himself alive, and so he gets in the way of working. And on his trap lines there is always more work to be done than he can possibly accomplish. The automatic claims of solitude drive him farther, faster, and his family needs the money the skins will bring, that wife and her children far away. They say that Labrador is no place for a lazy man who likes to sit down and smoke his pipe. In winter he has to jog to keep warm and in summer the flies have him on the dead run.

There is pride in it, too. The majority of yarns in this country where reading is an accomplishment and conversation an art, are tales of physical prowess. It is part of the code to drive 'er and make light of hardship. Working to the limit of physical endurance becomes a habit. It produces strength and strength begets strength until men accomplish superhuman feats.

January 3.

LAST night while were were asleep the God of the Wind, who must certainly be brother to the Man of the Woods, unsheathed his enormous crooked-knife and sculptured all the face of the river. With his hair flying behind him, rippling and snapping, he swooped down from behind a cloud and moulded and carved and scooped a bigger masterpiece than we can walk over in a whole day. Everywhere the snow is fluted in long points that slip away to the southeast. It is like a careless work by some master who cannot do wrong. All the little hill crests between the purple valleys are sharp and hard, all the razorback ranges of miniature snow-hills die away in long points, like a sandbar dying away in water. At first glance one might say they were all alike, but really they are individual creations as different as a million people's faces, and each one is a bit of strength adding its power to the might of the whole design. Under one's eyes they move and flow and rush, just as the Winged Victory in the Louvre moves. And when you look close and see it is not moving you know for sure the illusion is this later impression of stability, and the truth is the windblown rush of speed.

Over this surface of delight we walk without snowshoes

and our light, soft moccasins are like wings. The hollow crust is hard and musical, squeaking and ringing under our flying feet, now high, now low; we play tunes with our feet on the hollows and ribs and think of a harpist plucking the long and short strings.

How can we be anything but happy, breathing the icy air, skimming down the river feeling strong as steel, watching the sunrise come. The sky is a bright, penetrating blue, growing in intensity. The tops of the valley catch alight with gold and mauve. Slowly the color and light steal down the slopes, painting the miles of treetops and cliffs and snowbanks till only the surface of the river lies sombre. Suddenly, the sun like a searchlight stands on a mountain and the river is a carpet of gleaming gold dust, rippled with purple hollows. We cast long violet shadows and we feel like dancing and yelling. Soon the gold turns to silver and our noses and chins will stay warm without rubbing. The wind-lapped snow is a silver salmon's back curved into the sunshine. We never get tired of the winding river and its changing, singing wrought surface.

It is by these wind-moulded points of snow that the men find their way when caught on a wide lake or out on the bay in a blizzard. They never carry a compass. Just before the snow closes down blinding thick, they notice to which quarter the drifts are streaming. This one little bit of knowledge is all they have to comfort them in a blinding white prison where the walls have gone mad and the cold is so intense it will kill them if they go astray. Quietly they note how the banners of the wind are flying. The streamers of the drifts have some slight permanence, say five minutes. If they notice new drifts forming over the old and pointing in a slightly different direction, they know the wind is changing and change their course accordingly. It is a safer guide than keeping the wind on one side of one's face. It is their compass, and it can't be bought and it can't be lost out of one's pocket. Like all good things, like knowing how to swim or how to make a fire, it is there, salted down forever. When they strike the shore they will know immediately where they are, if they have ever travelled the region before; if not, they can generally follow it to a wooded spot where there is shelter and firewood and safety.

Miles above Mininipi Rapid the river showed patches of open water, a narrow black lane winding down the whiteness. At first the open spots were short, only a hundred yards or so long. Then the water slid under the ice again and the river was frozen all across. It seems strange to think that under our feet there is water, running faster than we travel. Later, the open channel ran for miles, bordered on each side by a pathway of hard ice. On this we ran and walked, ran and walked, sliding our feet along, never lifting them from the ice. Where the glassy surface was inclined now this way now that, we sometimes slipped and fell. The ice seemed hard and jarring after the soft snow. This is the kind of gait that makes one lame in the thighs. The sleds slewed and rumbled behind us, light as feathers and we made good time, about four miles an hour.

By the open torrent at Mininipi, where the river bends double and we had to face the cold wind, John showed me the spot where he and Juddy swamped early one spring, running the rapid in a cranky, homemade canoe. Slob and ice had jammed and frozen onto the bottom, making a shoal near the upper end where the water broke in huge combers. They were into it before they saw how bad it was. She filled and rolled over.

Juddy drifted ashore where the ice was low, and was able to climb out before he got too paralyzed to help himself. John caught onto a thick, ice-edge too high to climb, and hung there by his fingernails while the tide pushed his legs in under. Juddy could not see him, nothing showed above the ice but his slipping hand. John really thought he was done that time, but he bawled and Juddy finally came and pulled him out by the hair. They picked up the canoe down below. Fortunately they had a sled jammed in under the thwarts and that held the fur bags in.

That was almost as narrow a squeak, he asserts, as the time he drank a whole bottle of liniment. He was unconscious two hours that time. Rob has told me it is true.

It was very bad going beside the rapid, hauling the sleds along the steeply inclined "ballicaters" where snow concealed deep cracks that would break a leg as easily as not. The sleds rolled bottom up and tried hard to get into the water, but we finished with it at last and the roaring grew fainter and fainter behind us. However long and weary the miles may seem, we travel nearly twice as fast as we did on the way up, fighting the rushing water, wading in tide that made one dizzy to look down into it, poling and paddling till we were drenched in sweat, portaging and slipping over the rocks. Hauling a sled is not as hard as tracking ahead on hands and feet, inch by inch, while the line that runs back from one's shoulder, joining the canoe and the man in her to safety and the stable land, stiffens like wire, shivers water from itself and stretches thin to half its ordinary diameter.

It is strange, coming to the glade where we are going to camp. This is home for a little while. Everything grows closer and more intimate. The trees introduce themselves as individuals with peculiar crotches and forks and ways of leaning and lifting their heads. There is a friendly birch whose bark will light our fires, here a tufted silver pine on whose boughs we will lie. Heretofore, the woods have been just woods, endless hillsides of dark green seen from the river. Now we have picked a little patch of them to be our own, and when the fire gleams in the dusk and the axes ring, the glade, our glade, welcomes us. It is as though a door had been opened.

This is the clearing on Mininipi Island, like a room, like a home facing the river. When we came ashore, dusk was falling. Harvey and his crew kept on for Mininipi tilt, a half-mile below, where they were going to camp. A light snow was fluttering down. " 'Tis only grievin'," Donald said.

"How about a scoff," suggested Dan, "before we gits to work?"

We lay on balsam before the leaping, golden fire, safe, secure, snugly guarded by friendly trees. We forgot about making camp. All of us silent, gratefully achey, we found content in our thoughts or lack of thoughts; everything seemed pleasant, and the greatest pleasure of all was just to sit. Kay leaned on one elbow, looking into the fire, tired legs stretched out. Snow fell, drifting through the black trees so breathlessly, marvellously silent. It is the same startling quiet that the aurora wraps itself in when the darting, beating lights burst the firmament to pieces, without a sound. The fire snapped and a snowflake or two sailed into

274

the flames with a whisper. The slight sound strengthened the spell.

I looked at Kay, marvelling for the thousandth time that she can be a woman, sensitive, intuitive, keen to perceive the slightest shades of feeling or the truth, yet in body strong and calloused to hardship, almost as rugged as a man. She sensed that I was looking at her and smiled, her eyes shining in the firelight.

Oh, the happiness that fills us is as strong and quiet as Grand River. Just as the river never stops flowing down under the ice, so this ecstasy will flow forever in our hearts, carrying us with it to a limitless sea of hope and understanding and sympathy. In this life where one can conceal nothing, not even from oneself, it seems we have found ourselves out for the first time, found what we really are and what living is. It is like getting to the bottom of things, as though from this as a starting point we could live true. All of it has not been pretty, but the gem-hard beauty of these months has freed the soul like some sweeping tragedy that is too splendid and transcendent ever to be tragic.

Last night I thought this life was a brutalizing ordeal, a long, long chain of pain that one numbed oneself to endure. Tonight I think that we have touched the earth's core and found meaning. Whatever it is we sought, we have found. We hold it in our hands, dreaming by the fire.

January 4.

FROM force of habit we wake up early. But we do not have to get up, for it is Sunday. We lie in our bags and listen to the fire crackling. Through the holes which falling sparks have burned in the roof we watch the slow

275

snow wriggling down. The dear old dirty-white tent must be glad to stay in one place a whole day long and two nights. By the stove lies a hook-ended, willow poker, symbol of permanence. Week-day nights we rake the ashes to the front of the stove with a split chunk, not bothering to cut a poker. But Sundays we indulge in this bit of willow furniture quite as one might sign a lease. Whenever it is plunged into the coals it comes out breathing incense.

Mininipi Island is a pretty spot, but a bad place for dry wood. There is none on the island and one has to go across the ice and way up a hill on the main shore to find a good stick. It was long after dark when we made camp last evening and Donald, whose turn it was to get wood for Bill's tent, didn't bring in any too much. As we snuggled in our blankets this morning we heard a stir in their tent close beside ours. They had burned their last chunk of wood and were drawing lots to see who had to poke out into the cold and shoulder home another stick. Bill got the short end, and we heard him creak away on his racquets. We hugged ourselves in the warmth and curled our toes. "Ho, ho, Morty Roberts," John roared after him.

Morty is a famous character in the bay, a funny little Scotchman with a heart of gold. His accustomed footwear is a pair of rubber boots, even in winter, and the boys claim he goes to bed in them and has been seen snowshoe walking to his traps in the famous long rubbers. Up the river he is noted for his happy-go-lucky way in his younger days. An old pair of socks suited him for mitts, a five-gallon oil tin with a door that bent open and shut was good enough for a stove, a ragged tarpaulin for a tent, sticks tied to his clothes instead of sewed-on buttons, a tin can for a kettle, a rotten boat and shotgun shells wadded with grass. He hardly ever cut up enough wood to last the night and made a regular practice of getting out about two o'clock in the morning to look for more.

For going codfishing down the bay in summer Morty has an ancient motor boat. Every fall when it gets hauled up on shore the village speculates whether it can ever be made to float again. Every spring it goes into the water again, and sometimes without even a coat of paint. Occasionally it sinks at the mooring, but the water is not very deep and Morty quickly does a little salvaging and *put-puts* off again. They say that it takes the whole Roberts family for crew when the boat sails off down the bay. One squeezes himself into the little engine house and sits with his back against the planking and his feet on the engine block trying to steady it, so that as it spits and skips it will not jump off its bed. The lag-screws that hold the engine to its bed were rusted out long ago. Another stands just in front of the wobbling flywheel with a finger on the make-and-break spark contrivance, pushing it up and down with great rapidity as the engine revolves. The spring is broken and as soon as the vibrating finger is removed the engine stops. The Mrs. is up forward trying to stuff rags into the nose where the stem is rotted off from the planking, and the youngest boy is pumping for dear life. It is one of those built-in, homemade pumps that goes up and down in a wooden well. The water pours out onto the deck and is supposed to run over the side through the small scuppers. But the deck is full of cracks an inch wide and the water all pours back into the bilge again.

"Hey Paa," yells the boy in the engine house, " 'tis wunnerful hot on the fit in yere."

"What odds, b'y, what odds. She'll sink soon and that'll cool 'er off," calls Morty encouragingly as he stands at the tiller scanning the shore for a good place to beach her before this catastrophe comes to pass.

This afternoon we got to yarning and Bill told us about some of his and Donald's earliest trips in the fur path with their father. The boys used to complain that their feet were cold—at first. Their father would cut a willow and tell them to pound their toes with it. If they wouldn't do it, he did it for them.

Their father, Robert Baikie, of Mulligan River, is an interesting man, a skilful hunter and a clever carpenter. We got fairly well acquainted last spring when he came up to the fair at North West River. I was trying to make a komatik and he showed me how to bevel the runners and put on the shoeing and lash the crossbars. While I planed and sawed and filed he told me lots of things. When Robert was a little boy, *his* father used to take him out on the bay in the spring, darting seals at the blow holes. They went out on dog teams and he remarked something that has often occurred to me—how like a boat a komatik is on good going. The prow lifts and falls over the rolling ice, the track streams out behind and the sledge runs as smooth over the limitless expanse as a sailboat in a steady breeze. Sometimes in spring there are pools of water on the ice which the dogs gallop through. Sheets of spray fly from the nose, and the illusion is even more real. The bay is all gleaming, blinding whiteness in the sun and every man wears the darkest glasses he can get. Their faces get burned almost black, and some become snowblind even with glasses on.

Out at the grounds each man has a certain hole or group of holes to watch. When a seal comes up, he spears it and hangs onto the line that is attached to the barbed head of the spear. Bob's greatest fear, he used to dream about it at night, was that a big old harp would drag him down the hole some day. Consequently he evolved a plan. Whenever the water in the hole commenced to rise and fall, or whenever he saw the shadow of a whisker in the blue ice water, he made a little noise with his boot on the ice and the frightened seal went down again and came up in a hole some distance away. He never let any one know, and he was very much ashamed. "I was a fine seal hunter, them days," he told me.

Bob Baikie remembers when Indians used birch bark canoes entirely, dressed in smoked caribou skins, had birch rind or caribouskin *meetchwops* and no tin camp stoves. They used to try to make their winter camps near a tumbly brook where the ice was thin. They always carried as part of their gear a caribou's curved shoulder bone with which they could scoop rocks out of shallow water. They made a pile of rocks in the centre of the wigwam and built the fire on that. The rocks got red-hot and kept the tent warm all night.

When Indians are on the road in winter nearly all the family haul sleds. Even the old women and the girls of twelve and fourteen have their sleds. The old men come behind on a track that is like a sidewalk, sometimes hauling, sometimes not. In the middle are the women with their sleds and toward the front the strong men. Out ahead, sometimes half a mile or more, often lost to sight, goes a boy about fourteen or fifteen years old, breaking trail all day long. John Michelin says he has travelled with them and no one ever gives the boy a spell even when it's rimey and bad going. And the worst disgrace that can befall an Indian boy is to falter and have to come behind. It sounds impossible, but Indians do many impossible things and haul loads that would kill a white man.

John laughingly told us that the longest, fastest day he ever made down Grand River was with an Indian family, and one old squaw was hauling one heavily loaded sled and towing another on which perched her old man.

Another winter John and his half-brother, Stewart, fell in with two Indian families and travelled with them for several days. The first morning they started off at daylight and went and went and went. When it was well past noon, Stewart said to an old man with a scrawny whisker and straight black hair down to his shoulders that maybe they had better stop and boil up; the women might be hungry. The old man eyed him gravely and said, "The women are not hungry, but you are."

As always when yarning we came around to the subject of "outside" and the wonders of bridges and steamshovels and subways and washing machines. Things, things! I told them that people outside had so many marvellous machines that they had to spend all their time fixing them and got no peace at all. This information bored them. Dan said that if a government was poor he didn't see why they didn't print off a couple of boat-loads of bills and then they'd be rich again. John said he didn't see how anybody that was born in a country where the apples grew right on the trees could ever be fool enough to leave it.

John says if Kay and I ever go back to the city he would like to come out and see us some day, but he knows he'd never find us, he'd get lost in among the big buildings where you can't see the sun. He can find his way at night in the wilderness through a driving blizzard, and he says in a scared voice, "I'd get lost. You'd live at some number you say, in a block. I don't even know what a block is."

Sunday is the day for picking up loose ends and doing a little fancy cooking. Kay made some "figgy cake," which is simply the eternal bannock with a few raisins baked into it.

Our only washbasin is the small tin bowl used for mixing our bread dough. We soak our calloused feet in the mixing dish full of soapy, warm water. John says he doesn't think it's very medical, but he supposes footy bread is better than cracked heels.

All of us are chafed pretty raw about the groin from so much walking, and some of us have an awkward gait. I put on my underwear inside out, and it is considerably softer.

Our hands are stiff every morning and swollen a bit about the knuckles. John says it is always so when you walk a lot. The Indians carry a stick or a gun in their hands and this prevents the swelling.

January 5.

Long before dawn we were footing it down the river again, stumbling in rough ice, carefully skirting open water. The river is more or less all rapids here for miles. The ice was treacherous and weak in many places where the water rushed underneath. Several times Bill hesitated, wondering whether to wait for daylight or risk going on. We all cut sticks to try the ice with and felt taut and uneasy.

When you are tapping on bad ice and the stick goes through, it is terrifying, particularly in the dark. It is like

281

being a blind man only one step away from destruction. The stick goes down, down, miles into nothingness. You never imagined it would go through, you were hoping against it so hard. There is no security anywhere on earth, for the earth has opened to swallow you. One more step and you would have been struggling in the swift, numbing water. And now where will you go? You try to make yourself light and walk like a cat that would step in water without touching it. The little black hole through the white ice seems like a window of death. You draw back as from the brink of a cliff, alone in strange country at night.

Daybreak was showing over the hills, gray and dirty and more dismal than the night, when we hit Horseshoe Rapid and met Harvey "and them." The river was a jumble of pans and ice blocks and splinters fifteen and twenty feet high. It is narrow here and the tide is very swift. Often on the trip home this stretch makes trouble, and some years it is impassable. Ice and slob get jammed down below and form a dam. The water backs up and backs up, spurting up through every crack and creeping out over the ice at the shore line until the pressure from beneath becomes so great the river bursts. Then it freezes again, a weltering mass of jagged, broken, twisted ice that makes one think of fits and convulsions. It was horrible in the gray coldness.

Harvey and the rest were out on the jam, poking at it with sticks and retreating again to the shore, looking in the half light like bears nosing for food among the tilted ice slabs which shut them from sight and let them appear suddenly again. Their sleds were huddled on the bank.

Surely, I thought, we will have a time hauling toboggans through this.

Between the tilted, jumbled pans the ice was very weak. There was mush ice and shell ice and snow and cracked ice. Harvey's crew came to this point yesterday morning intending to travel all day, though it was Sunday. But they found the river had burst and frozen only the day before, and the young ice between the thick old chunks was not strong enough to bear their weight. They had to camp and wait till this morning. And the jam apparently did not improve much with age.

We all wore our snowshoes so that we would bear up better on the weak places. The sleds twisted and wriggled and capsized and creaked as we lifted and yanked and shoved them, doubling and winding to try to find a level way through the maze. Twenty feet away a man was completely hidden. The dear old snowshoes bent and groaned on hollow places where only the heads and tails were supported, bars split and the *babische* was cut and broken where sword points tried to pierce the web. We fell a great deal, and the sled nearly turned itself inside out. Sometimes, going over the top of a pan that was turned up on edge like a kicked-over table, the toboggan bent to the shape of a perfect wicket; but the juniper wood, bendy and tough as whalebone, stood the strain. The trail was littered with splinters and curls of orange wood shaved from the sleds by knife edges of ice.

Neither Kay nor I could manage our snowshoes, now on a glassy incline of forty-five degrees, now in a miniature crevass, now on a peak or the edge of a pan. We fell and fell and fell, while the sled threatened to smash itself to atoms. The boys got on better, to such an extent that we commenced to get left behind. Kay picked her way ashore and tried to get along the bank, but the steep slant, deep in drift and snarled up with willows, forced her to take to the ice again.

At the end of several painful miles, we decided to take off our snowshoes and risk it. By jumping from one old pan to old pan and carefully testing the unavoidable in-between spaces, we got on better for a while. The farther down the river, the weaker the ice; here and there were growing pools of water and by each bank, running brooks. It seemed as though we were cut off from the shore. John, about 200 feet ahead, got up on a pinnacle and yelled, "We got to hurry, she's going to bust again."

We could not hurry and we got left farther and farther behind. By and by, Kay put a foot through a soft spot and went down right to the thigh, catching herself with one hand on the sled and the other on a solid pan. A little later I did the same thing. We hurried on, hoping to catch up. I had no idea how the river would burst, whether it suddenly exploded under one's feet or gave some warning, whether it started up above and worked on down or came from below or went all at once. With each of us the wet foot grew more and more numb, and finally became quite insensitive.

However great the need for haste, anything was better than frozen feet. At a spot where the shore brook was narrow we got ashore on stepping-stones of ice, wetting the sled a trifle, but not seriously. There was quite a current in the running stream that flowed on the ice. On the side of the bank we built a fire, got dry socks and duffel slippers and moccasins off the sled and sat on a blown-down tree to put them on. The temperature was at least twenty-five and quite possibly thirty-five below zero. It seems impossible that there could be open, rising water under such conditions.

Nevertheless, it is a common occurrence on nearly all rapid northern rivers. It generally follows that the colder the winter, the more the river jams and rises.

The ice groaned and writhed in its bed. Where I had cut a hole testing it with the axe, a gusher spurted up a foot in the air and spread out in a pool, four inches, half a foot, a foot deep.

We lost twenty minutes saving our feet, then scrambled into the crystal jungle again. The rest of them were lost to sight, but we tried to follow their trail. Here and there we found inches of water over their footsteps and the shavings and splinters broken from their sleds were afloat. Frequently, where they had gone straight across, there were small ponds that we had to follow around. We still went without snowshoes. As we hurried faster and the sled got bent and buffeted worse than before I felt like praying that it might hang together in our time of need. My sled, that I made from a tree, can you stand this merciless battering. We'll be stranded, we'll be helpless if I didn't build you true.

This went on for hours, the water getting deeper and the ice getting weaker as we progressed. The only unexpected sight was a bit of black in the white, which, as we drew nearer, proved to be an abandoned sled. I recognized it as Russell Groves', a thick, heavily made one. Apparently Russell and Henry and Cecil had a bad time too when they passed along here. It must have been three or four days ago. The sled was broken across the middle, half the crossbars ripped off and its nose bashed in flat. A dirty, canvas wrapper lay partly across the wreck, one corner of its spotted, ragged edge lifted back by the wind as though to reveal the smashed face of a dislocated corpse. It almost made us frightened, that silent sled. I cast about in my mind as we hurried, which articles of our load we could carry and which we would leave if my toboggan broke. But there was nothing we could leave. Long ago we lost or threw away everything but the starkest essentials.

As I have many times before, I felt keenly my ignorance of the river's ways. Not to know, not to know what the warning signs were, whether there would be any warning, whether we were in real danger or only imagined our peril! The shores were steep mountains, dark with forest.

The patches of water on the ice rose still higher and the streams by each bank ran swifter. There were places where we could not have gotten ashore. The ice seemed hung between the hills by a thread. Open holes commenced to show, exposing the speed and power of the tide beneath the ice pack. It is hard to describe the evil of those black, liquid windows across which the water swept to dive out of sight with an ugly ripple. The ice around them was solid enough, but to us they were cross sections of horror. The water looked colder than the space behind the stars, oily, almost gelatinous, and jet black. Impossible to think of this as the pure green, blue or gold, the magic liquid that purled over the sandbars on sunny afternoons in the fall.

Gradually the tension in us relaxed as we slipped and crashed and progressed. We resolved to stay as near the shore as possible and make a dash for it if the river broke. And if it didn't, we wouldn't worry about it. The open holes were foaming torrents and they grew bigger until the river was nearly as much open as frozen. It was strange to clamber around the corner of a big ice block and find the current grinning right alongside. As the going became more menacing, we grew more assured. I suppose it was that we had been hungry and taut with worry and haste for too long and we simply relaxed as one will under protracted strain. The sled turned over at least five times every hundred yards. The gun got wrenched off, the stove worked out from under the lash line, a corner of the tent dragged behind and the kettles commenced to spill all over the ice. I lashed them all on again good and tight and took my time about it.

Then at last on the point of a bend ahead, smoke rose among the trees, and we heard some one shout, "They're coming." Hunger made our knees weak. We had been travelling as fast and hard as we possibly could since four o'clock in the morning and it was now exactly noon.

When we arrived, the rest were finished, had had their tea and a smoke, were lashed up and ready to go. "We seen your fire," said John, "and we thought you was hungry and gone ashore to boil up. We thought you was crazy too, to stop with the ice crackin' like that. Another few hours and we'd a had to git off the river and take to the heels."

We explained that we thought it inadvisable to let our feet freeze, considering this was a walking trip. We could have made better time in the hills with sound feet, no matter how bad the going, than on the river with frozen ones. We said no more about it, but as a matter of fact, the minute we got our feet wet we thought of the possibility, remote perhaps, that these most important extremities might become incapacitated and so force us to be hauled the last few days into the village. This being the most ignominious fate we could think of, we took no chances with it. We have set our teeth so many times, trying to hold up our end, I honestly believe we would shoot ourselves before we'd be hauled home.

They were surprised that we had come all the way without snowshoes, as they had worn theirs all the way.

All eight of them stood at the heads of their sleds, the icy hauling lines looped over their shoulders. " 'Tis all right from here," said John, waving to the expansion below, where the river widened to a white plain four or five miles in breadth. "You kin follow our track. So long."

And off they went, Harvey and John and Bill, the three mighty ones, in the lead. John with his powerful head and neck thrust forward, his short massive legs pushing him on like the driving rods of a locomotive; Harvey with his arms hooked back around the line and then drawn forward so that his mittened hands could clasp across his chest, walking bolt upright and thrusting first one shoulder ahead and then the other to propel the sled with short jerks; Bill with his head bowed and the strap across the top of his head like a tumpline, arms wound straight back in the line, walking with quick little steps and shooting his hips ahead much as Harvey did his shoulders; Arch walking easily, with no visible effort, not looking very strong until you studied him and saw that he, being the oldest, knew best how to save himself and could, perhaps, outlast the lot; the rest strung out behind, all the lines of their bodies expressing power and an indomitable forward drive. I wished in that moment I could draw, for their attitudes were significant, each one entirely different, an individual expression of strength and fatigue, will, hope of home, love or hate of the struggle. Each man's walk was his life and character epitomized, made splendid and grand because of its utter truth.

John had left us some warm tea hanging on the blackened kettle-stick over the fire. We gulped it down and ate nearly all our bread, for we were very hungry after eight hours marching without food. Although it was cold, we stretched out on the brush by the fire and laid our heads in our arms for a few minutes. We knew the boys had the bit in their teeth and if we reached the camping place at all that night it would be thanks to this short rest. It is really a dreadful thing to be behind on a trip like this where we haven't quite knowledge or skill enough to be entirely independent, and so must race on, all hurry and desperation. Some days we have been way ahead and it has been pure pleasure to go fast or slow, hunt partridges, stop or run just as it pleased us. The boys are not speeding for our particular benefit. They are travelling just as they would if they were alone, and that is what we want them to do. When they get within striking distance of home they always make long days. John says if he can get to Porcupine Rapid tonight he is going to make Traverspine the next night. That will be a distance of eighty miles in two days, worn thin to start with, hauling a sled and travelling on poor grub.

We found pretty good going on the lake expansion, as is nearly always the case where the wind can sweep. The boys were completely swallowed up in a shimmering mirage made by the sunlight on the snowy ice. The far shores were distorted and lifted half way up the sky where they flowed like a snake wriggling over uneven ground.

For hours we ran and walked, and as the afternoon waned the track on the hard crust became increasingly difficult to follow. Feet left no mark at all; the only indication was a spot of shiny snow half the size of one's hand, polished here and there by the passing of a sled as it slid over a hummock. Often we lost the trail completely. Then we would spread out and zigzag to pick it up. Kay did most of the trailing as she was freer, not being bothered with the sled, and she grew amazingly good at it, skimming over the snow now far to the left, now far to the right, bent forward searching the surface like a hunting dog on the scent. We did not wish to lose the trail, as we expected there would be bad ice where the river narrowed at the end of the lake.

The sun set very red and cold and a high wind rose behind us. In the fading light we lost our one indication of the track. Dusk found us at the narrowing of the river on new black ice. It commenced to crack with that peculiar radiating sound and we edged away from an opening that sent shivers down our backs. Looking around we could make out more patches of black, smoothly sliding water, hardly distinguishable from the black ice. We kept quite close together and went very carefully, tapping the ice with the axe handle and at the same time scanning both sides of the river for that blessed sight, blue smoke or a light.

"If we don't see them around this point," I said, "we had better get ashore or it will be too black to find a decent stick of wood." We were very glad the tent and stove, axe and sleeping bags were on our sled.

The wind was roaring a gale now and the wriggling drift, swept down from the lake, whispered against our feet. The temperature was dropping, we felt empty and weak again.

There was no sign of the camp around the point; nearly all the shore was hillside that dropped steep down to the river, but we could make out a cove in back of the point, sheltered from the wind and level enough to provide a place for our tent. Whether or not we would be able to find a turn of dry wood in the darkness we did not know. At any rate we had to go ashore somewhere. It was too dangerous to wander any longer among the black ice and the black water. Both of us were thinking about a fire.

On a last chance before turning into the cove I unlashed the shotgun and let go three blasts into the air. My hands were almost too cold to get the third shell into the breech. The barrel burned like a red-hot iron when I touched it by mistake with my mitten off. The shot sounded very lonely, and more like a call for help than we could have wished. Then we waited, two—three—four long minutes, listening.

"Look, look," we both said at once. A shower of sparks rocketed over the trees, once—twice. It was down below, only a quarter of a mile away. We never heard a single sound from the answering gun on account of the force of the wind. They heard ours and did not see it; we saw theirs and did not hear it.

While we were picking our way with the utmost care toward the direction of the flash, we heard two sliding steps —just two, and John stood in front of us all of a sudden out of the darkness. Hunters always appear like that in the night. There is not a sound. All at once they are there. They do not do it purposely, or to be dramatic, or even knowingly. It is just that they spend their lives seeing before they are seen, hearing before they are heard, and at last it becomes an instinct, a magic presence like an enchanted, invisible cloak. His beard parted in a grin that showed the white teeth. "Hello," he shouted in the flying wind, and we could hardly hear him, "Whar come from today? I'll

291

show you the way in. 'Tis bad." We went into camp on the dead run, winding in and out between the water.

"Whar come from today," is the inevitable greeting of an ancient Indian named *Sou-saka-shish*, whose attempts at English John can imitate to perfection.

Bill's tent, lit up and cozy with the sparks flying out of the funnel, was pitched close by the shore, right within the foundation logs of a ruined tilt. He crawled out the door and came over the snow to us in his shirtsleeves and stocking feet.

"I heerd you shoot," he said, "and so I out gun and down onto the point like the Old Feller was after me. 'Tis bad out there in the dark."

"Yes," we agreed, "it is."

"Come in, come in and git a warm. Don! Shove on the kittle again and move your big fit." He held up the tent flap and ushered us in with a magnificent gesture like a king swinging open the bronze portals of a great palace. The warm sweet air hit us in the face as we crawled in. There will never be a finer palace, nor a more princely host. "Me and John'll put up your camp," Bill stated, reaching for his leggings and moccasins and mitts, eyeing us ever so unnoticeably. But I caught him and his face wrinkled into the friendliest smile.

A couple of minutes in the warmth and we had to reach outside for snow to rub on our hands and feet. The sips of tea burned all the way down, pleasantly, like a shot of brandy. We were as nearly frozen as we cared to be. By the time I was thawed out enough to be of any use John and Bill had brush cut and the tent and stove up. The only thing I could do to help was split two chunks of wood. We had picked the nearest spot as the best place for the tent. It proved to be on the side of a hill where we slept half standing up; and the brush was great limbs of a white spruce. But none of us cared about that, the camp was up quickly and that was what mattered. The stove fell off its legs a couple of times when it was red-hot, but we didn't care about that either. The main thing was that it was red-hot.

This is Porcupine Rapid, Garth McLean's ground. His tilt is high up on top of the first bank above us, and Harvey and his crew are staying in it tonight. John went up there to play cards after supper, but we were too tired to climb up and have a look at it. While Kay was sewing a tear in a legging and I was sleepily baking some bread, Bill came in to patch his moccasin, sitting cross-legged by the stove, and tell us a little about the place. Arch dropped in for a little while too, to listen sympathetically to the tale of our mishaps.

The old tilt where Bill has his tent pitched was abandoned long ago, because the water rises right up into it in the springtime. The only other high place was right up on top of the bank, so Garth built a fine big cabin up there. It seems that Garth is very neat and particular about his possessions, and every year he grumbles at the Height of Landers, just as Jo Blake does, that they leave his tilt "all anyhow" when they pass by. He has gone home for more than two weeks now. Bill told us they found a note waiting in the tilt. "We always does," he informed us.

This year it said, "Cut your own wood and leave things alone. And mind, fur boards is harder to make than to burn." This made them laugh, for they would as soon burn their own mittens as some one else's fur boards.

One February, Bill told us, he was on his way up to Goose Cove for the spring hunt. He was travelling in company with Garth and his brother Jim. The evening they got to Porcupine, they found Indians had been by and ransacked Garth's tilt in passing. They had taken nearly all the flour and tea, left all the boxes of odd nails and cans and bits of fur and feathers and cartridges upside down, heaped a pile of old bones in the corner and nailed most of the fur boards to the wall. Jim and Bill thought it was lovely. Garth boiled over. After supper when Garth had calmed down a little, Jim found it very dull.

Two old pairs of footless stockings had been hanging in the rafters for years, waiting to be thrown out or converted into gun-rags. Jim cocked his eye at them and said in a sympathetic tone, "Well, Brother, they didn't take your stockings anyways." Garth was so mad that he wouldn't even say good-bye to them when they left to go on in the morning.

This has been one of the bitterest days we have ever experienced. We have no reason to be glad; we dread the morning, we are trained too fine, almost fed-up. And yet, as we fall asleep everything is all right.

January 6.

IN those books of arctic exploration which Stefansson describes as mere catalogues of hardships there are seldom any accounts of the inconvenience of a nose, particularly a runny nose. Perhaps a nose is hardly suited to tales of arctic feats. One wonders how Eskimos manage their noses so well, how it is in the long years of evolution that they have not contrived to grow fur on them or lose them entirely.

The greatest hardship of the trip to me is a raw, red nose which drips like some damp rock in a cave, simply from the cold, not from a cold. No one ever has a cold on trips like this. Colds grow only in places where every known means of science is organized to prevent them.

The wet nose in question, going before me like the prow of a ship, tends to get frostbitten. This is unpleasant. Moreover, there is the difficulty of handkerchiefs. I have only two, and one of these has the middle burned out of it. If kept in trousers or inside coat pocket, they tend to stay at least pliable. But to reach them requires the removal of mitts, which is not always feasible. Often it is preferable to allow the icicle in one's beard to lengthen. If the handkerchieves are kept in an outside pocket where they can be reached with mitts on they are very satisfactory for the first twenty minutes in the morning. After that they have been dampened and they freeze as hard as a brick. Any one who has blown a sore nose on a brick, not once but ninety times in a day, begins to feel heroic or ridiculous. The two are much alike.

A little song,

> "Jesus sends the weary,
>   Calm and sweet repose,
> Helps the tired traveler
>   Blow his runny nose."

has a comforting, melancholy quality, and when hummed between cracked lips in the teeth of a wind it soothes the spirit with the petroleum jelly of self-pity.

Camped tonight in a little ravine back from the river. We are sheltered from the wind but even so the tent is surging and straining at its ropes like a sail, for there is a blizzard on. Out on the river one cannot see ten feet, there is only the wind and the swirling, lashing snow that swoops out of the darkness, thickens and swoops again. Our flour will last only another day. We have plenty of beans and peas and a bit of tea and sugar and butter, however. One good day will get us to the first house at Muskrat Island where Carl Hope and his family live. The boys have all gone on, trying to make Traverspine. Late this afternoon we saw them like black pin points far ahead on the wide river. Perhaps it is that we have been weak, bogged down and been left behind. Perhaps it is that we are going to enjoy the last few days setting our own pace.

At the boil-up this morning John and I had a conference. I told him we could get along all right by ourselves from here down as the river is broad and safe, and if he intended going on half the night to Traverspine, we would rather camp early and come along next day.

"You sure you'll be all right?" he asked.

"Yes, sure."

"Well, there's no bad ice, only above Muskrat Falls. Around the falls the winter portage is on the south side. There's a great big blaze on a tall spruce. You'll see it. I got a little flour on the sled. You take it, and you got a couple of pounds of peas and beans haven't you? Well, b'y, I'll have Edna cook up a quintal of codfish and a barr'l of potatoes all ready for you when you gits there."

We flew along with them for a long time still, feeling that perhaps, now that we didn't have to, we would go on with them to the bitter end. The going was perfect, wavy snow packed hard as iron, squeaking and ringing under our feet. It is like a special dispensation direct from Providence to be allowed to skim along without snowshoes for a whole day and a half. The river here is a mile or more wide with comparatively low shores. The high hills on either side are miles and miles back from the river across rolling country, a wider view, something more expansive and less grim than the deep valley in which we have been travelling so many days.

At Sand Banks we stopped to have a look at Stewart Michelin's tilt, nestled in the bank close by a brook. It has a door with hinges, a board floor scrupulously clean, three windows, a feather mattress on the bunk, a cast iron stove, an iron poker made from an old gun barrel, a great big oven half way up the stove pipe and two flour barrels in which to stow odd gear; in short, a most luxurious establishment. There are no iron stoves and barrels in the tilts way up above, beyond the rapids and portages.

From here, off to the southeast we could plainly see the snowy tops of the Mealy Mountains, the mountains of the bay, the mountains of home. And from here the trappers began to leave us. Bill said, "Me and Don and Dan aren't goin' to drive 'er all night neither. Maybe we'll see you."

By two o'clock they were the merest specks and at half past the sky was growing darkly overcast and we were looking for a place to camp, hurrying while there was yet light. Snow commenced to fall, faster and faster and the wind rose till the moving, flickering blanket made us feel that the world, the solid air and sky were all going by us like a rapidly moving strip of film and we alone were stationary.

The south bank is not a good place to camp, for the winter wind sweeping across the wide river has stunted and killed the trees. Nevertheless we found a fairly sheltered spot over the bank and down in a hollow; a small dried-up arm of the river it appeared to be.

My axe, a small one that Arch lent me for the trip down, was in bad shape; the helve was cracked to splinters just below the head and all ready to break. It worried me, for one cannot make camp nor use the stove, in fact we are hardly equipped to live for very long without an axe. If the head breaks off when one is chopping hard and flies into the deep snow it can easily lose itself. John and I pawed and sifted the snow for more than an hour one time this winter looking for an axe head.

I used it very gingerly putting up the tent and cutting enough wood to light a fire in the stove. Then Kay arranged the brush, took in the sleeping bags and put on the kettles of ice while I went off to see if I could find a straight-grained birch, back from the river. On the way I took care to note a slender dead spruce that would do us for the night's firewood. It was pretty dark, but I found a small birch that was good enough, cut it down and brought back a split piece the length of an axe handle. To have the new stick cut and split was a relief. The old helve was so weak and wobbling that I broke it off with my fingers.

Kay had everything stowed away in the tent or rolled up in the sled wrapper outside so that nothing would be lost if it snowed deep. Already our track in from the river was covered. Sometimes we pretend we are Indians and speak only in the few Indian words we know. Kay says the play is dangerously life-like, for every one knows that Indian women do most of the work of making camp.

Inside, it was as cozy as could be. The kettle was boiling

and some split peas were on to cook. We had a snack of bread and tea and Kay started to mix up some bread for to-morrow while I got my crooked-knife out of the progbag and set to shaping a rough helve. Our firewood was almost all burned up and I had to hurry. I sank the axe blade as deep as possible into the end of a chunk of wood by hammering on the poll with another chunk. Then we put the poll of the axe head into the coals. The wood of the old handle that was wedged in the eye soon dried out and shrank in the heat, and when it started to char it could easily be pushed out with a stick. All the while the blade had been embedded in green wood and, in addition, we kept sprinkling snow around it to keep it from getting hot enough to lose its temper. Next we toasted the birch stick over the fire to dry the frost out of it and make it lose a little of its brittleness. A small split in the top of the new helve, made by hammering on the back of the knife, a wedge shaped out of the old hardwood handle, a little pounding, and the job was done.

Outside, it was black as ink, but I knew where my firewood stick lay and it didn't take long to get it home and chopped up. The axe hangs in the top of the tent, "seasoning." In the morning the handle will have shrunk loose, but we can fix that. We have just put away an enormous meal of peas porridge hot mixed with our last small cube of pork. Of the different kinds of supplies we brought, split peas have been the best—nourishing, quick to cook, light to carry. Much more appetizing than beans and more easily digested.

Out on the river the wind is screaming. One cannot stand upright against it and the snow stings like flying sand. Let it blow, we can't stop it, but we are snug.

299

Yesterday the blizzard continued and the drifts
mounted; we thought it best to stay where we were.
This morning the snow had stopped falling at last, though
the sky remained overcast. We were up good and early as
we wanted to spend the night in a real house at the Hope's.
We knew Martha Hope would have some redberry jam for
us and maybe some potatoes. Shameful to say, the prospect
made us shiver with delight.

The snow lay very deep on the river. What a contrast!
Day before yesterday we could trot along leaving hardly a
mark on the hard, slippery snow. Today a man could not
travel a mile in an entire day without snowshoes. We sank
nearly to the knees with them on, and the sled tunnelled
along behind like a hoary old mole. It was one of those
days when you have to "lean at it" and the scenery goes by
very slowly and often not at all. The trappers stick together
for days like this so there will be plenty of men to take their
turns ahead. We hadn't gone half a mile before a sudden
warm wind blew strong from the south, a prelude to one of
the strange, January "milds" that get everything wet and
sticky and slow travel almost to a halt. Any one on the
trail would infinitely prefer a temperature of thirty or forty
below.

Kay went ahead breaking trail all the way, and I came behind with the sled. It was the only way we could get ahead.
The soft, loose snow falls in on top of the racquets at each
step and one lifts tons of it in a day's walk. Both of us
found our jobs were all we could handle even at first, and
the snow grew more sticky each hour.

At noon we were just above Muskrat Falls, sitting on the

sled, panting and worn, watching the cascade tumble and foam through the shining jumbles of ice at the sides of the chute. The path around the falls was marked by a big new blaze which we felt sure Bill had put there for our benefit.

Toward two o'clock it began to snow again, great clogging flakes like dumplings, and we wondered whether we would spend the night at the Hope's after all. I had an idea the house was on Muskrat Island. Kay thought it was on the mainland. In any case we knew the island was a narrow piece of land more than a mile long and if we took the wrong side we would surely miss the house, especially in the snow with darkness coming on.

All at once a little above Erwin's Island we thought we could make out a black speck that moved, then two. They were running to meet us and waving their arms. We ran toward them for a long time. At last we could see they were smiling and then we had them by the hands, Mr. Carl Hope and his son, Lawrence.

"Hello, hello, well, well, so you got yere. What's the news? What wonderful hard haulin', eh? Well, Miss, and you walked all the ways down Grand River, breakin' trail too."

Carl is about fifty-five years old, gray, slightly stooped, one of the kindest men in the bay. His eyes are so dim he can hardly make out the sights of a rifle, but they are improving a little. The trouble probably came originally from getting snowblind so many times. He is quite generally known as "The Governor" on account of his serious, responsible manner and his large, official-looking moustache. He was dressed in a brown flannel shirt, a white coat of some thick cotton stuff with green braid sewed all around the edges, a cap with mink fur ears, tied back across the top on account of the warmth, woollen trousers a half an inch thick, leggings, moccasins and a huge pair of bear-paw snowshoes.

As though to offset his father's, Larry's eyes are black leaping fires that sparkle and flash when he talks. He is an Indian-looking boy, thirteen years old, slight but very strong. Last year he was in the school, but this year it was time for him to start learning to be a hunter. "Reading books," as some of the old people quite rightly say, "is no good if you got nothing to eat."

"You done well to stay where you was yesterday," said Carl. "Yes, we knowed you'd be along today so Larry and me come up to have a look around. We wasn't sure you'd know where the house was to, and Martha said you might be almost out of grub."

They had come five miles up the river just to look for us and help us in with the sled. Carl wanted to haul my toboggan for me, but I couldn't bear to let him. I thought to myself, I've dragged this thing 300 miles and I'll finish the job if it kills me. He understood perfectly.

Nevertheless, I did receive help. Larry came behind, pushing with a big stick against the back end of the sled, I came next in the harness, Kay and Carl went ahead making a good track. Still we progressed but slowly for snow stuck to the sides and bottom and even to the head of the sled. Every little while we turned it over, knocked the lumps off and scraped it clean. Carl dug down in the snow and pulled up a piece of the old icy crust. With this he scrubbed the wood and it made the sled run freely for a time; then we had to do it again. A hairy sealskin lashed across the sled

302

bottom runs smooth as silk on this kind of going, but we did not have one.

"What time did the boys pull in to your place night before last?" I asked Carl. "Did John really get to Traverspine?"

"Naw," Carl said, " 'twas half past ten when we heerd 'em yell coming up the bank. Nobody'd go on with John in the snow. They all stayed the night."

The snow was falling thicker and it was quite dark when we finally reached the end of the narrow channel between Muskrat Island and the south shore. On the mainland we saw the lights from the windows of the house, warm and yellow; if only we could haul up the bank we would be there. Four dogs came down to sniff and snarl at us. "We should have took them along, Paa," Larry said, panting.

Everything was soft and moist and silent, all of us were completely whitened, the path was muffled, the wood pile was an enormous white mound, the low roof of the house was more a dome than a peak; soon, it seemed, the house, the world, would be swallowed up, engulfed, erased under the silent, slowly drifting whiteness that filled the darkness.

I think the Hopes are part Norwegian. It is said Carl's father deserted from an English man-of-war in Nova Scotia and wandered "down along" in fishing vessels. The name was impossible to pronounce. People said they hoped to be able to twist their tongues around it some day. The Hope is all that has lasted. Their house, twenty-five miles above the mouth of Grand River, has come to be a haven of refuge for winter travellers. They are the hosts of Grand River.

When we went inside, the savory odors from the stove

told us that Martha was planning to live up to her reputation. She stood in the middle of the kitchen, her three little girls around her. Effie and Drucilla, the two eldest, came and shook hands, looking at us very solemnly and then smiling ever so faintly with their big black eyes. Agnes, the youngest, a fair-haired child of three with pink and white cheeks like apple blossoms, could not quite summon the courage.

Martha made a great fuss of Kay. She carried her off right away and brought her back with a skirt on, of all things; a plaid woollen skirt instead of moleskin breeches, and in place of sealskin boots a pretty, new pair of moccasins all embroidered with beads.

Every now and then Martha would come over from the stove and stand in front of Kay, doubling her hands up in her apron, her eyes dancing bright and then hiding themselves under her heavy brows again. "My, my, Miss, you walked all the ways down Grand River. How ever did you do it. And John told me you was a proper trapper now and how you baked rose bread fer'n when you was way up there."

She hurried back to the stove in her quick, alert way, darted her head into the oven and out again like a bird, the steady flow of glad, friendly talk never slowing for an answer or an oven or anything else.

"My, my, Miss, tell me, did you like it up above? Did you like it, true? I knowed you would. I said to Carl, didn't I Carl, most women, and from outside too, wouldn't like it but she'll like it. I always wanted Carl to take me up the river but he wouldn't and now his eyes is too bad altogether. I think us women could be most as good hunters as the men if we was a mind to leave them with the washin' and the babies an' that. Sometimes I do leave Carl and go off all day after part'idges. I likes my new gun wunnerful. John told me you was a real good shot. Oh my, yes, I got him into a corner and I axed him all about you. I s'pose you killed hunderds and hunderds of part'idges up there, yes, I only got a hunderd so far. They'm wild seems like it this winter, wunnerful, wunnerful. An' you come all the way down with that crew of men, runnin' and walkin' all day long like as not, and all of them bad enough bound fer home and John worse 'n any of 'em.

"John has only been married about a year you know," Carl drawled.

"Yes, I know," went on Martha, pouring the steaming, fragrant tea, "but he's always been one of the head fellers fer drivin' 'er; all the Michla's is like that. Robert and the Englishmen come yere winter before last and he had them near done out. You looks twict as good as they, Miss. Yes they'm in a hurry no mistake. Why, I mind one year Stewart Michla got in with a company of them, John and them from up above, comin' home. Stewart were only comin' down yere from Sandy Banks. He come in a hour after the rest of them was finished their tea and gone on. He said he weren't goin' to sweat *hisself* to death fer no crew a wild men that got to go clear into Canady to trap a few weasels and samson foxes. And you know, Miss, Stewart he kin leave most anybody if he's a mind.

"Come on, set in, make yerself a meal now," Carl interrupted.

We all drew in our chairs to a table with a white cloth, china cups and plates and saucers, shiny silver. We couldn't get used to sitting on chairs at all, at a table with china cups. We had grown so used to our own black, flattened kettle, to sitting cross-legged on the brush with a tin cup and a tin plate, using one sheath knife between the two of us that we had almost forgotten there were other ways. I felt that surely I would never get used to this kind of business again, and at the same time I had to resist an impulse to put my fingers into a jug of molasses that stood in the centre of the table.

There was baked, stuffed partridge, three-quarters of a bird apiece, thick brown gravy and pieces of pork, potatoes with the taste of the earth so keen and sweet in them that if they had come from different gardens I am sure I could have distinguished the individual environment of each separate one. Once upon a time I considered potatoes an inevitable and boring part of every lunch and dinner. But not now. I have no doubt I was a dreadful spectacle at this point.

There was actually more fresh crisp white bread than we could eat, and besides, there were four bulging top-heavy loaves of molasses bread with raisins and pork fat baked in them. Dumplings and molasses too, and all the sugar we wanted for our tea. Last came the redberry pie and the fourth cup of tea. After the third piece of pie I shook my head, but Martha said, "Make yourself a meal, now. I know you're shamed to eat any more, but we'm used to this. Everybody's starved comin' out of the river. Carl, gimme the plate."

Martha has an enviable reputation as the Mrs. Malaprop of the region. They say that when Carl was away at the

Mission hospital in St. Anthony having his eyes treated and a cataract removed he sent a letter home. Martha and Suzannah Best were trying to read about the operation.

"What is this word?" said Suzannah. "He says he's had his eyes separated."

"No," said Martha, squinting at the letter, "it's evaporated."

The boys claim that she has dozens of unique expressions: *numinum* or *lunilum* for aluminum, *Gem 'n Dora flour* for the brand name Glenora Flour, *Irishman* for nourishment. John swears that she has told him to set up to the table and have a little Irishman and that she told him Lawrence shot a goose that was right blue with vexation when she meant starvation.

Most of these expressions have been exaggerated; many of them, the boys admit, they have made up themselves. I only set them down as an example of the amount of fun the trappers in their tilts on Sundays far from people can wring from little things. Maliciousness is farthest from their thoughts. Martha and Carl represent an outpost of home to all the Grand River men, the first house, the first good meal, the first warm night, the first woman, the first children; a man is as good as home when he gets to the Hope's. Dirty, frostbitten, ragged, lean, their beards and eyelashes full of frost, their sleds battered and splintered, sometimes with a hole worn right through the wood,—these are the guests the Hopes receive. And sometimes they have had some starving ones stagger in.

Out of their meagre living the Hopes provide scores of enormous meals every winter. Each man that stops could easily eat four large potatoes, a whole loaf of white bread, two partridges, five cups of tea and an entire redberry pie, except that a Labradorman does not consider it seemly to eat as much as he would like in some one else's house. Some of them, I am certain, *never* eat as much as they would like even when at home, having trained themselves since boyhood to do with little food. Most of the trappers if they have any flour left on their sleds, bring in the bag and empty it into the Hope's barrel. Even this is more pay than the Hopes want.

As the men come by in December and January they pass the word when the next bunch will probably be along. Martha tries to prepare for them. Sometimes she gets up at four o'clock in the morning to bake a dozen loaves of bread and cook up a pie or two. She likes to have meat for them, and she spends whole days hunting it.

When the hunters start back up the river again in February, the Hope's is the last house, just as it was the first coming down. By the time they get to Muskrat Island they have discovered or remembered the odd things they forgot in the complicated business of leaving home. Perhaps a man forgot his tobacco. Carl has some. Maybe the hunter can't find a needle in his progbag. Martha has plenty. Maybe a new pair of moccasins has proved too big. Martha takes in the heel in a jiffy. In the morning when it's time to shove off on the long haul, Martha has a loaf of bread or a bun of 'lasses cake tucked in the sled load somewhere.

Carl and I sat by the stove and smoked our pipes while he told me about his last trip in on the south path. His eldest boy, Jensen, age sixteen, is in there now and expected out some time this week. Carl says he worries about him some on sudden dirty days, but he has taught the boy always to leave a little flour in each of his six tilts and to kill partridge on the way in if he can and hang them up for the return, in case of a big batch of snow or a twisted ankle. This is the first year Jensen has been hunting alone. For the preceding five years he has been furring in company with his father, learning not only to be a trapper but also to be a part of that remarkable Labrador father-and-son relationship, the mutual respect and spartanism and silent sincerity that often grows like a flower beside the winter trail.

Little Apple Blossom is always sad when her brother is far in the country. When bedtime comes for her she gets up on a chair, pulls a sweater of Jensen's off a nail and carries it away to put under her pillow, or perhaps to put on like a pair of trousers. Without this, sleep is impossible.

Pretty soon from the small bedroom that is boarded off at one end of the kitchen she calls, "Paa!"

"What darlin'."

"Come here a little bit."

"Oh, it's a secret is it," says Carl, smiling. He leaves his talk of fur and bears and Indians and goes into the bedroom. Through the boards come whispers, and then a low sweet lullaby, unconsciously gruff, consciously gentle, sad and half unmusical and very pretty. It runs along, as masculine and beautiful as the roar of surf on a beach at night. It sinks to a murmur and little Apple Blossom is asleep.

Back by the stove Carl lights his pipe and goes on with the fur and Indians, no awkwardness, no embarrassment, no explanation.

To us, fresh from the woods and as naïve as children, it is the purest poetry, a wistful scene out of some charming play. Where will we ever see again life that is art and art that is life like this.

January 9.

WHILE we were sleeping a high wind from the northwest brought the cold again and swept the river. All night the river was a channel of flowing snow streaming straight through the air like whipping pennons, whirling up above the trees in vertical maelstroms, hissing against the boards of the house. When we looked out the door before going to bed it was as though a big snowstorm were on, but it was only drift caught up and carried by the wind as a rapid stream carries sediment.

The drift was still rolling this morning, but not quite as high, for the gale has hurled millions of tons of snow into the woods on both shores and left itself hardly enough to play with.

The sled creaks over the frozen ripples, the snow is icy hard on the crests and softly luxurious like an ankle-deep carpet in the hollows. We've our hoods up, dickies belted tight and our overalls on. Nothing can keep out the cold and the drift that wriggles its white hands into every crease and seam.

One last time we turn and wave to the house and the three Hopes standing by the bank, half hidden already in the drift. The memory of our little time there is a bright, beautiful miniature painted in a silver locket.

Martha said we should not go on in a wind like this and Carl too, but half-heartedly. Martha wanted company and she wonders if we are competent to take care of ourselves, it is so easy to get frozen on days like this. Carl understands better, I think, that we are not the same people we were in the fall. We haven't the faintest resemblance to born hunters, but we have learned a number of things about taking care of ourselves since September. At least we have a good idea what we are capable of and what is impossible for us. And from now on we will be able to improve and grow more independent of help. It is only by travelling absolutely on our own, foreseeing the risk, learning to see and remember landmarks and the woods signs, planning out the grub, knowing how to use the food, clothing and shelter that nature provides and thus travelling far and light, that we can ever know and be part of this land. In a few years we may be able to go up and down Grand River by ourselves with average safety. Perhaps the time will come when we can go off over the hills in any direction we like and know that we can sustain life for a month or two in winter by some uncharted lake and find a way back.

And then again, perhaps we shall not be able to make a living here, perhaps we shall have to go away. It is quite possible, for the fact that we admire these people does not mean that all at once we can equal them. Sometimes I wonder whether our very small margin can possibly see us through while we are learning the ways of such a different environment. It takes time and capital for people with a background like ours to learn to live here, just as it would for a Labradorman to learn to make a living in New York. There are whole sections of skill and knowledge and habit that every Labrador child acquires almost automatically; and we may never be able to acquire some of them. When these considerations loom large I try to say to myself that it does not matter even if we should have to go away. For we will come back again. And we shall never be in despair again now we know there are truth and simplicity and beauty, that they can be found, not so much in a geographical place as in the way of life such places bring about. Whatever happens, we have an aim henceforth, and it is to live all our lives as we are living now.

There was a time only a year ago when we thought a twenty-mile walk in February was a considerable feat. And so it was, and so it might be again—the last we might ever take if we were to be caught out in the middle of the bay in a blizzard. But it is different now. Twenty miles on reasonably good going near a guiding shore line is only a stroll. And at the end of it we can sleep soundly and with perfect comfort on a board floor. Somewhere in us there has been a gain.

In a way, that twenty-mile walk last February, the first time we had ever been very far from the trees in winter, was the beginning of this trip. The temperature was forty-one below zero early on the morning we left North West River. There was no wind, but even the breeze of our walking cut like a knife. Out on Goose Bay with nine miles of ice to cross and an island in the middle, it commenced to snow, lightly at first, then heavier so that the island disappeared. There was still time to go back, or we might go on and try to strike the island, not a very big one, by our compass. We debated in our inexperienced way. Kay said at last, "I'd rather be lost in a snowstorm than be a mollycoddle all my life," and we went on. The snowstorm died away and the sun came out after a little while. Yet it did us good to have taken a chance.

Today we wish we had a big, runnered sledge with a mast lashed and guyed to her and a tarpaulin up to the wind. The wind is square behind us, like a strong hand in the small of the back. With the gun and a corner of the wrapper I have fixed up a low, triangular sail on the sled and she almost runs herself. If we had a komatik and a big sail we would be doing thirty miles an hour, the acme of speed in these parts. For many a Labradorman a long run before a gale on a sailing komatik is the greatest speed he ever attains in his life. It does seem unbelievably fast after weeks of walking. Arch Goudie told us the fastest he had ever travelled or ever wanted to travel was coming down Grand Lake in a blizzard with a squares'l rigged to the komatik, steering by trimming the sheets, careening by the big rock headlands on one runner, hardly able to see a thing in the thick snow, with his eyes watering and the sail in the way. When he got to the foot of the lake the dogs were twenty miles behind.

Before sunset, for it is only fifteen miles to Traverspine, we were turning off the main river into the narrow stream where the three houses stand on a high bank. True to his word, John had codfish and potatoes cooked for us. He looked like a boy again with his beard shaved off, and everywhere he went he carried his little girl in his arms. Robert was just home from the woods, looking worn, but the same iron, friendly personality as always. On three trips in The Long Path, which goes in from here and over the south hills eight tilts distance, he has caught more fur than most of the Height of Landers. While Kay was talking and playing with Robert's children he showed me a beautiful cross fox and a silver.

We were to stay the night at Robert's, but first we went to supper with the old man, Uncle Jo. John was there and his wife Edna and their little girl, also old Mrs. Michelin, whom they all call "Mer," and one of the old man's grandchildren, Ewart, a handsome, strong little chap of ten. He can cut wood almost like a man, and he has kept them in rabbit and partridge meat all winter. He has his own little snowshoes and axe and gun as well as one big dog and a small sledge. With this outfit he drives around to the traps near the river, standing up on the sled and cracking the whip.

Uncle Joe told us he was extra glad to see us because he never thought he would again. It is one of his greatest pleasures to have some one new to talk to and as for us we are only too glad to listen. After supper he was telling us a yarn about the old days when he was a boy. One of his teeth was apparently bothering him as he talked, for he kept reaching in his mouth and pulling at it. Finally he stopped his story and went into the next room. We heard him rummaging in a box of tools and then he said, "Mer, where's them plyers?" She got them and we heard him sigh twice and then again, deeply.

"Yes, teeth is a bother sometimes," he said, throwing the tooth into the stove and spitting a little blood after it. "I'm real glad to git clear of that one. 'Tis only the second one I ever lost, too." He told us that he had been able to keep his teeth so well because he didn't wear them out by rubbing them with a brush. All the same, he rinses his mouth with salt water and runs a thread between all his teeth every day.

About half past eight Robert's young son Lewis came in, to show us the path up to their house in the dark, he said.

The stars were out and the snow crunched beautifully. Lewis was telling us how he shot a horn owl off the top of the woodpile.

LATE in the morning we pulled out for Mud Lake, only six miles away by a shortcut called the back channel. As we were going down this narrow strip of ice overhung with trees, we met a handsome Indian boy. He told us there were five families of Inus camped at Mud Lake. We talked for five minutes more, but neither of us had any idea what the other was saying, so we gave it up and I said *Miami* and he said *Good-bye*. It reminded me of Amundsen's description of a winter at Herschel Island where he says that the white sailors from the whaling vessels caught in the ice all wore Eskimo clothing and the Eskimos all wore white man's clothing.

In spite of its name, Mud Lake in winter is the prettiest of the settlements. There are ten or twelve houses on both sides of a wooded channel that winds in half a mile or so from Grand River. The white ribbon of ice is like a sunken road. Around each bend, one after another of the white or weathered gray houses shows up among the dark trees, each one surprised to have been found in this narrow channel no different from a thousand others that are uninhabited. There is a small white church and a graveyard that is growing in size, like all graveyards.

Last summer in there I helped dig a grave in the sandy soil and I read the burial service over a little girl who died in the epidemic of dysentery. She had been a happy kid. I left out the part about thanking God for taking her out of

315

this vale of tears. The old days of childhood reasoning seemed the sanest after all, the days when I would have said, "She died in pain. I don't thank God for that. If he came down from Heaven and managed the whole business why didn't he keep her well, why did he torture her? I don't believe it if the minister says God hurt her for days and nights because it was good for her and for her mother. I don't believe God had anything to do with it at all. If I did I would hate him, whether he killed me for it or not." It was a pretty day and the sun was checkering the graveyard with cheerful light, everything was fresh after a rain, a day that makes life sweet and death hideous. We tried to sing a hymn, *There's a Friend for Little Children Above the Bright Blue Sky*, but none of us knew the tune and it merely sounded as though we didn't believe a word of it and were ashamed to be pretending in the presence of such devastating truth.

The rough coffin rested on battens across the open hole. There came into my mind the memory of a fur trader from way North who told me he always used to recite Gunga Din as the service at Eskimo burials, and the look of his face as he laughed. Around the board casket there was a piece of old rope. When the box was lowered into its resting place in the wet sand, the rope had to be removed and drawn up. *We had to save the rope!* We couldn't even let that frayed old piece of line die in the grave with the little girl. The futility of it, the pettiness of our importance almost knocked me down. The world would not allow us one second's respite with our grief; experience would not let us pitch the rope into the grave and go away somewhere to cry alone. We had to put such luxuries as sorrow away from ourselves and remember that tomorrow a boat will have to be towed or a sled will have to be hauled and rope is hard to get. It made me angry that we have to live by such terms. The rope was a symbol of the defeat of the defeated, the chaining of a slave who has already learned better than to run away. What good would it have done the four-year-old girl if we had put the rope in with her? None at all.

And yet, how fine it is of the unspoiled Eskimos away North to put in the grave the precious knives and spears of their kinsmen. We sniff and say that an Eskimo who dies for lack of a knife that sleeps beside a skeleton is a fool, never supposing that his custom may be the acceptance of a challenge, a wail of grief and a battle cry of defiance to life, to death, to Nature kind and Nature cruel, to the shadowy future and all the engulfing incomprehensible. He doesn't care for his own future when he stands beside a grave. But we, we think always of the future; that is the root of civilization. In this respect primitive races are certainly finer than we; that they can ignore the certain sufferings of tomorrow. It enables them to live today, which is more than civilized men can do. It is inexpedient, it costs life, but it is brave. Life is so uncertain, they know how to treat it. To a certain degree, in certain ways, they provide for the future, of course, but beyond a certain point they will not go. It is not always ignorance that stops them. Many of the Indians we have met, and even some of the trappers—John particularly —have a fine disdain for the future that makes our foresight, our anxiety to provide every possible comfort and safety, our desire to insure against the future and establish that unattainable ideal of society, Security, show up by contrast as ugly and greedy and small. Smart, yes; but not glorious.

I was not thinking all this business as we tramped up the channel. I was only thinking how good it would be to see Uncle Johnny and Aunt Sally Blake and sit by their stove in their fine old house and drink a cup of tea. We wondered if they would be as glad to see us as we them, and we were sure of it.

Uncle Johnny was on his way out to feed his team of dogs that he keeps in a log stockade in a grove of poplars back of the house; a frail old man with white hair and a drooping, snowy moustache, carrying a steaming, odorous pail of corn meal and seal fat. The door to the house has had a wobbly knob for some years now and it turns round and round quite ineffectively. John Michelin, who is a favorite and often visits there, says the best thing to do is to turn it seventeen times to the right and thirteen times to the left and then kick for Sally to come.

They told us right away we must stay as many days as we could. Aunt Sally was particularly impressed with Kay's trousers. She said they were very sensible and she couldn't see why all the women hadn't taken to them for winter time long ago, especially for fishing out on the ice. Uncle Johnny sat on the old board sofa at one end of the kitchen and told us the news. While he talked he stroked his black and white cat, of whom he is very fond. This winter she caught six prime weasels around the house and in the sheds. He skinned them and traded the pelts for cans of condensed milk for her. "Yes, kitty, you'm smart all right." And she purred contentedly.

When tea was ready, Aunt Sally brought out to show us a small, brightly colored pitcher shaped like a bird with its bill forming the spout. Last summer she saw it in a Montgomery Ward catalogue and sent all the way to the States for it.

Twenty years ago a lumber venture on a large scale failed at Mud Lake. There was a smithy and a big bunk house, barns and two mills, also half a dozen winter logging camps in the country round about. Way back of Traverspine there is still an old tumbled-in logging camp and in the bunk house there are two barrels of double-bladed axe heads, now so rusted as to be worthless. So it has gone with peavies, chain, blocks, harness, steel cable, axes, bolts, pipe, fittings, tools and hundreds of thousands of dollars worth of other valuable equipment. Most of it the Labradormen could have used. But it did not belong to them and they would not touch it. Now rust and rot have spoiled almost everything. At the entrance to the Mud Lake channel near the point where it flows into Grand River two enormous lumber scows lie rotting in the bank and just below them, two leaning, pitiful steam tugs. On the shore there is a huge lumber storage shed, now empty save for old saw blades and belts and horse sleds and scattered remains of the big steam sawmill.

In the days of the lumbermen there were horses and a hundred or more men, a bridge across the channel and a woodroad way in to the hills. Now the bridge is gone and the road is grown over so that it will soon cease to be a path. The people in Mud Lake remember the lumbermen by name and their sayings and fights and dances and songs, their timber cruises and gigantic booms of wood as though it were yesterday. In summertime one finds all around the paths and in the woods and in the grass of the cleared fields bits of old iron and pipe and brass steam fittings. The children take some of the more fantastic shapes of metal to put in wooden boxes and play motor boat with.

Uncle Johnny was Skipper John Blake in those days, piloting the lumber steamers up and down the bay and the tugs and barges out to meet them by the changing treacherous channel to Sandy Run. There was plenty of milled lumber then. The lumbermen built Uncle Johnny's fine two-storey house for him and he paid for it out of his wages. He was always a clever trapper and a hard worker, and now he has enough to get along on. They say that in the old days before the lumbermen came he was very saving and whenever he saw a person throwing something away he cautioned them, saying, "Save he, b'y." At boil-ups away on the path when he cut off a piece of bread to eat he always held the bannock over the open mouth of his grub bag. By and by there were enough crumbs to thicken a good mess of partridge soup. However that may be, his savings have enabled him to be very generous to a number of people who consider such thriftiness unseemly.

At evening Jo Broomfield, one of the Company's men, drove in with a ten-dog team and a komatik loaded with flour for the Indians. If we would bide here till Monday he would be going back light and glad to give us a ride.

January 11.

W E decided to stay and wait for the team. Meanwhile we have visited every house in the village. The women all know Kay very well as she has treated many of their children when they were sick. She even "found" some of them, that is, was midwife at their birth. One of them is

320

named after her. Women talk to women mostly, and men to men. There is not much mixing of the subjects, children and fur. Everywhere they ask us to have a cup of tea or stay for a meal. We always accept, no matter what time of day or night, for we get hungrier the more rested we become. We have never been so lean and hard and hungry. Our belts are three holes in, as contrasted with September, but the calves of our legs have grown so big with muscle that our once-loose leggings can hardly be pulled on. In the past five weeks we have walked 600 miles, three-quarters of it on snowshoes and much of it with sled or pack. The accumulated hunger cannot be appeased. We never get enough; we simply eat until we are ashamed to eat any more. Then we stop, but it is not because we are satisfied. Every evening when the sky commences to grow dark I find myself wondering if we hadn't better hurry up and look for a stick of dry wood.

January 12.

SWINGING down the channel with the toboggan and its load lashed like a toy on the komatik, sitting on and waving good-bye to each house, nothing to pull, not even one's own feet, and the dogs breaking into the lilting surges of a gallop every time Jo cracked the thirty-foot sealskin lash—what luxury! Out across Goose Bay and by Rabbit Island with the sledge dipping and slipping over the snow in such effortless waves of progress it seemed we must be dreaming.

But soon we commenced to get freezing cold and the rest of the way we spent our time running to keep warm, then jumping on to catch a breath and running alongside again.

Our clothing is just right for walking and hauling, for travelling so it is as important not to sweat as not to freeze. But for riding one needs three times as much clothing as we possess, and even that is not enough.

Jo smoked his pipe and only ran a little now and then. Sitting on a hairy caribou skin near the nose of the sled he watched the bay and the dogs with his deep blue eyes and told us about everybody in North West River. It has been a bad winter for the Indians on account of the scarcity of caribou. " 'Tis them have killed up the deer," he said, "and if they'm starving now, 'tis their own fault. But they don't know no better, I s'pose."

Very rarely he spoke to the dogs in a quiet voice—*heder-reder-reder* (left), *uk-uk-uk* (right), *whurst-st* (go on), or knocked on the sledge with the short wooden stock of the whip to make them go faster. The leader obeyed every soft-spoken command immediately, for there is never a better managed team than Jo's. He used to be dog driver for Revillon Frères when they had a post across the river and for years since then he has been driving the Company's dogs. Every one of these dogs he has raised from puppyhood and he is always the one to feed them. No one else has driven this team all winter, and so they are not spoiled by being constantly shouted at and whipped and urged on. A week of that kind of driving and they will not obey anybody.

From out on the bay the village is a toy town with houses smaller than matchboxes set at the base of a hill the size of a loaf of bread. As we purred in closer to the Company's red roof and tall flagpole, the hospital and its long wharf nearly snowed under, the school, and all the small houses with their plumes of faint blue smoke, the dogs commenced

THE AUTHOR ON ARRIVAL AT NORTH WEST RIVER
IN JANUARY, AFTER A SNOWSHOE TRIP DOWN
GRAND RIVER

Photograph by Fred C. Sears

BERT BLAKE

to hump their backs and dig. We came up over the bank onto the hard-trodden path at a gallop.

The kids were just coming out of school and Kay and I tumbled off to say hello to them—the little roly-polys with bronze cheeks and Japanese eyes, the spare tall Indian-like ones and the fair ones with blue eyes, the ugly and the beautiful, all of them bubbling over with cold air and laughter. At first they did not know us, and then they hopped up and down in the snow at the sight of Kay's trousers and my beard. They wanted to touch us and take us by the hand, they ran around in circles and tumbled and laughed and babbled ten thousand exclamations, questions and statements at once. "Oh Mr. Merricks, Uncle John's goin' to take me up Grand Lake fer a week in the spring. Oh, Ernest and me's pardners this year 'n' we play goin' up the river. OO, Miss, I thought you was a man. Pearl's learnin' to sew boots. Dru kin read good now. Where'd you come from? D'you see Paa up there? OOO look b'y, what a whisker, cripers!"

The doors of the nearby houses opened and people slipped out through the snow to shake hands and say a greeting. We were home again; not returned to a quaint village, but really home.

In the evening, after supper in the cozy Grenfell Mission hospital, we sat by an open fireplace.

"Well," said one, "what was it like, all in all?"

"It was tough, but it was glorious."

"But honestly, what do you think now?"

"Well, it was a glimpse into a life we never knew before. It is unbelievable what a trapper can accomplish. We knew before that they were remarkable men, but now we know they are supermen. Away in the country they are absolutely ruthless with themselves; they will not even take time enough to eat and sleep; pain, cold, fatigue, hunger cannot bend them. They are there to get fur and they get it. Yet they are kind and full of fun. Stacked up against their iron self-discipline, their fortitude and honor and knowledge of nature, our little store of civilized facts and worldly cleverness seems very small. We would like to be more like them and less like ourselves. What do we think? Well, we think it is a life that is too much physical and not enough mental, and yet we think it turns out a man more fit to live and know and understand and love and laugh than a life that is too much mental and not enough physical. And yet this that we speak of is of no account whatsoever. It is the land, the long white lakes, the forests and mountains and rivers, the space and the northern lights and the cold and beauty. Nothing within the scope of our comprehension is as worth knowing as the heart of that. Even if there were no reason, no benefit, even if it were not an antidote for every poison that complex living distills, even if it were not strengthening and sparkling, this would still be so."

PART III
BITTERSWEET

WHEN we were rested from the trip down Grand River I should have liked to go up the Nascaupee River to Seal Lake with Bert Blake on his spring hunt. But Bert has three boys who, together with him, fur all his extensive ground, and this time I wanted to tend a path myself and see what I could accomplish, not just look on.

There were not many paths available, but finally my good friend Henry Blake, who is known as one of the best of the North West River hunters, offered very kindly to take me away with him to Winnikapau Lake where I could fur one of his trap lines on shares. He said he could not promise that I would make much, but that he would teach me all he could. After the first round I would have to do the best I could alone.

Much as we both regretted it, Kay could not go, for a sled cannot transport as much gear as a canoe, and my dog and I could hardly haul enough grub to nourish ourselves.

She boarded with Mrs. John Groves at Goose Bay. It is twenty miles by ice from North West River. There is only one other house and that is empty. But the Groves have been very kind to us, they have a fine big house and Mrs. Groves was glad of the company while her husband was away on the spring hunt.

Kay spent many days hunting over the hills and tending rabbit snares. Mrs. Groves liked fishing through the ice and the two of them would go off for the day with an ice chisel and a grub bag, a little sled and a dog or two. Two or three times Kay walked to Mud Lake and to North West River; she did a little nursing and tried her hand at learning to make sealskin boots and caribou moccasins. In the evenings she knit for us a thirty-fathom trout net and read *Jean Christophe* for the sixth time.

February 10th, the cold morning when I left at sunrise, it was a wrench to go away. The first hour over the wind-swept ice with the sled already running hard and the dog behaving badly was as black a time as I can remember. But it is the same with the trappers; when they start away again in winter the first few days are unadulterated misery. It is a little like going to war. Toward the beginning of February all the trappers figuratively tighten their belts and clench the muscles of their jaws. It is time to start back into the woods again on the long, bitter haul to the furring grounds. Each man is conscious of an enormous Presence that begins just back of the house, the wilderness that is waiting. He hates it and loves it, he fears it and defies it and understands its grimness and its bounty. His utmost endurance and the fortitude that is a steel-strong habit in the long days will not change its sphinx-like face by so much as an ice crystal. But in the mystery of paradoxical sensations that the wilderness rouses, each man senses that he has been made whatever he is by the great Unknowable where he is going. It cares not whether it kills him or makes him rich, but he knows the great Unknowable well enough to have borrowed and armed himself with a little of its own immortal carelessness.

Henry and I and a man named Edward Michelin were together most of the way up, seventeen days of the most abominable weather that ever was; thaws, blizzards, rains and gales of wind at thirty below. Edward had two pairs of snowshoes we used to josh him about, a big pair called his "winter snowshoes" and a little pair called his "spring snowshoes." Both pairs had been so often mended with seal-skin and salmon twine that the original mesh was practically non-existent. He was very proud of them even though he did put his foot through one now and then. Henry used to tell him they weren't fit to leave on a limb for the jays to peck at.

Ed had a catamaran [a light sledge with wide runners] and a powerful hauling dog to help him. The dog was named Cabot after William Blake Cabot of Boston, explorer and scientist who has made many trips in this country. Henry had a toboggan and a little Indian hunting dog called Dash. The dog was very small, but sometimes he could haul a little bundle of clothes and a grub bag done up in a sealskin. I had a toboggan for myself and another small one for my husky dog. She followed along behind on the track, or was supposed to. My dog's name was Diamond, but Henry called her Old Drybones before we got home again, she was so thin.

With the varying weather we had all kinds of going, crust that broke and hooked our snowshoes, light, powdery snow in which we sank above the knees with our racquets on, but most of all sticky snow that clung to the snowshoes, making them weigh about ten pounds apiece, and put the brakes on our sleds till we could barely move them. Sometimes they came so hard it seemed as though we were just rocking from side to side in pain and not stepping ahead at all. We'd start out in the morning and it would be such hard hauling I'd say to myself, a man can't keep this up all day no matter who he is. And in the evening we'd still be at it.

Labradormen are odd with their code of never giving in. Evenings about half past four we'd stagger up a bank, build a fire and boil a kettle of tea. After we were finished we'd start picking up our grub bags while Henry said, "Well, I s'pose we'd better go on a ways," and Edward answered, "Sure."

Then, casually looking around he would remark that it looked like a pretty good place to camp.

Henry'd say, "Yes, it is a pretty good place for wood and brush." At this point they'd both turn to me and ask me if I wanted to go on or camp.

I joined in the farce always and said, "It's up to you, I don't care. I'd just as soon go on if you want." Really I didn't see how I could crawl another inch, but I've found by experience you always can, somehow, especially after a cup of tea.

Then Henry or Ed (generally they alternated, one to-night and the other tomorrow) would say, "Well, I aren't tired, but if you fellus want to we may's well camp. My! we've only come a little piece today."

The drama never lacked spice, for sometimes they did pick up and go till long after dark.

Up by Mouni's Rapid I got snowblind. For three days we had been walking on a crust that tripped us if we didn't watch our snowshoes all the time. Every look at the forested green hills to rest our eyes meant a fall. My glasses were fancy things from the States, with sides in them and fur to go against the face. Of course they steamed up from the warmth of my face inside and the cold outside. I couldn't see where I was stepping with them on, so I got disgusted and took them off. The third evening the pain suddenly knifed me. It was a very mild attack, but the light from a candle in the opposite corner of the tent would stab me through the head like a long needle, even though I had my eyes covered with a bandanna and my two hands. I was almost totally blind for one day and blind in one eye for three days. A pair of "glasses" such as the Eskimos have used for centuries would have been much better. They are pieces of wood about an inch and a half thick, carved the shape of eyeglasses. They are pierced by two tiny eye holes. The outer part of the hole is cut away, funnel shape to enlarge the range of vision. The sides of the funnels are then blackened with charred wood to dull the light that enters to the eyes.

It was a February of unprecedented mildness. The river was open almost everywhere along by Mouni's. We crossed on a rotten bridge of ice, tapping ahead of us with sticks. Now and then the stick went through and we stepped elsewhere. The bridge disintegrated as we walked on it. I doubt if any one could have crossed behind us. Next morning it was gone.

Ed left us there to go on up to his place at the Big Hill. We had to stop a day and a half to look at some traps Henry had left set by the river in December on his way home.

Our last day up that interminable Lake Winnikapau there was a crust on top and sticky snow underneath. At every step we broke through a hole nearly two feet deep and could hardly pull our racquets out to make another hole. We took fifteen-minute turns ahead. At the end of each period the man who had been breaking trail would sit on his sled gasping and rubbing his legs while the sweat ran into his eyes and the shivers coursed up and down his back. The other fellow went on, punching holes in the crust, floundering, stumbling, often falling, beating his snowshoes with a stick at every step to knock the lumps off them. It was easy enough to catch up to him, and then came the turn ahead again. If we took off our snowshoes we sank almost to the hip and the bottom six inches was water on the ice. The hauling lines ate into our arms and chafed our hands in the mittens raw.

For hours we never spoke, afraid of the words of weakness we might say if we opened our lips. Henry's sled had one crossbar broken off and it was running badly. He was also suffering from indigestion. I was ahead for a long stretch and I commenced to leave him behind. When two men are travelling under such terrific stress, it unfortunately but almost inevitably becomes a contest with considerable temporary bitterness. I know it is so with Labradorman and Labradorman. Perhaps it is more so with a Labradorman and an outsider. I cannot explain it, nevertheless the feeling is tremendously powerful. As I commenced to draw away I looked back and saw that Henry was pale and had his teeth in his lip. A gust of blinding passion shook the sanity right out of me and I thought as my teeth ground savagely, "Now I can leave you if I want. You have left me behind so many times on these sled hauling trips, all you Labradormen; you have always been superior, now it is my turn for once. Ah God, I don't care if his sled is running harder than mine and he's sick. I wouldn't care if he had a broken leg. No one has ever cared if I was lame and my load was lashed on crooked and my hands were freezing. It's a fight and nothing counts

332

but results. I can leave him, I can leave him. I don't care why! The fact remains!" I had no intention of leaving him or even showing him that I could. It was simply that I knew for the first time in my life that I had the power. I could have held up my fists to the sky and screamed with evil joy. I never thought how these Labradormen have taught me and hauled stuff for me to make my load lighter and waited for me and been kind in the midst of the cruelest suffering. For a moment there was not one spark of goodness in me. I found myself trembling and afraid.

Henry hauled up alongside and we stopped and ate bread and sugar to keep us going. After that he was as good for it as I was.

All afternoon the same stony headlands looked down on us, two specks in a pit of mountains. They eyed us, as distant and unattainable as the clouds. Poor Diamond commenced to falter and drop way behind on the track. I put more of her load on my sled, but still she lagged behind with her little sled. When she got a quarter of a mile back she would lie down in the snow and stay there. I had to run back and get her and drive her ahead of me and try to catch up. When I had caught up it would be time for my turn ahead again and I was so done out from running I could hardly stagger.

At nine o'clock in the pitch dark we reached Henry's cabin, which is built in a level grove of birches close to the shore at the foot of a mountain. The mountain looks as though it would one day kick the cabin into the lake. But for a protecting spur of rock, avalanches would have done so long ago. We dug out the door and went in. For a minute we sat in the cold dark with our heads in our hands not thinking

333

of anything, not even of lighting a fire in the stove. We were too tired to cook the meal of bacon and peas we would have liked, but after a mug-up of bread and tea it was fine to curl down into the bag and pull the soft duffel blanket up close and drop off to sleep with the friendly fire snapping and the light from the damper hole dancing black and gold on the logs.

In the daylight the huge thirty-five-mile lake, with its jagged edge of sheer blue mountains rising up to the sky, made that cabin seem too small even to exist. The weight of the mountains and the length of the lake crushed its being, its consciousness of itself, to absolute nothing. Once at evening, when the ice was turning purple, I came over the top of the mountain and looked down over the trees at the lake. I won't forget it ever; our high-rimmed, isolated world was Godlike for a moment and unearthly in the hugeness of its desolation.

Then again, on some clear days it was like opera scenery, and on stormy afternoons it was like death. Sometimes at dusk I would be coming home across the lake. Perhaps Henry was at the cabin skinning fur and had the candle lit. It used to make me laugh out loud—the cocky, cheerful cheek of that one yellow pin-point light at the foot of a crouched, black mountain as high as the sky.

Henry furred the path that goes into the country three days' walk to the south, and I furred the trap line that extends three days to the north. He took me with him once in each path, setting up the traps and trying to teach me as much as he could in the short time. Then we went our separate ways in opposite directions, always arranging, however, to meet on Saturdays or Sundays at the cabin by the lake.

The north path was all long, narrow lakes and hills, a chopped-up, broken country of woods and open ice and long views over endless trees and snowy land. About every quarter mile there would be a trap. Setting and baiting and fixing them barehanded is cold work. Otter and beaver traps are the worst, for they are set in water. The smell of the rotten fish and beaver castor bait never left me. I always had to hurry to get to whichever one of the little 6 x 8 tilts was the end of the day's journey. I didn't know the way well enough to find them in the dark.

It's very strange and illuminating to be alone in the woods 150 miles from a living soul, not knowing the way very well, with darkness coming on, the wind rising and the sky aching to belch snow. All nature seems to be brooding, watching. Sometimes the atmosphere was so hostile, I wasn't really afraid, but I had no idea of ever getting out of it alive.

One of those lowering, hostile days I had to stop all day at the little tilt on a hillside by a lake that Henry calls Red Water. Diamond was having puppies. Three little beauties they were, two brown and white ones and one black and white like herself. I had a heavy pack and no sled. They couldn't walk and I couldn't carry them. Diamond was so thin I doubt if she could have fed them long. We had nothing to feed them on and very little for ourselves and Diamond. We couldn't haul them 200 miles down the river and care for them all the way. I had to kill them, though I would almost as soon have killed myself. I took Diamond down the hill to the shore and tied her to a tree; then hurried back up, and laying the puppies' heads on a log, I smashed them with an axe handle. I looked up, shivering, smeared with blood, and there stood Diamond, silent, between two trees watching. She had slipped her harness. *The Hound of the Baskervilles!* flashed into my mind. I don't know why. I suppose because the story sickened me with horror when I read it at the age of twelve. Diamond didn't fly at my throat. I took her down the hill again and tied her fast with fumbling fingers, then buried the pups a long way off in the snow. I think I know the grisly feeling of being a murderer, a Macbeth or an explorer who shoots the dogs that have slaved for him. If a horn owl had called, I think I'd have been off the handle.

After all, confidence comes when the strangeness wears off. There were sunny days, too, swinging down narrow, cliff-bordered lakes for some of which I invented names each time I came to them, Rabbit Ribs, Paradise Alley, Hour Glass, Puddle, Hole-in-the-Clouds, Shuttle, Never End. There were brooks where the water never stopped singing down under the ice, and a beautiful hillside above a fair-sized stream that I think was Michikamau River, where I could look way off to the ridges that lean against the sky near Michikamau Lake. Those days I forgot to remember blizzards and was glad to see nothing in the traps, dreaming all day to the snowshoe rhythm of old friends and when I was a kid and how Father used to read us *Robin Hood* and *Roland* and I used to look forward to it all day. At night the cozy fire and the northern lights, and the bursting sensation of being tired and young and strong, absolutely on one's own to live or die.

Evenings after the wood was cut up and supper cooked

and eaten there was always the work of thawing and skinning fur, baking for tomorrow, mending snowshoes and getting everything ready for the start at daylight. I never stretched out on the bunk before eleven o'clock or midnight. Then the cold woke me up to stoke the stove two or three times before dawn. In the path one can carry no blanket nor sleeping bag.

We were short of grub most all the time and seldom killed all the partridge, rabbits or porcupine we wanted. There was some old caribou track, but we didn't see any caribou and you can't eat track. Occasionally we'd manage to kill enough meat for a big feed that would satisfy our hunger. Especially for Sundays we tried to do this. But in general the mainstay was bannock and not enough of that. I tried to bake about half what I knew I'd want. The brain keeps saying, "If you don't skimp you'll starve altogether," and the stomach answers, "Let's eat and the devil with tomorrow."

The second of April we pulled out for home. My total was five mink, three marten and twenty-five ermine. Very poor.

Henry had to haul home the canoe that he came up the river in last fall. A couple of days before we left, he cut down a straight spruce and hewed out a catamaran to haul the canoe on. Winnikapau was sticky again and it took us a day and a half to get to the lower end. Henry, the dog and I all hauled on the catamaran, with my sled, the sleeping bags, tent and stove, guns, kettles and grub all piled in the canoe. Below the lake the river was open for a long way. It was sunset when we got to the water, put the catamaran aboard and started walking down the river with our arms instead of over the ice with our legs. Before the long twilight was over, the swift current had bowled us down to Mouni's, a distance that took us three days on the way up.

Ten miles below Mouni's we paddled next day before we came to ice. In the afternoon in a snowstorm we met Victor Goudie and Gordon Goudie, two young fellows with a komatik and dog team on their way up to get their canoes and bring them down for next fall's hunt again. We were looking for them, for they were to bring two dogs up, to help Henry haul his canoe home. The dogs were there and while he was unfastening their traces from the bridle, Victor told us he had slipped off the ice wall beside Mininipi Rapid the day before. He caught hold of the ice and hung on, but he couldn't climb up because the edge was too steep and the current was pulling his legs downstream. Gordon climbed down to the edge of the water, got a good grip and gave him a foot. Clinging tight and almost pulling Gordon in, Victor hauled himself out. They had a note from Kay for me and a box of raisins for Henry.

We hauled where the river was frozen and paddled wherever there was a mile or so of open water. Lots of places the ice was covered with water and getting bad. Our sealskin boots were getting leaky and worn-out. Places where the ice was bending under us we'd run along with one hand on the canoe, so that we could hold on and it would float us at any minute if the whole business went through. We hauled across lots of yellow, slushy places we wouldn't have dared try but for the canoe-on-the-sledge, our amphibian rig. Generally when we were paddling in the canoe, we let the dogs follow along shore.

We nearly got a ducking in the Horseshoe Rapids. It was

sleeting and freezing on us as we paddled down toward them, the water very black and filled with floating slob, the hills lost in slanting snow, the canoe and everything in it draped with wet, white flakes; such a vague, strange, miserable, magic afternoon. I looked back at Henry in the stern, covered with snow, a fur cap, ragged beard, icy mitts on an icy paddle; sliding down that black river he looked the picture of an old-time voyageur. We had three rapids to run before we got to Horseshoe tilt, a cabin tucked away beside a brook deep in a valley of enormous hills. Down ahead the rapids were roaring and the broad water narrowed to a raging channel between sheer ten-foot walls of blue and green ice. We picked up speed until it seemed we were falling through this chasm. Ahead of us the water broke at the brink of the rapid's slant. The incline was so steep we couldn't see over to make out where the worst rocks or the smoothest water lay.

We were rushing down the grade when we saw about fifty yards ahead of us the big white plume that curls up over a boulder just under the surface. We dug our paddles to get clear, but an eddy drew us right down on it. At the last second Henry stuck her straight for it, for if she hit broadside she would roll over and over like a barrel. We were flying and the water looked very cold. Just above the rock there was a deep pocket where the water dipped and then flew into the air over the rock. Into this hole we plunged, stood almost straight on end, put the bow right under and filled the canoe a quarter full. But she rose to it ever so quickly and we shot up over the rock and never touched. We must have had an inch or so to spare. We spent the night at Horseshoe tilt and I was glad, for I was freezing.

From there on it was all ice. We were up before sunrise every morning, always conscious of the sky and watching what the weather would do, hating the warm sun that came at noon to rot the crust, hating the rain or the snow or the east wind because they were our enemies that chained our feet and slowed our sleds. Mostly we had sunny days, and our faces were burned nearly black with the glare from the snow. The dogs could haul the loads, for they and the sleds bore up. But we sank through the crust, and it was run and walk, run and walk all day long to keep up. In these long spring days of five o'clock dawn and eight o'clock dark we made thirty-five-mile runs. The last days we were both limping so badly we sometimes had to take turns riding in the canoe a little.

That last morning when I parted from Henry at Traverspine to cut across the six miles of woods for Goose Bay and Kay, I was glad. Then I could limp as much as I wanted. I was crusted with dirt, ragged, hungry, my sled was broken and patched, my dog was as lean as a fence rail and most of all I was weary with the cumulative weariness of walking, hauling, running, paddling, cooking, getting wood and water, patching boots for endless days and nights. All the last few days there had been no beauty in nature, only adverse or advantageous travelling conditions. The great high hills beside the river half-lost in snowstorms, the lovely purple snow that sparkles with gold dust in the sunrise, the blue sky and sunset clouds were very little to me compared with a good crust that would get us along. Getting along—that is the fixed idea, waking and sleeping. All for a dream of comfort and food and relief from walking, walking, walking. It wasn't all quite crushed out of me, but almost. I was

340

good and sick of the life in the woods and could hardly bear the thought of ever going up the river again.

It was thinking something like this when I came in sight of the house at Goose Bay across a wide arm. All the white plain of the bay and the mountains and the sunshine and sky made me stop. I sat down on the sled and cleaned my ragged, black fingernails, though I was trembling with haste. And the clean, long distance and the familiar hills broke on me like a beautiful blue and white wave. And I thought aloud, "I can never go away and leave this. I never will."

And now I am home and Kay is here. There are clean clothes and comfort and leisure. I've eaten and slept for two days continuously.

The world of books and thoughts again. I had forgotten it. The world of quiet sunsets through the window and the snowy mountains deepening, darkening.

PART IV
HOME

July 25.

WE are living in the other house at Goose Bay. It belongs to John Groves' brother, Charlie, who has moved to the village to give his children a few years' schooling. When we set up housekeeping here in April it was still winter, the bay was frozen tight and ptarmigan used to feed in the willows close by our water hole.

The house is a gray, weather-beaten structure with a sharp-peaked roof and a crooked stovepipe that is capped with a Chinaman's hat. Charlie couldn't decide what to charge us for rent, so he gave it up and decided to charge us nothing at all. "If the roof leaks, you will fix it," he said, "and that will keep the house from rotting. 'Tis better lived in."

There is green grass and a potato patch, raspberry bushes and a huge stack of firewood logs in the clearing of spruces. Our boat is drawn up on the white sand beach where the clear northern water laps and roars by turns. Way across the bay a chain of blue and white mountains humps its mottled back up to the sky. On sunny days after rain we can see the shine of a cascade in the mountains sixty miles away.

The stars come out and the northern lights creep up from the edges of the world to mirror themselves in the bay. The wind shifts and fog and lashing rain sweep in from the bergs on the coast. The sun rises pink over the mountains and sinks again in the forested western hills. The geese fly north

345

and salmon come to the river mouth. Twinflowers and wild iris appear in the woods, and blossoms on the potatoes. How good it is to be part of the rain and the work and the changing days.

John Groves and his wife live a quarter of a mile away across the point. They have given us bear meat, shown us the best places to fish and hunt ducks, taught us in a tactful, amused way, and enjoyed the teaching.

The biggest room in our house is the kitchen-living-room with its built-in cupboard in the corner, beams and a gunrack overhead, curtains at the little windows and bearskins on the floor. In the centre of the room stands a big, black "double stove," a treasure that came from Quebec long ago. It looks a bit like a locomotive rampant, but we have great affection for it. The first night we had no bed. We had a barrel of feathers, however, and of them and some canvas Kay made a mattress while I nailed together a bedstead of boards, using squared-down logs for legs. With a couple of caribou skins and our old sleeping bags under the mattress, it does very well. Having no pump as yet, we use butter tubs for water buckets, and every day I fill a barrel in the kitchen with water from the shore. Our washtub is a sawed-off barrel. One day we had it half in the water at the shore to swell when a big tide set it afloat. By the time we took notice, a strong breeze had drifted it so far that we could just make it out with the battered pair of opera glasses which we use to scan the bay. It was a long row, but worth it to see the fat old tub rollicking and bobbing along before the wind like a jolly old lady on a holiday. Until spring came we had no spout tea kettle and only a little butter, as the Company's supplies were practically exhausted. By springtime there is

SHE LOVES THIS LAND FOR ITS OWN SAKE

always a shortage of something, and some springs even such necessities as tea and cartridges and tobacco are lacking.

Just before the break-up we caught plenty of trout and smelt through the ice, and I spent two weeks cutting wood a little way up the river that winds in back of the house. There were nearly a thousand turns to haul out to the bank for next winter's supply. A turn is a log that one man can handle, and if it is easy to shoulder it only counts for half a turn. Labradormen spend, on the average, a month a year working at wood. It must be cut and hauled to the shore, hauled home with dogs on the spring crust or boomed home by water in summer, then sawed and split and stacked. That is the price of a year's fires. It's devilish hard work, but it's never futile or unworthy or petty, and it makes one very strong. I've spent some lovely times in early spring making the white chips fly from the still-frozen trees, or booming logs, long lonely summer days, on the river, making the water carry on its back tons of wood for puny me. But even better is the roaring stove within and the roaring wind without on howling winter nights. Every birch chunk was cut with your own hands. And if it hadn't been cut, you would be frozen to death.

In May the ice started to break up and the ducks and geese from the south circled down to feed on the ponds of open water. John, over across the point, can imitate the call of geese and draw them half a mile out of their course if it is evening and the ragged V of kronking birds is looking for a safe resting place for the night. They circle overhead, a shotgun's roar splits the sky and a bird tumbles out of the flock while the rest sheer off screaming. We were out in our white canoe hunting ducks almost every sunrise and again at evening, for we needed the meat. Crouched behind a low white screen which is fixed crosswise on the gunnels of the canoe, one paddles with a short paddle, very silently. If it is done right, the birds think they see only a drifting white icepan of which there are thousands on the water. More often than not we inadvertently bumped the side or rocked the canoe and our meal of meat fled away. But we will learn; everything takes time.

These were the loveliest days of the year, Labrador spring-time, with the blue water, and the white ice drifting down the bay in the silver sunshine. In late June there is hardly any darkness, and the sunlight lingers, touching this part of the world as though it were too fair to leave. At night, from eleven till one, there is half-darkness while the sun's pale flush moves along the northern horizon. All the rest is day-light. Lambert de Boilieu paints it well in his *Recollections of Labrador Life*—"Night and day hold each other's hands upon the hilltops. . . . No sooner does the sun set north by west, than, like a giant refreshed, it rises again north by east."

John Groves launched his motor boat and set his seal nets in Sandy Run, ten miles away. I often went with him to help haul them, as cold and wet a job as there is. The water is icy and the twine of the heavy, snarled nets cuts one's freez-ing fingers. One haul we got thirty seals. The carcasses are dog feed and the skins are boots and moccasins and mitts, strong thongs and rugs and parkas. The livers and hearts and tongues are delicious and the meat of the young ones is good eating. John showed me a clump of birches on Sealing Point at the south side of the run. It marks the spot where he and Charlie had their tilt when they were boys, seal fishing alone springtimes nearly thirty-five years ago. The tilt burned and birches grew up on the site.

When the ice was all gone Kay and I set off for North West River in our little boat to get a barrel of seed potatoes and the mail. We picked a day of fair wind and moved off from the beach with both our two sprits'ls drawing and the boat leaping like a colt. In the afternoon, as the wind blew harder, the boat heeled until sliding water was lapping over the gunnel. We sat on the windward side and sang, and the mountains seemed to smile. We were a couple of miles from land but we bent the steering oar and never luffed because the sun was out. When the sun is out we are never afraid. It was good to see the village of white houses nestling on the river bank, and to come ashore and talk again with the men and women and children we care so much for. The river in spring flood was a brawling rapid by the town, the boats were anchored under the point, and a schooner out beyond. With a few strangers who were ashore from off the schooner we felt shy and ill at ease, as though we should put up our defenses and yet had no defenses to put up. We seemed to have lost our masks; we could not carry on a conversation that revealed nothing, and we did not wish to learn again.

It took us two days to get home against a head wind. Toward evening of the first day we rowed for hours and hours trying to make Rabbit Island. Often Kay helped me or gave me a spell, for we had two pairs of oars. The wind came stronger with the darkness and the bay grew rougher, so that we pitched and pounded and could barely crawl ahead. We were soaked and hungry and Kay had to bail all the time. Finally the island almost disappeared. In the increasing blackness we could just make out its darker gloom

349

and we felt very much alone in a tossing boat with the wave crests grinning at us. It looked as though we could not make it and I thought of putting up one sail without the sprit and running all the long way back to Sandy Point, where we would have to get ashore in the darkness through the breakers. It is a bad place, for the water is shoal far out. But we pulled for half an hour more and gradually inched in under the island and so to the beach on the sheltered side. In a little while we had the tent up among the trees and a fire crackling in the tin camp stove. The balsam brush floor poured out its sweetness. We put the kettle on and ate. Rain came and drummed on the canvas while a big sea roared against the inky island. In the cozy tent we hugged ourselves with delight to think we had gotten there by our own strength, no motor, no advice, just us and a little callous and muscle against a breeze that was slow about getting boisterous.

When morning came it was raining and pretty rough, but the wind had veered and we went on, very happy.

Since then we have been on much longer trips alone in our boat and camped the night in coves and brook mouths and by lake shores that are like visions of paradise.

The potatoes are up and a few of them are big enough to dig and eat. The corks of our net bob on the water just off the house, and from it we get more trout and salmon and pike than we can eat. Three tents of Indians are camped not far away and we give them lots of fish, for they have no net. Sometimes they bring us a rabbit or a duck. Their glade is piled with chips and curled shavings. They have cut the straightest-grained spruces and are busy making canoes.

Occasionally we wish one of our old friends from the States could come and stay a while, one of the rare ones who never has and never will "knock under and go with the stream," some one in an old hat who would fit in immediately. We'd fish and look at the mountains, or go off up the river picking berries. Then home on the current like a leaf, not a sound until the grating on the sand. We'd sit on the floor and smoke our pipes and talk and laugh and roll on the bearskins. Fried trout for supper. We have no extra cup, but a very neat one can be manufactured from an old tin can, or perhaps we'd make a wooden bowl.

A few of the trapper families have been to see us, come for a cruise they call it, and some have had a meal and spent the night. A boatload of people came in from North West River one day and Carl Hope paddled over another time with young Effie. He stayed two days because there was a storm on. Effie said she was coming again to stay a week with us. We have been in these people's houses so often we like to have them come and stay in our home. We like to talk and show them pictures in magazines and when they go we are sorry. And yet we are glad to be alone again.

Just now the midges and mosquitoes are very, very bad; worse than any one at home can imagine. But they will go away again. We have made a great big mosquito netting tent which we use in the house, a house within a house. Though the windows and doors are all screened, the mosquitoes come in through the wood, up through the floor, down the stove-pipe and out the damper hole of the stove, in under the eaves. Often we keep a pot of lightly smouldering bark in the kitchen. The thin haze of smoke is not unpleasant to us, but it temporarily incapacitates the mosquitoes.

I have been making some paddles and an oar and a table and some birch spoons. The hardest part is picking a straight-grained tree or log, for knotty, crooked wood is a waste of time. One learns to do better and better with axe and crooked-knife. Every completed object is my own, made with my own two hands. I don't owe any one anything for it, either in skill or in time. Such as it is, it's *mine*. The fragrant, wavy-grained, satin wood—if it weren't any good to make useful objects out of, I'd have a block of it just to carry around with me to smell and touch at any time of the day or night.

Every bit of work we do seems worth doing. We catch our fish and eat them, we build things and use them, we shoot our meat and row our boat and boom our firewood down the river, saw it, split it, and burn it. If we want jam, we pick some redberries or some raspberries. Most of the things we can't make or find or improvise we have to do without, and this makes our creations of tremendous satisfaction.

Every day is our day, all our own, to make of what we will. There is no one to intrude and bring on an attack of self-consciousness. Here in Goose Bay, if we wish to be alone and unharried by a million other people's noises and projects and lives, to work out our own, we can be. There are people whom we can help and be helped by, there is everything we dreamed and at one time despaired of ever finding in life and the world. We feel so close to things that at night we could no more fall asleep without going outside to touch the wind and the dew, look at the dark trees and the sky, listen to the bay, than you could go to bed with your shoes on.

Sometimes we take the afternoon off and go out on the sandbar to swim in the shallow water that the sun has warmed. The breeze blows the flies away and we lie in the sand. Now and then we paddle way up the winding river and pole a little rapid to the gap between the hills. Only a few people know where this river rises, two weeks' walk in winter in to some high mountains. Even these people do not know where the mountains would lie on a map. In the late afternoon, floating home, no one comes to look at us except a family of ducks with young ones that cannot fly yet.

This evening the bay is very quiet. We have been sitting on a driftwood stump in the sand. A dying spruce leans out over the still water, looking down untroubled at itself. As though the edge of the bay were breathing, a faint shining ripple runs along the beach. Way off in the sky across the bay the tops of the mountains are glowing in the last sun. We lay our fingers in the water and dig our bare feet deeper into the sand to be closer to the earth's heart, we love it so. And a feeling of gladness and sorrow comes over the water to us like a wave; gladness that the earth is so free and wide and life-giving and generous; sorrow that so many millions of men are unhappy, neither knowing nor caring for these things.

THE END